Swati Sengupta studied English at Jadavpur University and then worked as a journalist for various newspapers in Kolkata. She now freelances for newspapers and writes fiction and non-fiction books. Her published books include *Half the Field is Mine, Guns on My Red Earth* and *The Talking Bird.*

OUT OF WAR

Voices of Surrendered Maoists

SWATI SENGUPTA

SPEAKING
TIGER

SPEAKING TIGER PUBLISHING PVT. LTD
4381/4, Ansari Road, Daryaganj
New Delhi 110002

First published in paperback by Speaking Tiger 2016

ISBN: 978-93-86338-15-0
e-ISBN: 978-93-86338-17-4

10 9 8 7 6 5 4 3 2 1

Typeset in Adobe Garamond Pro by SÚRYA, New Delhi
Printed at Sanat Printers, Kundli

For
Ma & Baba

'How much can we ever know about the love and pain in another heart? How much can we hope to understand those who have suffered deeper anguish, greater deprivation, and more crushing disappointments than we ourselves have known?'

—Orhan Pamuk, *Snow*

'If you are neutral in situations of injustice, you have chosen the side of the oppressor. If an elephant has its foot on the tail of a mouse, and you say that you are neutral, the mouse will not appreciate your neutrality.'

—Desmond Tutu

Contents

INTRODUCTION

~

'Every movement is a kind of psychological warfare. It is also an individual battle—fought by human beings, with deeply personal longings and passions, no matter how small they may appear from outside. No political movement can be so overwhelming as to completely overshadow an individual and his or her emotional demands.'

Communist Party of India (Maoist) politburo member, Koteswar Rao, alias Kishanji, who spearheaded Maoist operations in West Bengal's Jangalmahal (the three districts of Purulia, Bankura and West Midnapore), was killed in an encounter with the police in the Burisole forest area of West Midnapore on November 24, 2011.

It's a long drive in unruly traffic and takes me past numerous dhabas where people eat hot and spicy egg curries with boiled rice and guzzle down bottles of beer to knock off the scorching heat. The road bends and narrows to become paths through green fields dotted with mud huts, until gradually the narrower earthen tracks navigate surreptitiously through forests.

I travel to homes on hilltops reached by negotiating sharp rocky paths. Homes from which the heady smell of mahua comes wafting through the air, until it blends with the smell of khichuri boiling on an earthen oven inside the compound of a primary school.

These are roads less travelled—red earth glowing in the sunlight at dusk, the full moon and quiet, star-studded nights, the busy cacophony of village bazaars, cow markets, rooster matches, football and hockey games being played on large swathes of greenery, long walks, pillion rides on two-wheelers over bumpy earthen tracks.

I visit homes where chickens run amok, crows caw on neem trees, cows, buffaloes and goats doze off in the summer heat, mud walls and wooden doors dazzle with colour and paintings. Herein lie entrenched the dreams and aspirations of the comrades and their families. I listen to tales of neglect and their morbid resignation to fate.

I meet some of these men and women, now removed from their previous lives in the forests where they were part of Maoist groups. I meet them in 'safe houses', in silent, cold rooms interrupted only by the hum of air conditioners. Here, these beautiful young men and women, dressed in smart trousers and shirts, or salwar-kameez, glittering bindis, dangling earrings, polished fuschia nails and red lipstick, talk about their dreams, about the excitement of falling in love and about the joy of becoming parents.

Then there are visits to dormitory rooms filled with pots and pans, sarees, shirts, undergarments and baby clothes, a radio playing in the background, the smell of breast milk and puffed rice.

Gurgling waterfalls, chirping birds, blaring horns from buses with people perched on top, criss-crossing small towns and quaint villages, the smell of marigold garlands and coconut oil, bumping along on dusty and rickety roads, the breathtaking beauty of rocky mountains, songs and dances by tribal women and men, the air filled with their giggles and full-throated laughter—this has been my journey, after I set out to listen to their stories.

* * *

The Naxal movement takes its name from Naxalbari block in West Bengal's Darjeeling district bordering Nepal. This area became the centre of a peasant uprising in the 1960s. India was then plagued by a severe food crisis. Starvation deaths were common and land was owned by a very small group of rich landlords. With such wide chasms between rich and poor, such sharp divisions in property and food distribution, the poor faced exploitation of the worst kind. There appeared to be no escape out of this rut.

On March 3, 1967, a group of peasants surrounded a plot of land in Naxalbari and, in a symbolic show of power, lifted the harvested paddy from the granary of the jotedar. The uprising continued for several months, marked by several similar incidents. A share-cropper was beaten up by the armed agents of a local landlord, which was followed by armed bands of men seizing the land and food grains.

It reached a flashpoint on May 24 when peasants armed with bows and arrows killed a police inspector.

The following day, an enormous police contingent swooped in on the protestors and gunned down eleven of them, including six women and two children.

This was, in a nutshell, the beginning of the Naxalbari movement. A group from the CPI(M)'s Siliguri unit, which included men like Charu Mazumdar and Kanu Sanyal, led from the front, along with Jangal Santhal who mobilized the tribals.

Subsequently, in 1969, this group split from the CPI(M) and formed the CPI(Marxist-Leninist). Mazumdar was hugely influenced by the revolution in neighbouring China brought about by Mao Tse-Tung and his army of peasants. He believed the situation around him was much the same as that in China, and it was important that the government should be overthrown by an armed, militant peasants' movement.

Soon, this Naxal movement became synonymous with an extremist movement which made exploitative landlords and policemen in different parts of the country fear rebellion from among the poor, landless and oppressed. A powerful armed protest against the unequal distribution of wealth, class divides and exploitation was thus born. It was the people's assertion of power against the oppressor state and rich landlords.

While the CPI(ML) was the original Naxalite party, the People's War Group (PWG) broke away from it in 1980 under the leadership of Kondapalli Seetharamiah. Its base was the Dandakaranya (now Chhattisgarh) where powerful guerilla armies were formed. Later though, the PWG merged with CPI(ML), Party Unity (PU) and Maoist Communist Centre (MCC) and this entity is now the Communist Party of India (Maoist). The words 'Maoists' and 'Naxalites' are used interchangeably even by the police and the Naxals themselves, as well as the media and in this book.

The Maoist movement took on many forms in different states such as Andhra Pradesh, Madhya Pradesh, Maharashtra, Chhattisgarh, Bihar, Jharkhand, West Bengal, Odisha, but it has always been linked with people's movements for the rights of the poor over land and forests. Over the years, it spawned various avatars and rippled across different parts of the country and often took extremely violent forms.

As recently as April 11 to April 13, 2015, thirteen-police personnel from the Chhattisgarh Special Task Force (STF), Border Security Force (BSF) and Chhattisgarh Armed Force (CAF) were killed in three separate incidents at Sukma, Kanker and Dantewada [one BSF jawan in Kanker, seven STF personnel from BSF at Sukma and five CAF personnel at Dantewada].[1] Eighteen heavy vehicles were set on fire by the Maoists. A Janmilitia Commander, Sori Rama, alias Kanna Karigumdam, surrendered and claimed that thirty-five Maoists had been killed in the battle between the STF and the Maoists in Bastar on April 11.[2]

Perhaps the deadliest massacre unleashed by the Maoists in the history of the movement in India was on April 6, 2010.[3] An ambush at Chintalnar in Chhattisgarh's Dantewada left seventy-four security personnel from the Central Reserve Police Force (CRPF) dead and another fifty injured. The attack took place when the police team was conducting, what in the armed forces' parlance is known as an 'area domination exercise' (a pre-emptive exercise that involves keeping a vigil over an area that makes the armed forces assert their power and authority so the Maoists would fear their presence and stay away). It was a planned attack executed to perfection by a 1000-strong Maoist force.

On May 25, 2013, Maoists attacked a convoy of Congress leaders in Chhattisgarh's Sukma, killing eighteen persons,[4] including former state minister Mahendra Karma (the Congress leader behind the infamous Salwa Judum initiative), Chhattisgarh Congress chief Nand Kumar Patel, and injuring former union minister VC Shukla (who died later).

In 2015, as reported by *The Indian Express*, on June 14,[5] the Ministry of Home Affairs (MHA), in reply to a right-to-information (RTI) query, said that over 15,000 people (including 12,177 civilians and 3,125 security personnel) had been killed in Naxal violence in nine states (Andhra Pradesh, Bihar, Chhattisgarh, Jharkhand, Madhya Pradesh, Maharashtra, Odisha, Uttar Pradesh and West Bengal) between 1980 and May 31, 2015.

State forces too have had their share of ruthless killing. The same report mentions that 4,768 Naxals were killed during this time. Between 2011 and 2016 (till June 30, 2016), 9,698 Naxals were arrested, according to the Ministry of Home Affairs.[6]

State terror in Chhattisgarh has been what nightmares are made of. The state, central governments and police unleashed the Salwa Judum in Dantewada in 2005. Tribal youths were armed and deployed through this vigilante group in the name of counter-insurgency and resistance to what was termed 'Naxal atrocities'. The Supreme Court declared it illegal in 2011,[7] but by then there had been rapes, killings and thousands of the poor had been left homeless, after their houses had been burnt. As of January 2007, according to official figures, 47,238 people were living in twenty Salwa Judum 'relief camps' or base camps as they were popularly called. Out of the 1354 villages in Dantewada district, a total 644 villages were affected by Salwa Judum.[8]

In November 2011,[9] the party's politburo member Koteswar Rao (alias Kishanji) was killed in an encounter in West Bengal (which was alleged to be fake),[10] dealing a severe blow to the movement in that state.

The Maoists have a major party meet every five years in which central, regional and state-level members participate. The ninth such party congress was held in 2007. (No party congress has been held since then, presumably due to the constant attacks on the CPI(Maoist) by the state forces.) In 2007, there were around forty central committee members and fourteen politburo members,[11] while in 2016, only eighteen central committee members and seven politburo members remain free.

According to a report of *The Economist* (in 2006), the Observer Research Foundation in Delhi was quoted saying that the Naxalites had 9000 to 10000 armed fighters with access to about 6500 firearms and perhaps a further 40,000 full-time cadres.[12] Similar figures were mentioned by other newspaper reports around this time, quoting other sources.[13] The number of cadres has come down since, and was said to be between 10000 to 20000 or less in 2013. A majority of cadres (approximately 60 per cent) are now women.[14] The number of members has been steadily reducing over the past few years.

But these mind-boggling numbers only begin to indicate the extent of the matter.

* * *

In the past five decades or so, the Naxal movement has undergone massive transformations—not just by adopting innovative and better use of technology, but also in their approach and tactics.

In their approach, there has been a shift from targeting individual exploitative landlords to causing large-scale violence in order to draw attention. Recent operations in Chhattisgarh also indicate that the Maoists have chased after and killed policemen, while earlier they focused on causing damage from a distance and fleeing. There is also more frequent use of technology (for example, the use of remotely triggered improvised explosive devices) and of innovative tactics to target a greater number of policemen (such as placing bombs behind Maoist posters or burying them underneath Maoist flags inserted in the ground).

This focus on large-scale killing is the most controversial aspect of the war—in fact, many within the CPI (Maoist) have quit the party over the years, saying they were perturbed by the scale of terror and killing. Some others I spoke to talked about how upset they were about the fact that 'the ultimate end is less of a priority'.

If the scale of war has increased, it has been so from both sides. Tactics used by the State have changed too. In the recent past, the central and state governments have been pumping in crores of rupees for what is being termed 'holistic development' of the backward areas where the CPI (Maoist) is active and where the movement is considered a 'threat'. The sheer volume of funds pouring in solely for security bandobast is instructive: apart from each state's funds, the Centre's allocation for 2014-15[15] was a whopping Rs 207.08 crore under the Security Related Expenditure (SRE) scheme, which reimburses states for funds spent on families of civilians/security forces killed in violence, the surrender of Naxals, training and operation of security personnel, community policing, 'security-related' infrastructure for village defence committees and so on.

In addition to this, the Scheme for Special Infrastructure (SSI), with Rs 445.82 crore released during the Eleventh Plan period (2008-09 to 2011-12), for closing 'critical infrastructure gaps' that cannot be covered under existing schemes, includes everything from upgradation of roads to preparing camping grounds, helipads, enhancing security and so on in the affected states. From 2013, the funds are shared by the Centre and the states on a 75 per cent: 25 per cent ratio, with an outlay of Rs 373 crore, "for upgradation of training infrastructure" (this scheme has been discontinued from 2015-16)[16]. Another of the Centre's ambitious plans has been to increase road connectivity in thirty-four 'Left Wing Extremism (LWE) affected' districts, building 5422 kilometres of road at the cost of Rs 8490 crore, according to the MHA's annual report of 2015-16. As of 31 December 2015, 3887 km of roads have been completed at the cost of Rs 5341 crore. The government is also planning construction of another 342 roads (5466.31km) and 126 bridges with an estimated Rs 1800 crore in 44 districts of nine "LWE affected states"[17].

There's also the sanction for building 400 'fortified police stations' in the core Maoist areas of ten states with Rs 2,00,00,000 for each police station. The plan has been operational since

2010. As of 31December 2015, 278 police stations have been completed and work on another 122 is under way (according to the Ministry of Home Affairs annual report of 2015-16). There is a plan for fortification of another 250 police stations in a second phase at Rs 2.5 crore per police station.[18] In August 2014, the plan for setting up mobile towers at 2199 locations in these same ten states was cleared by the government.[19]

Government plans for security forces have been massive—fifteen Counter Insurgency and Anti-Terrorist Schools (CIAT) for training police personnel have been set up; special anti-Maoist forces are being upgraded along the lines of the Greyhounds (a force under the Andhra Pradesh Police that specializes in anti-Naxal operations); thirty-six India Reserve (IR) battalions have been mobilized 'to provide gainful employment to the youth, particularly in the LWE affected areas', apart from ten Specialised India Reserved Battalions (SIRB) that will soon be set up in different states.[20]

The sheer number of police personnel deployed to fight the rebels is also jaw dropping: one hundred and sixteen battalions, including ten battalions of Commando Battalions for Resolute Action (CoBRA) and one Naga India Reserve battalion, of Central armed police force are assisting state forces in Chhattisgarh, Jharkhand, Bihar, Odisha, Andhra Pradesh, Telengana, Maharashtra, West Bengal, Madhya Pradesh and Uttar Pradesh.[21]

The situation has all the ingredients of a devastating war. Rocket launchers, grenades, state-of-the-art weapons, national and state level intelligence agencies in place, and debates on whether aerial bombing by the Army should be used to crush the rebels.

Finally, Rs 19.3 crore was allocated in 2015-16 for what the Ministry of Home Affairs, Government of India calls the 'successful Civic Action Programme (CAP)' that 'aims to build bridges between the local population and security forces'.

'Under CAP, efforts are made to project the human face of security forces so that they can win the hearts and minds of the people'.[22] The government also plans to make effective its other existing programmes such as the Pradhan Mantri Gram Sadak Yojana (PMGSY), National Rural Health Mission (NRHM), Ashram schools, Mahatma Gandhi National Rural Employment Guarantee Act (MGNREGA), Indira Awaas Yojana (IAY), Scheduled Tribes and Other Traditional Forest Dwellers (Recognition of Forest Rights) Act, 2006 and several others, in these areas.[23]

All this is 'to *wean away* the potential youth from the path of militancy or Left Wing Extremism' according to the MHA report from 2012-13. (Italics mine).[24] Terms such as 'weaning away' and 'Left Wing Extremism' are ingrained in the way the majority looks at the marginalized: this is how those who fight a war from a 'legitimate' platform view those whom they have declared outlaws. So it is not difficult to figure out why these terms are used so casually in government reports.

The State finds no dearth of justification for this war. It is interesting to note the MHA's observations in its annual report for 2012-13: 'There is a growing belief that the ideological paradigm offered by the CPI (Maoist) is completely out of sync with the aspirational matrix of present day Indian society and the world.'[25] In 2014-15[26] it went on to say:

'It is a belief of the government of India that through a combination of development and security related interventions, the LWE problem can be successfully tackled. However, it is clear that the Maoists do not want the root causes like under-development to be addressed in a meaningful manner since they resort to targeting school buildings, roads, railways, bridges, health infrastructure, communication facilities etc in a major way. They wish to keep the population in their areas of influence marginalized to perpetuate their outdated ideology. Consequently, the process of development has been set back by decades in many parts of the country under LWE influence. This needs to be recognized …to build pressure on the Maoists to eschew violence, join the mainstream and recognize the fact that that the socio-economic and political dynamics and aspirations of 21st century India are far removed from the Maoist world view.'

Many also question whether this alternate rule outside of democracy is acceptable to a nation where 66.4 per cent of the eligible voters, or 55.1 crore individuals, voted in the 2014 Lok Sabha polls.

Are the Maoists really not open to development? Why do they continue to use arms despite so much bloodshed? Abhay, spokesperson of the CPI (Maoist) Central Committee, said in a statement (a press release dated June 11, 2013) that:

'…The ruling classes are appealing to the youth to give up violence and pursue their goals through legitimate and democratic means… The glaring fact is that youth have taken up arms as a historic task of the oppressed masses to shape their future with their own hands relying on their own strength and their own people after decades of recurring and frustrating failure of the Indian State to respond to their usage of "legitimate and democratic means to gain their genuine demands and rights." Appealing to them to give up arms for "legitimate and democratic means" is not only putting things upside down but also a cruel joke. Youth have not taken up guns because they fancy them or in an atmosphere where there was no dearth of legitimate and democratic means or because they don't value democracy. It is quite the opposite.'

Why is there so much anger among the people living in and around the 'Maoist belts' of the country? That these are also mineral-rich areas, inhabited by the poorest of poor tribals is certainly a factor. These are the other reasons:

On 18 August 2015, writer-activist Arundhati Roy read out a note at a press conference at the Press Club of India, New

Delhi, to express solidarity with Soni Sori, Linga Kodopi and
the people of Bastar.[27] It said:

> '…the policeman who Soni Sori says supervised her torture—
> which included, among other things, pushing stones up her
> vagina—in police custody, was awarded a Police Gallantry
> Award by the President of India, on Republic Day in 2012.
> Many people were outraged and condemned this. Personally,
> given the state of affairs in this country, I thought it was an
> honest declaration of intent by the Indian State. I only wish
> the award citation had been honest too. In cases like this one,
> the citation could have said: "This Award is hereby conferred
> on Officer XYZ for bravely supervising the torture and sexual
> molestation of a dangerous Adivasi school teacher."'

She also went on to say:

> 'The mining companies are getting restless. The MOUs that
> were signed handing over Adivasi land to them have not
> been actualized because of the resistance from local people.
> Operation Green Hunt continues as Operation No-Name.
> The Salwa Judum is being re-constituted. Once again SPOs are
> beginning to kill villagers and call them Naxalites. Anybody
> who criticizes or impedes the implementation of State policy
> is called a Maoist. Thousands of Dalits and Adivasis, thus
> labeled, are in jail absurdly charged with crimes like Sedition
> and Waging War against the State under the Unlawful Activities
> Prevention Act (UAPA).'

Granted the reality of the State's use of torture and violence,
questions also need to be asked of those who have taken this
path of protest. This however, is not an argument that justifies
police action against villagers and the Maoists, nor does it
negate the State's motives behind usurping tribal land to set up
factories, coercive action against tribals, sham hearings, so-called
consent of poor tribals to giving up their land, and the overall
corporate influence on governance. But the pertinent questions
still remain: Has the violence always been only a matter of self-

defence? Would the Maoist movement in India have been more acceptable to the people in this country had the violence been scaled down? Most importantly, can violent action be continually justified simply because it is a 'reaction'?

The Maoists have been saviours to the poor and provided them with food, livelihood and security where the government failed to deliver. Those leading the movement set up schools, educated children and the youth, brought the poor together to grow crops, focused on healthcare, hygiene, drinking water and so on. This was hugely appealing in the most backward area— especially in the mountainous and forested Dandakaranya— where many villages remained outside the government's basic knowledge, much less intervention. This terrible apathy led them to join the Maoist movement during the 1980s and '90s. They were attracted to the Maoist ideology and its pledge for social service. To the lowest rung of cadres—the dedicated foot-soldiers—this was considered far more significant than the use of arms in the armed violence, perhaps because of the immediate, palpable change it brought into their lives.

However, it cannot be denied that now there is an overlap of revolutionary ideology and criminal activities. There are factions, clashes within the movement, murders (in the name of killing informers)— and these are some of the reasons cited by Maoist foot-soldiers for backing out of the war zone.

The nature of the Maoist leadership and recruitment have both undergone a sea change as well. At its inception, the movement was primarily strengthened by the urban intelligentsia. Educated youth from Kolkata's colleges and universities joined the movement to fight for the rights of the poor, leaving behind the prospect of bright careers and the comfort of home. But the armed Maoist soldiers fighting this war now are a different kind of soldier, many of whom have even had associations with crime and the underworld.

In 2005, in Andhra Pradesh, Kadapa-Anantapur district

committee member Bathala Aruna—alias Jyothi and Bharathakka—who had surrendered before the police, said she was worried the Maoists were admitting cadres solely on the basis of acquaintance and did not bother much about their commitment and philosophy (*The Hindu*, October 23, 2005).[28] There is also evidence of forceful recruitment, by the Maoists.

Questions have been raised on the method of levy collection—how demands often turn into extortion. Finally, there is strife within the party ranks, with breakaway factions and groups being formed, just as in other political parties.

In this war, a majority of those killed are themselves the poorest of the poor—whether they are tribals from forest and mineral belts, those living in villages, towns or part of the police contingent. It would be foolish to dismiss all these deaths as collateral damage in the war. If one cares to visit the homes of jawans who died in this war, one would see that there is not much of a difference between the homes of slain Naxals and the police jawans. How then can the killing of thousands working in the armed forces by the Maoists be justified? On the other hand, the top leaders from both sides remain untouched by the brutality of the war. This has been the argument of some Maoist soldiers themselves.

On the other side of the issue, what of those children whose parents were killed by policemen, women who have been raped by the armed forces, and others who have nowhere to place their valid demands? Can they still vent their anger through non-violent means? Maoist ideologue Varavara Rao asked me to always remember that there is a difference between Gandhians and Maoists. 'This is an armed protest, an armed struggle,' he said, making it a very open and shut case about the violent path being a given in this struggle for justice. Under the circumstances, is it even valid to argue a case against violence?

As for a nation where the death penalty still exists, what else can be expected of a government other than crushing a movement through violent means?

As one gets embroiled in this argument, perhaps the only valid ground for debates, questions and opinions come from the fact that those who had once taken up the armed struggle are themselves rejecting this path. Had this path not thrown up ethical and moral questions they could not themselves answer, or shown stumbling blocks that they hadn't foreseen, would these soldiers have given it up?

What are the reasons behind armed guerillas rejecting guns? Those who were not left with any option but to be part of an armed war—why now are these people giving up the violent path? Does it have something to do with the failure and/or irrelevance of the movement? Or is it simply the success of the government and police that they have been able to win the psychological war?

* * *

Every movement is a kind of psychological warfare. It is also an individual battle. After all, it is being fought by human beings, with deeply personal longings and passions—no matter how small they may appear from outside, no matter how inconsequential it may seem in the momentous war. No political movement can be so overwhelming as to completely overshadow an individual and his or her emotional demands. If, at the core of it, a movement needs to suppress or kill these emotional longings, then those at the helm need to remember that such a movement can only be for a chosen few. Extreme personal and emotional sacrifices along with intense dedication for an uncertain and prolonged period cannot be demanded from a vast group of people. It might work only when there are no alternatives in sight. But if there are alternatives, then the soldiers will quietly slip away.

In such a situation, it would be easy for the State to find quick-fix solutions by spending a few crores to get some people to surrender and fulfill these cravings of the heart: buy a plot, build a house, get a salaried job, get married, have children, send them to English medium schools, look after aged parents and above all, lead a life outside the eye of the storm. However superficial, however short-lived, the lure of money can make a difference when what you can buy with that money is happiness. After all, neither the State nor the Maoists have ever focused on the individuals prior to the armed clashes.

This raw nerve has been touched by the government through its 'surrender scheme'. What the State has long denied the individual, and what the Maoists never addressed, has become the main thrust of a government programme. People who never got enough to eat, are being given Rs 2,50,000 and jobs with monthly pay ranging between Rs 10,000 to Rs 20,000, as well as government quarters to live in. At first glance, it may be too difficult to resist.

An individual's decision is also an important factor simply because we all demand love, respect and want to be treated equally. No matter who we are, no matter how little we matter to the rest of the world. I think it is very important to look at individuals in order to understand a movement. That is what I have tried to focus on in this book. I have looked at how an individual felt about the movement when she or he joined the Naxalites. In many cases, it was not to fight injustice, not to bring equality in the society where the individual lived, not to prevent the government from taking over their land, but to escape the suffering from hunger at home. Some individuals turned to the Maoist movement because of the prospect of regular meals at the squads when there was never enough to eat at home. This was not always the case, but certainly there were many who felt that way.

And what exactly happened when they were in the squads? They got to eat, and in addition, the guns handed to them made them feel empowered. But after the initial novelty wore off, the person gradually grew detached from the movement, often for very simple reasons. These were, in many cases, episodes that had hurt their pride. Under the circumstances, they became all the more aware of the fact that neither the State nor the

Naxalites were their friend. And that the only friends were just other individuals like themselves—their parents or spouse or children. It is in this manner that the personal won over the political and individual equations became far more central to the lives of these soldiers than the larger war they had set off to fight. In many cases, they were not even aware of the larger war they were fighting.

There is an anguish that comes from feeling small against those who want to assert their superiority—whether in terms of money, class, caste and so on—and that creates a detachment. It would be wrong to think that innocent villagers have felt angry and hurt only due to police torture. Not getting the same kind of food that a senior colleague is served might have made a junior cadre angry. The anger may not have led him to give up arms and surrender immediately, but it hurt his pride, the anger kept simmering till he no longer wanted to remain in the group.

Maoists are not jehadis. They do not have suicide squads. Therefore, the dedication and commitment is far less than the fervour and spirit of those who fight against the State or broadly, a system, on religious grounds. Whether this lack of extreme dedication is due to the leaders' incapability to inspire the recruits adequately, or whether the ultimate end proposed by the CPI (Maoist) leadership is a bit fuzzy, is for the top Maoist leaders to analyse.

Through my interviews, I have constantly seen that this 'lack' of commitment has led the soldiers astray. They have been easy to woo by the State. Some admitted their lack of interest in the movement, said they were fatigued and expressed fear of death now that they are no longer part of the movement. What is there instead, is a desperate urge to live and to savour life.

This book is about the lives of those who are no longer part of the Maoist movement. It is the stories of Maoists who have 'surrendered' and/or drifted away from the movement. I have looked at their personal lives in order to figure out the whys. It also includes the story of someone who had worked closely with the Maoists as a part of a frontal organization and would prefer not to be identified as a Maoist. I could see the person's apprehension (like many of her colleagues based in cities) that the Maoist tag could ruin lives forever in the 'legitimate' world.

* * *

Surrenders have been taking place for decades now, but it was around 2009 that the central and state governments began to discuss a major increase in the compensation package. Since April 1, 2013, the Centre introduced 'Guidelines for surrender-cum-rehabilitation scheme of Left-wing extremists in the affected states'[29] prepared by the Union Ministry for Home Affairs, from which, it suggested, the states could take cues from. Most states have subsequently altered their own schemes and issued notifications.

According to the Centre's guidelines, its twin objectives are '*to wean away* the hardcore LWE cadres who have *strayed* into the fold of the LWE movement and now find themselves *trapped in that net*,' [italics mine], and also, 'to ensure that the LWE cadres who surrender do not find it attractive to join the LWE movement again'.

According to the MHA, the scheme has been introduced, 'keeping in mind the specific geographical and social landscape to help those Left Wing Extremists who want to abjure violence, surrender and join the mainstream. It is part of a multi-pronged conflict management and resolution strategy and is required to be implemented along with firm legal action by the police against those who follow the path of violence. The scheme will aim at providing gainful employment and entrepreneurial opportunities to the surrendered LWEs so that they are encouraged to join the mainstream and do not return to the fold of the LWE movement'.

Under the scheme, a grant of Rs 2,50,000 is offered to state committee members, regional committee members, central committee members and politburo members. Rs 1,50,000 is for area commanders, sub-zonal commanders, zonal commanders, or anyone selected as a hardcore Maoist by the state screening-cum-rehabilitation committee. The offered money is kept as a fixed deposit in a bank for three years and can be withdrawn after that by the person who has surrendered. This however, is subject to 'good behaviour' certified by the State. The money may also be kept as collateral security against which loans for self-employment are taken. The sum however, varies in different states, as it is the state governments which ultimately implement the scheme.

There are incentives for the surrender of arms as well, that range from Rs 35000 for LMG (light machine guns), GPMG (general purpose machine guns), pika, RPG (rocket propelled grenade), sniper rifles, rocket launchers and similar weapons; Rs 25000 for AK-47, 56, 74 rifles and Rs 10000 for pistols, revolvers, SLR (self-loading rifle), carbines, Sten guns, .303 guns. Other categories include explosives, remote control devices, improvised explosive devices (IEDs), mines, wireless sets, satellite phones, detonators, grenades and so on—anything and everything the Maoists use for operations against security personnel can be exchanged during surrender for money. Here too, the sum varies across states.

The guideline also says that those who surrender will be lodged in a rehabilitation camp where they will be offered training according to what they choose or have an aptitude for, and meanwhile get a monthly stipend of Rs 4,000 for thirty-six months. If a surrendered rebel gets a government job before these months elapse, then the stipend is discontinued.

Across the country, an estimated 300 Maoists have been surrendering on an average almost every year since the 1990s. The surrenders were mostly from Andhra Pradesh. Before the guideline was introduced by the Centre in 2013 and states implemented their own 'rehabilitation packages' roughly around the same time, the compensation was very little, and most surrendered Maoists usually got small plots and/or tractors for them to earn a livelihood. At the time, the money offered on surrender varied between Rs 5000 and Rs 20,000 depending on whether they had arms to offer as well. Now, the 'incentive package' has been increased many times over, even if it varies marginally from one state to another.

The Maharashtra and Chhattisgarh governments have each announced Rs 1,00,00,000 reward on the CPI (Maoist) general secretary Ganapathy. Andhra Pradesh has a reward of Rs 25,00,000, Jharkhand government Rs 12 lakh and the National Investigation Agency (NIA) Rs 15 lakh (*Mail Online India*, 2014).[30] Anyone providing the state(s) with information that leads to his arrest gets that amount. It also means that when a person surrenders she or he gets the amount announced as reward plus the amount one would get for the surrender.

Chhattisgarh and Andhra Pradesh governments have announced rewards for surrender of top Maoist leaders. The highest reward is Rs 25,00,000 for a central committee member, Rs 20,00,000 for state committee members or special zonal committee members, Rs 8,00,000 for district committee secretaries and Rs 1,00,000 for squad members.

As recently as in 2014, Andhra Pradesh Police offered Rs 20,00,000 to GVS Prasad alias Gudsa Usendi, spokesperson of the CPI (Maoist) Dandakaranya Special Zonal Committee who surrendered in January along with his wife, Santoshi Markam. Prasad is from Warangal district of Andhra Pradesh while his wife is from Kondagaon in Chhattisgarh.[31]

Otherwise, the immediate grant varies between Rs 2,50,000 (Jharkhand/Odisha) to Rs 1,50,000 (West Bengal), the monthly stipend varying between Rs 2,000 to Rs 4,000 per month (West Bengal) to Rs 3,000 (Jharkhand).

* * *

In this book, I have focused on the stories of those who surrendered, the reasons that led to the surrender and their lives afterwards. I have also taken a close look at the methods and context of the surrenders.

The surrender of Maoist soldiers has become a major cause

of worry for the Maoist top leadership. In an interview for the *Maoist Information Bulletin* (reported in *The Indian Express*, April 19, 2015),[32] CPI (Maoist) general secretary, Muppala Lakshman Rao, alias Ganapathi, has said, 'More than three-fourth of the mass surrenders are due to targeting of active cadres by means such as severe torture, rape, destruction of property, psychological warfare, threat to kill or maim etc.' The report quotes Ganapathi saying that the People's Liberation Guerilla Army (PLGA) and mass organizations 'are kneeling before the enemy. Yes, there is increase in such numbers (of surrenders) recently and a few from state, district and area committee levels have also surrendered.'

As a solution, the general secretary of the CPI (Maoist) called for 'supreme sacrifice' at all levels and expansion of the movement to newer areas and strengthening their presence in existing areas.

Those that have surrendered felt 'free' to talk about the darker side of their association with the CPI (Maoist)—they could talk about disgruntlement, worries and anger among the cadres about the movement and its future. A few rose up to the middle level in the party hierarchy and all of them present a counter-narrative to the glorified view of the Maoist life. I believe this counter-narrative, through the stories of those who have moved away from the battlefield, is important as it can give a detached and more balanced view to understand the movement.

There are also people who surrendered, yet did not opt for the government money on offer because they were afraid they might be killed by their former Maoist colleagues. What happened to these people? Why did they surrender? What was it, if not the money, that made them leave that life behind? I try to explore all these reasons as well.

Why do surrenders take place? How much is a surrender a matter of 'choice'? A large number of surrenders are, in fact, arrests. Journalists know this from their police sources.

According to a former member of the Maoists' Kolkata City Committee, it is primarily due to intense police/State pressure.

He alleged that the arrested are routinely stripped naked (whether male or female), and physical torture is not uncommon (to put it mildly). After a point, this pressure can get to you. In the depths of forests where those at the receiving end are poor, illiterate tribals, the torture is many times more cruel and intense. It is tough to stand up against the enormous State power, and even more difficult to continue the fight.

Then there are other reasons such as differences of opinion on various issues (discussed at length later in this book), fatigue and the urge to get back to a normal life. A changed political scenario—especially a change in the seat of power—may also contribute to surrenders, as has been the case in West Bengal. Some have simply left behind the life of an armed soldier because of the anguish of painfully long absences from home. Some others could not justify the violence. There were also those who were lured by the State's offer of money, but along with it there was also the desire to live a quiet and peaceful life with their loved ones. Usually it is not just one of these above factors, but more than one that contribute to a person's decision in surrendering.

One of the important things for me to look at was not just the feelings of each person immediately after surrender, but how they felt about the movement a few years after drifting away from it. Did they get what they were looking for? Is that all they can hope for? Are they terribly disappointed? If so, why?

At the same time, I question whether the security issues of surrendered Maoists have been addressed by the states that have publicized the surrender schemes. Does the loss of a few lives even matter to the government?

Despite 'surrendering before police', some former cadres narrated stories of police violence, explained what had led them to take up arms, and the pains of surrendering before the same brutal police force.

A surrendered Maoist in Chhattisgarh, whom I met at Kondagaon, told me that the camaraderie in Maoist camps is often a bit of a sham that is put on display during visits by writers and journalists. The milieu is hardly as equal, fair and congenial when the visitors have left, he said. It is a bit like our family secrets and clashes being hidden under the carpet when we have guests at home. But these secrets do exist.

I leave it to the readers to decide which of the versions they would choose as *real*. To me these are different versions of the same story seen from different perspectives. The narratives here are simply the view from the eyes of those who otherwise matter little to this world, and who are caught up in a deadly war.

* * *

I have interviewed Maoists who were operating in different parts of Chhattisgarh, West Bengal, Odisha and Maharashtra. I also travelled to Bihar and Jharkhand hoping to talk to some of the surrendered Maoists there, but was denied access to the surrendered persons by those who had 'control' over them: the police. But the travels helped me understand the various dimensions of the Naxalite movement and the way it differs in different states.

In all the cases, I took pains to talk to the surrendered cadres one-on-one unless language became a problem (which it was to an extent in Odisha, where I spoke to them through interpreters when it became difficult to understand each other). I kept in touch with them after the interviews were over, and called on the phone to find out how they were doing. In most cases, they weren't doing very well.

To me, the narratives are human stories that tell us about the plight of being poor in a growing economy governed by majoritarian politics. It is about the futility of the poor and the tribals' very existence in a country where they are always afterthoughts in policymaking. I look primarily at the concerns and worries of ordinary cadres who belong to the lowest rung in the party hierarchy; the lives of those poor women, men and children who had once joined the movement but are now disenchanted.

Part I

THE YOUNG ONES

~

'When battles are fought, its reins are in the hands of experienced leaders; and the young ones are hardly aware of the larger picture. Suman told me that many youngsters like him were shocked at how the movement unfolded before their eyes. "It wasn't the simple, straightforward battle of good versus evil that I had perceived it to be," he said. "I had joined the war thinking I was part of the sea of poor people fighting the cruel government, but I soon found out that there were shades of grey in this conflict."'

This picture has been taken from a video shot inside a camp by a Maoist cadre. The boy playfully aims the gun at the person shooting the video. This boy is said to have once pulled the trigger and killed a cop but there is no confirmation on this.

1

Suman Maity (alias Saontha)

It's early November. There's a slight nip in the air, and people are lazing about with their first cup of tea—the sweet, milky, thick tea popular in large parts of rural India. Somewhere in the distance, there are rows of mud huts with thatched roofs and saal trees.

Here, within Lalgarh police station, where I had spent the night in a tiny, eight ft. by seven ft. room, new living quarters for police personnel are being constructed. Cement, sand, stone chips, bricks lie scattered around. It is on its way to becoming a 'fortified' police station under a central government scheme where Rs 2,00,00,000 is being spent per police station. Or perhaps it is being done up with state government funds, I am not sure, but there is a lot of activity all around to enhance its security.

True, it is less a police station and more a fortress: the boundary wall is nearly twelve feet high with the additional buffer of barbed wires; these are further covered with aluminium sheets, making it impossible for anyone to catch a glimpse of the station from outside. On top of either side of an enormous iron gate—the main entrance—there are watch towers guarded round the clock by armed policemen.

Inside, there is a tiny temple in one corner of the clean, earthen compound. Where life exists on the brink of death, prayers are somewhat of a necessity. If nothing else can, surely divine miracles should be able to save the policemen from a Maoist attack?

Lalgarh, 180 kilometres from Kolkata, is a cluster of 118 small villages in the West Midnapore district of West Bengal. It had been in the national headlines in 2008. A CPI (Maoist)-led agitation against the then Left Front government in West Bengal, had created a virtual 'liberated zone' here. Tribal villages over a 300 sq. km area had become heavily armed with bows, sickles, arrows and a huge back up of sophisticated and indigenous firearms. Lalgarh had geared up for an armed confrontation with the State. And a war did take place—a protracted, bloody war whose scars have not faded completely yet.

Armed Maoist cadres who were already living in the forests and trying to create a major impact for over a decade were finally successful in creating a free zone in Lalgarh. Roads were destroyed, government vehicles were burnt and hundreds of villagers took up arms and voluntarily joined the Maoists in an enormous show of protest against the Left Front government's apathy and misrule.

This continued till the death of CPI (Maoist) politburo member Koteswar Rao (alias Kishanji) in November 2011. In this time the Naxal movement was the most successful it had ever been in West Bengal since the Naxalbari upsurge of the 1960s. Between 2009 and 2011, in West Midnapore district alone, forty police personnel, twenty-six Maoists and 276 civilians were killed, twenty-five civilians and eight policemen were kidnapped, sixty arms were looted from police and 122 firearms were snatched and looted from common people (this last figure alone indicates how many licensed arms civilians had been carrying). During this time, over 1,100 Maoists were arrested and nearly 500 arms were seized by policemen—what is known as 'police recovery'.

The Left Front government—led by then Chief Minister Buddhadeb Bhattacharjee—grappled in the dark seeking the perfect plan to win the war against the Maoists. But it is never easy to overpower a movement that has the support of ordinary people and the Left Front that had ruled West Bengal for over three decades, had become unpopular (the 2011 election results were soon going to confirm this) and cut off from the people. Their leaders were unable to take firm decisions for fear of further losing their domination. Things went out of control, especially because the opposition Trinamool Congress was breathing down its neck. The Trinamool Congress was at its most powerful and popular since its inception and was backing the people's agitation that also had the support of the CPI (Maoist). It was the perfect recipe for a disastrous end to the thirty-four years of continuous Left rule in West Bengal.

The Left Front government had earlier introduced a 'rehabilitation' scheme for the surrender of the CPI (Maoist) cadres, taking its cue from other states. But it was no surprise that this had few takers in 2010. Once the Trinamool Congress came to power in Bengal, it wasn't long before the ruling party and the Maoists drifted apart, and soon the relationship turned bitter. CPI (Maoist) politburo member Kishanji was killed in an encounter with the police, and the Maoist movement began to lose steam in Bengal. It was from here on, that Maoist cadres began to lay down arms, and surrenders followed one after another.

A year from Kishanji's death, when I spent the night inside Lalgarh police station, it wasn't the same volatile place that I had visited a couple of years earlier while reporting on the agitation as a journalist. This time, I was going to meet a teenage boy who was living in the police quarters just opposite the Lalgarh police station.

It was morning and this boy was getting dressed to leave his 'home', the police quarters, for a few hours. He had been up at the crack of dawn and had studied for two hours at the tiny reading table in his room. Then he took a bath, performed puja, and grabbed a quick breakfast of ruti-torkari (chapati and curry). Dressed in smart blue denims, a white full-sleeved shirt, with an orange tilak on the forehead, seventeen-year-old Suman was ready to head out for tuition classes. With acne marks on his chubby face, sharp eyes and a smile that appeared every few minutes, he looked every bit like a teenager one might encounter in any village or small town in the country. But the story of his life was the stuff edge-of-the-seat thrillers are made of.

Even for the 300-metre stretch from the Lalgarh police station to his tuition classes, he had to ride pillion on a two-wheeler driven by a brawny policeman. The man's job was to protect the youngster, who could not step out of his tiny room without a police escort. These elaborate arrangements had been made because Suman's life was under threat. But smiling an endearing smile, he said he wanted to believe that his life now was much better than the past few years.

In the police records, he was a former Maoist sub-zonal commander in West Midnapore. His best known alias was Saontha. When I sifted through a bunch of papers, I could see glimpses of that past life—a black-and-white picture of a thin, strong lad whose tired eyes looked accusingly at the camera. There is rage, not fear in the sharp eyes. Now, when I sat next to him (he had come to meet me inside the police station premises), I could see that the anger had somewhat mellowed.

As a young boy of thirteen, Suman had given up his family, friends and school and become an armed Maoist cadre. He was quick to transform himself into an exceptional and brave soldier who rose through the ranks due to his unusual courage and intelligence. He became part of the innermost circle and a constant companion of Kishanji, the power centre of the Maoist movement in Bengal for close to a decade.

* * *

Suman's story would be impossible to tell without travelling several years back in time. The place: a village in Lalgarh. The year: sometime in 2006.

Suman's father, a sharecropper, would travel ten kilometres on a bicycle every day to work on a two bigha plot and his mother worked at home all day. Suman and his younger brother went to school and were doing well in studies. They lived a hand-to-mouth life, but still, those were blissful days, Suman told me, as we settled down to have a long chat. He resorted to that smile every now and then—it gave him the confidence to go on talking about his anguish and distress without giving in to tears.

'I was good in studies. But we were so poor, my brother and I continued to wear our old shorts even when we were quite tall because our parents couldn't afford full length trousers for us. I used to wear shorts to school even in class eight,' Suman says, blushing. 'I used to feel shy, but then, there were some others like me at school too. You see, most people in the area were quite poor.'

Things changed dramatically overnight when his father had contested an election in Suman's school for a guardian's forum as a Jharkhand Party candidate. In highly politicized West Bengal, battle lines were immediately drawn as it meant direct confrontation with the powerful ruling party, the CPM.

There are allegations that one of the clever strategies adopted by supporters and members of the CPM, then the ruling party in Bengal, was to lodge 'false' complaints against those who opposed them politically. This form of intimidation always helped the ruling party nip almost every form of opposition in the bud. Therefore, it didn't come as a surprise that a case was slapped against Suman's father—a false one, he says. 'Around this time, my father went out of town on work for several months, because the paddy cultivated seasonally was not enough for a family of four people. We had no idea where he was. We only knew that he hadn't fled, he was keeping track of the court proceedings and promised to be back before the next hearing,' Suman recalled.

But, one night, there was loud knocking and kicks on the wobbly door of their house. 'We are policemen. Where's your father?' the men at the door yelled. 'How do we know you are cops?' asked Suman, shivering with fear, but trying to show he wasn't buckling under pressure. He felt that CPM goons had come along with the police to ensure they were sufficiently terrorized.

The door had to be opened—there was hardly an option—and then the torture began. All he could see initially in the dark were human figures flashing torch lights into their scared, groggy eyes. Suman was slapped and kicked. Worse, his mother was kicked by policemen and pushed onto the floor right in front of his eyes. The boy was numb with disbelief.

'That did it. I began to hate policemen so much, that every moment of my life since then, I wondered how I could avenge the insult. I was plotting and planning, but didn't know how to strike back. We were innocent people, how could policemen humiliate us like that?' he said.

Around this time in Lalgarh, a potent 'movement' was brewing. Maoists had already been making inroads in the area for several years, but they were looking for that one opportunity that would give this movement a shot in the arm.

An IED blast along Chief Minister Buddhadeb Bhattacharjee's convoy on 2 November 2008 changed everything in Jangalmahal forever. The Chief Minister was headed back to Kolkata from the foundation stone laying ceremony of a steel plant to be set up by Jindal Steel Works (JSW), for which the company had signed a Rs 35,000 crore investment agreement with the West Bengal government for 10 million tonnes of steel and a captive power plant in Salboni.[1] Union ministers Ram Vilas Paswan, Jitin Prasad, and West Bengal commerce and industries minister Nirupam Sen were also part of the convoy. Though all of them escaped unscathed, six policemen were injured and some vehicles were damaged. It was a symbolic show of strength by the Maoists and a protest against setting up of a steel plant in the tribal dominated region.

The police reacted extremely aggressively to the blast. The raids that followed this episode involved inhuman torture. A woman, Chhitamoni Murmu, was blinded in one eye by a policeman, and she, along with ten other women were abused and beaten up during a police raid on November 6, 2008.[2] A one-member committee consisting of IAS officer R.D. Meena was set up several months later by the Bengal government. It concluded that police had indeed committed excesses on eleven women.[3]

The Maoist movement began to gather momentum and became inseparable from the 'people's movement' from here on. Hundreds like Suman were waiting for a strong support system that could help them avenge the CPM's bullying and torture, while the Maoists had been looking for the right opportunity to get their movement on track. Hundreds of people joined in, destroying roads, taking up arms against police and state administration. The anger had been simmering due to years of neglect and deprivation, and police atrocities added fuel to that fire, till it became a raging, volatile and powerful movement. Women, men and children took to the streets, arrows and sickles in hand, closing down roads with tree trunks, setting government vehicles on fire. Entry of any government functionary was forbidden.

A committee—the People's Committee Against Police Atrocities (PCPA)—was soon formed by the local residents of Lalgarh and beyond. With the Maoists' support in this people's movement, the PCPA soon came to be identified as a frontal organization of the CPI (Maoist) party and the difference between the PCPA and the CPI (Maoist) in the specific context of this movement became more and more blurred.

Suman was one of these hundreds of people who had absolutely no doubt about which side to take. 'No one had approached me. And frankly, I think in the Lalgarh movement, the Maoists did not have to coax people or plead for their support. It came from within. Women who had nothing to cook in their kitchens, men waiting in fields to get some work, the older lot depressed and resigned to fate—for most people, the support to Maoists came naturally,' he said. 'For me, this was an opportunity to take my revenge on the police for what they did to me and my mother. But I was frustrated because even as I had heard many were joining the Maoist movement, I did not know how to contact them. No one had approached me till then.

'Then, one day, one of my classmates asked me, "Tui Mao-badi-te jabi?" (Will you join the Maoists?). It was a phrase common among men, women and the youngsters of Lalgarh and adjoining areas around that time. I promptly agreed, and was taken to a place called Kumarbandh, where I stayed for a week. But they (the Maoists) did not enlist me. Disheartened, I went back home.'

But he was obsessed with the thought. 'My blood was boiling. I saw the situation as a golden opportunity to take my revenge against the police. I didn't want to come back. And since I knew their adda (den), I went there again. This time, I got lucky,' Suman recalled.

Suman was inducted and asked to begin training immediately. A rigorous training session began for the sixteen-year-old. It also meant that he could no longer stay at home. 'I stopped going to school, and my parents objected. Since I had always been a good student, my parents could not accept that I would drop out from school and involve myself in an armed war. But I was determined.'

From physical exercise to arms training, Suman went through it all. Just as he was a topper in school, he did well here too, and rose quickly in the ranks—from a novice to sub-zonal commander in Lalgarh and Salboni in no time.

'No state power can beat the Maoists in the psychological war. They (Maoists) work so passionately and live through such hardship, that their side automatically has an edge because at the core of the movement, there is dedication and selflessness. That means half the battle is won,' said Suman. 'And the common people's support is heartwarming. I have seen women carrying cooked rice and vegetables wrapped in plastic packets hidden inside their blouse, travelling miles to deliver the food to Maoist cadres. How can the police expect to win this battle that has so much love from the ordinary people?'

Inside the forests, there was the fear of poisonous snakes, insects and rats. Herds of wild elephants also move through the forests on the same route as the Maoists (from Purulia's Dalma hills to West Midnapore). Add to that the constant fear of policemen. There were times when only half a litre of water saved in a bottle was available for washing. They slept under the open sky most of the time, and, during monsoons the tents were likely to be swept away by the torrential downpour, so they had to be set up in a particular way. They also had to prevent water from seeping into plastic sheet 'beds'. Extreme weather, miles of walking every day, pangs of hunger—it was not easy.

'The Maoists had such huge support of the common people! Some of the poorest villagers would go through great pains to feed and protect us and informed us whenever police came in the vicinity—the work I did was dangerous and physically tiring, but still very fulfilling.'

Suman was brave and dedicated. He rose to the top very fast, and became one of the closest aides of Kishanji like Badal, Sushen and Sukanta. Suman, Badal and Sushen were sub-zonal commanders of Salboni, Lalgarh and Kotayali, while Sukanta was the zonal commander of the same area. 'I had many aliases. I was very smart—wherever I went, I took different names,' he smiled. Though only seventeen years old, Suman had already lived many lives, taken up many identities. The most popular of these names was Saontha, and it soon became a name people took notice of—for he was ruthless, cunning and spared no one. Those who feared the Maoists the most around this time, were the CPM men, especially the party's armed goons—who came to be known as *harmad bahini* (robbers).

In the forested regions of West Midnapore, Saontha was a terror. According to the police, he had led attacks on many police outposts, including one at Pirakata in 2009. Among the major attacks of which he was a part were two incidents in October 2009 and February 2010.

In October 2009, the officer in charge of Sankrail police station in West Midnapore, Atindranath Dutta, was abducted and a bank was looted by the Maoists.[4] Sub-inspector Diwakar Bhattacharya and assistant sub-inspector Swapan Ray were shot dead when they put up a fight. The Sankrail officer-in-charge (OC) was tied up and taken hostage. The police station was ransacked and firearms including rifles, revolvers and pistols were looted from the armoury. The Maoists demanded that fifteen tribal women who had been arrested earlier be freed if the state were to have the OC back. Finally the tribal women were released on bail by the Jhargram court, after which the Maoists set the OC free. This incident showed the enormous power wielded by the Maoists in the West Midnapore area around 2009. Suman was alleged to be one of the key players in this incident. While it is not clear whether he was himself present during the attack, Suman was part of the group of Maoists that released the OC. Suman's face was covered with a *gamcha* (a piece of cloth) during this time.

On February 15, 2010, one of the most violent attacks on the police in Bengal took place. In the attack on Eastern Frontier Rifles (EFR)'s camp by the Maoists, twenty-four jawans were killed.[5] Suman was alleged to be part of the team behind this attack as well, though he himself does not admit this. Apart from this, he is said to be involved in incidents of killing of several people in Jangalmahal though, again, he himself denies all this.

Despite the show of power and authority, and the fun of the

guns, the war presented another ugly side to Suman as well. It was not too long before he was ravaged by the fickleness of the adults, the cruelty of policemen, and deserted by those he considered friends.

When battles are fought, its reins are in the hands of experienced leaders; and the young ones are hardly aware of the larger picture. Suman told me that many youngsters like him were shocked at how the movement unfolded before their eyes. 'It wasn't the simple, straightforward battle of good versus evil that I had perceived it to be,' he said. 'I had joined the war thinking I was part of the sea of poor people fighting the cruel government, but I soon found out that there were shades of grey in this conflict.

'I was shocked to see that in tough situations when the police got wind of our movement and location, the seniors in our group escaped without informing us and left the young boys to fend for themselves. No one knew where those leaders vanished,' he recalled. 'And when the crisis was over, they were back without a hint of guilt. They never apologized either.

'It was shock and disbelief first. Then the negative thoughts grew on me. I wanted to run away from it all. But by then it was too late. I even feared dwelling on these thoughts because if anyone got a hint of what was going on in my mind, they would surely have killed me.'

* * *

One night in the summer of 2011, Suman and his comrades—Sukanta, his wife Kabita, Sachin, Bheem, Ashok and Subhas—were walking through the forests of Bagghora, all of them carrying rifles—carbines, SLRs, AK-47s.

Bheem was a bit unwell, so he took shelter at a house. The other six kept walking through the forest. But even as they were moving stealthily, all of them could sense danger around. They had a hunch that the armed forces were patrolling the area and it would be extremely risky to walk through the forests for too long.

It was pitch dark when they decided to stop for the night and set up tents. Crossing a village to move on to the next stretch of forest was too dangerous. They would be spotted and their presence would not remain secret anymore. Therefore the safest bet would be to camp right there.

Accordingly, two tents were set up. One of the six was on sentry duty and the rest quickly went off to asleep. Suddenly, towards dawn, Suman woke up—'in fact, all of us awoke almost simultaneously'—with the sound of footsteps on dry leaves. 'We froze.'

It took a few seconds to regain composure and then all of them put their hands on the triggers of their guns. 'There were three pairs of footsteps coming in a straight line a few metres ahead of us. How had the security forces come so close to our tents? This was impossible, we thought!'

They now feared that a few torches lit at night may have been a giveaway. 'It was time to fire. We took our positions—in a row one after the other. We started firing, but no one fired back. It was weird to say the least. In a moment, we realized, that the footsteps were that of a group of wild boars! Three wild boars had walked slowly towards our camp sensing that there were people which meant they could find some food.'

A sense of relief dawned on them as the first rays of light shone from behind the trees. It was the start of another day, and they hoped there would be no new danger till they reached the destination.

But to his horror, Suman saw that terrible damage had been done. 'I found blood on my hands and clothes. Had I been injured in the firing from the guns by our own people?' In a moment, he figured that it was not him, but Ashok who had been injured. He was bleeding profusely as a bullet had pierced his knee and come out from the other end. In the first few seconds, Ashok himself hadn't realized it. 'It had been shot from a gun from one of our teammates who was aiming at the wild boars.

A few seconds later Ashok slumped onto the ground and began groaning in pain.'

What should they do now? The wild boars had vanished and there was no immediate threat. But Ashok had to be treated by a doctor as quickly as possible.

'All of a sudden, Subhas alerted me—he nudged me and whispered into my ears that Sukanta, Kabita and Sachin were planning to escape, leaving the three of us behind. They had realized how dangerous it would be to take Ashok to a doctor. It was a long way from where we were stranded, it was already morning and carrying Ashok would be a terrible risk.

'I was shocked at Sukanta, Kabita and Sachin's reaction. I couldn't leave Ashok to die like that. He was in tears, afraid that we would leave him behind. But I assured him that whatever the risk, I would not let him die. I told Sukanta, Kabita and Sachin that they could leave if they wanted to and I took Ashok on my shoulders and began to walk. His full weight was on me. Moreover, I was wearing a bulletproof jacket, which made things even more difficult.'

They now split into two groups. 'Splitting the group was practical and convenient. Not only because the three of our 'comrades' were reluctant friends, but also because a small group of three is less visible.'

So they set off: Subhas, Suman and Ashok. 'I was carrying Ashok on my shoulders and Subhas was a bit ahead of us. We kept walking for miles, crossed forests, vast stretches of fields and eventually reached a village. Subhas made arrangements for a doctor. In the end, we did manage to save Ashok.'

Soon after this, Ashok quit the movement, and later he got married. Suman smiled, 'He now walks with a limp. But it gives me great satisfaction to think that we could save him in the end. As for me, I have a nagging shoulder pain which comes back from time to time even now, bringing back memories of that horror-filled day.'

As we sipped tea, Suman told me that this episode was a huge learning experience for him. 'The fear was so intense that it didn't leave scope for checking if there were wild boars or human attackers on the prowl. The job was so risky and some peers and comrades could easily dump you in the face of a crisis. If Subhas and I hadn't been there, Ashok would have been dead. It could have happened to me too.'

For him, this was yet another episode that made him stray from the path on which he had set out to build a new Lalgarh.

* * *

According to Suman, some 'middle level' leaders based in Purulia, Bankura and West Midnapore who had quickly risen in the hierarchies of the Maoists or the PCPA around this time had killed their personal enemies saying it was necessary for the cause of the movement. The victims were projected as the Maoists' enemies—they were alleged to be leaking information. 'Kishanji and other top leaders often had no clue about the real reasons behind some of these killings. But it led to bitterness among many about the movement,' he said.

'When I was going through such a dilemma, it suddenly struck me that I could surrender. But I was afraid—I could trust no one. How could I send my message across to the police? What if my comrades came to know and killed me for deceiving them?' Such was his inner turmoil that Suman prayed hard that he would somehow make a slip and get caught by the police. 'I just wanted to be arrested but feared that if anything went wrong, I could even be killed in an encounter.'

Finally, his prayers were answered. On 9 November 2011 a combined team of officers from the West Bengal Police and the Central Reserve Police Force (CRPF) launched a raid after sources informed an officer of the West Bengal Police that a group of four to five men were hiding in some homes in the Amdanga-Kalibasa and Nonasole-Pairachali areas, in interior Lalgarh.

They zeroed in on one particular house in Pairachali village. The cops began to move in from different directions. The area was surrounded by a heavy contingent and Suman came under police surveillance without his knowledge. In fact, he was sleeping inside a villager's home, his shelter for that night. He woke up with a start. 'My sixth sense worked. I was constantly alert about being followed by the police, and there was something in the air, the smell and sounds which woke me up. I had my AK-47 by my side (some Maoist leaders even sleep with hands on their firearms, but I did not). At that point, I had no idea what I should do,' he told me.

'I was in a dilemma—should I run away like I had so many times in the past? Or should I move half-heartedly—so the cops would be able to catch me?' He was embarrassed to say this, of course, but clearly, he did not know how to hide the truth even if it did not show him in the best light. 'I don't know if I was being deceitful by not putting in my best efforts to escape. After my initial dilemma, the only thing I prayed for was that I should not die in an encounter.'

He began to move towards the forest area, away from the home where he was hiding. But the troops were already waiting on the other side. Suman walked into the trap. And how happy he was that the trap had been laid there! He dropped his AK-47 and held his hands up in surrender. There was a loaded chamber, two filled magazines and an ammunition pouch with him. There were also three other comrades with him.

This episode is significant on many counts.

From the police's point of view, the arrest fetched a huge quantity of arms and ammunition from numerous forest hideouts after Suman's interrogation. This also turned out to be one of the first among a series of information inputs on the movements of some top Maoist leaders who were traveling between Jamboni and Binpur, sneaking in and out of Jharkhand through the forests (the names of these leaders cannot be disclosed for the sake of Suman's safety. It is with his permission that I use his real name here.)

So wasn't he a traitor, I asked him, despite the apprehension that this question might offend him. Suman knew himself inside out. He had asked himself this question and found an answer too. 'Not that my mind is completely free from guilt, but every human being has his own sense of right and wrong. I saw many wrongs with my own eyes being committed within the squads, and in my mind I had gone totally against this war.'

For Suman, life took a dramatic turn again. 'My father was called by the officers to the police station during my interrogation. For my father and me, it was a very emotional moment—we couldn't stop crying. As I said, my parents had never approved of my involvement with the Maoist movement. Like all parents, they too wanted me to study and do well in life.'

But Suman could never start again from where he had left off. 'Now, I cannot stay at home with my parents. Their lives—like mine—are also at risk. Once I was with the Maoists but in order to give up that life, I have now sided with the police. It is impossible to remain neutral in this war.'

During my first meeting with Suman, he was preparing for his class ten final exams through distance education. He would regularly take tuitions from two police constables of the CRPF at their camp close to the Lalgarh police station. Not just Suman but other local boys preparing for their school examinations and competitive examinations were also offered tuitions and guidance at different battalion camps. This was one of the ways in which the state and central armed forces 'helped out' the local boys—an almost foolproof way devised to win them over.

* * *

By the time I visited him a year and a half later, Suman had become a young man. It was an outstanding transformation but I wasn't quite sure if this new Suman was the result of the transition from adolescence to adulthood or because of the new life he had been leading. He looked more confident, though he was still struggling to fit into the environment and among the people surrounding him.

In blue denims, a navy-blue-and-white striped tee and sneakers, it looked like he had even been weight training! I teased him about this. He was also wearing a stylish pair of tinted glasses. He was constantly fiddling with his phone, had a Facebook account and kept in touch with friends over WhatsApp. Just like a normal eighteen year old, I thought. I was comforted by the thought—not by the fact that the guns had been replaced by a mobile phone—but because he seemed happy about his choice of life.

He explained how I could download WhatsApp so it would be easy for us to be in touch. 'You can even send voice recordings, video-clips at the snap of a finger,' he told me. 'It's so easy!' I wanted to take his photograph with my camera, but he insisted that the ones in his Facebook account were much better. 'I look terrible in this haircut!' he laughed. 'I'll help you copy the photographs into the chip of your camera if you aren't carrying a pen drive,' he said. Clearly, he was much more technologically savvy than I.

But I soon found out that a fancy mobile phone was a mere distraction to stay away from the worries of his uncertain life. He showed me his mark sheets from school—he had stood first in class, and his school-leaving tenth standard examinations marksheet showed that he had been short of distinction by just seventeen marks.

Yet he chose not to pursue his studies because he could not do any ordinary job. 'It *must* be a police job.' Without police protection, he could get killed.

He told me how, just a few weeks earlier, some unidentified men chased after his father, probably to assault or to kill him. His father was on a bicycle on his way home—it was around 7.30 p.m.—when four to five men who were hiding in a bus stop identified his father and chased after him, who then pedalled hard to get away in the nick of time. 'It worries me to think they (my family) are exposed to risk all the time. My brother travels to his college every day and can be attacked any time,' Suman said.

Are goons really after his parents? Can the police ever trust 'former-Maoists' completely? The state police and the CRPF had been constantly testing him and had kept him under the scanner—perhaps that was why he was yet to get a job. He was yet to prove his unfailing allegiance and integrity before 'the State'.

While some officers were fond of him, he was still under close scrutiny. An officer told me that Maoists are 'perhaps not harming him and his family deliberately'. He said, 'It is true that the Maoists do not have their earlier strength in West Bengal since Kishanji's death, but had they been up to some mischief, it wouldn't be so hard to attack his home and family members, to injure or to kill them. Saontha used to be a dreaded Maoist and he knows the area like the back of his hand. Probably, the Maoists want to spare him because if there is a turnaround, they hope they can get him back.'

Suman meanwhile was pinning his hopes on a government job. His father—who encouraged him constantly, told him that the sage Valmiki was once the dacoit Ratnakar—and that it was possible to be a 'good person' in society some day '*despite* the past'.

'If I do not get a police job eventually, I will have a loss of face far worse than what I faced when I was a Maoist,' he said. 'People in Lalgarh know I will be someone to look up to some day. The villagers appreciate what I have achieved today, and they expect more out of me.' Was it the proximity with the police that made people around him consider this turnaround—from a young Maoist soldier to someone 'close' to the police force—an *achievement*?

By this time, we had become so friendly that he told me about the girl he loved—and still loves—since childhood, but whom he lost because he fell in love with another girl at the Maoist camp. He lost her too as she married someone else. He spoke about the highly sexually charged atmosphere of the Maoist camps—the gritty boys and girls from different villages of the area coming together, moving around, staying together in camps and how they fell in love with each other. 'This affair of mine just happened,' he said, snapping his fingers and giggling. 'At that point, there was no one who remained single in the party. Everyone was pairing up with someone. There was the thrill and desperate desire of having someone of your own by your side when the atmosphere is otherwise so vicious; there was so much fear, sounds of roaring guns, hatred, blood and death engulfing us,' he said.

'The Maoist leadership, too, encouraged this. It helped the movement thrive. This was a huge additional attraction for young men and women to carry on with the armed war,' he said. 'The leaders never forced anyone into the movement. So if anyone wanted to return home, it was not opposed as long as no information was leaked.'

He took the girl home, eager to marry her and said he would quit the life of a soldier. But Suman's father wouldn't let the marriage take place without testing them a bit. He asked her to go home and urged Suman to find himself a job before tying the knot. 'I agreed.' They parted. She went back home and he set off for a city in south India, worked at a poultry farm and began to earn and save money.

'All was going well for some months, and I had saved up quite a bit of cash. Then suddenly one day, a friend of mine from the village called me and said I was needed urgently by my girlfriend. But it was just a ploy to bring me back. I had heard she was having an affair with someone else by then. I came and found it was true. Coming back was the greatest mistake of my life. I got sucked into the armed war again,' Suman said. He made his way through groups of armed CPM gangs who were guarding the area from Maoists and went into the forests again.

In his thick red personal diary, which he showed me, Suman had pasted photographs—of himself, his parents and his younger brother. They were a close-knit family and the brothers had vowed not to have separate kitchens even when they get married. 'Dada, konodin bhinyo hobo na, kintu!' his brother had promised Suman.

Ironic, since for years now, they had been eating food cooked out of different kitchens. His brother's vow was actually a vision of a better life they could lead some day in a distant, illusory future. Suman still lived on canteen food; he hadn't tasted meals cooked by his mother for days, and he had given up a part of his childhood and his entire adolescence to a bitter, raging war.

The diary contained secrets of episodes in the forest, photographs of his dear ones, dry pressed flowers, other memories and messages written in remembrance of his girlfriend.

That life was over for good. He had straddled both sides—the police and the CPI (Maoists), and in both cases he was fully convinced he had chosen them on some merit. He had been sure the Maoists were showing him the right path, so he followed them despite knowing that it would be difficult. But he found himself lost on that road, cheated and surrounded by people he could no longer trust.

After his arrest, he found affection among some police officers. He was delighted and moved by the fact that the cops were not just ruthless and inhuman people that beat up innocent villagers. That trigger was perhaps enough to make him a 'convert'.

But it had been a long wait. The officers who dissuaded him from the Maoist war were no longer posted in Lalgarh. They were working elsewhere in the state and could not do enough in their individual capacities to get Suman a government job.

'Between 2011 and 2014, there were several officers posted in the area who were able to work effectively to end the Maoist movement in Bengal. They took interest in some boys who were part of the war and motivated them to get out of the movement. But for those like Suman, who did not accept the rehabilitation package fearing their Maoist colleagues would retaliate, things became difficult,' said an officer.

Suman was hoping to get the job of a barber in one of the armed police forces, but things did not work out in his favour. There were cases pending against him, he was alleged to be involved in many armed operations against the state, and so on. But Suman believed this could not be a reason why he wasn't getting a job 'when those who officially surrendered with similar cases pending, have been recruited as home guards with the state police'. I couldn't disagree. It is not clear whether the government wanted him to remain grateful that he was picked up but also went slow on the cases slapped against him.

We met many more times since our first meeting at Lalgarh police station in November 2012. One of these meetings was at the upmarket South City Mall on Prince Anwar Shah Road in Kolkata. We ate Subway sandwiches and drank coffee, along with a police officer who had played an important role in Suman's arrest in 2011. The officer constantly pulled his leg about his former girlfriend and asked him what they used to talk about. Suman blushed every time the subject came up. The woman, who was part of the Maoist squad at Lalgarh and later married a young man in the same squad, had surrendered with her husband. They now had a child.

The officer rued that things only work as personal initiatives, not as part of an official policy. 'Many Maoists have officially surrendered. But Suman did not, because he did not want to be identified by his colleagues as a 'surrendered Maoist' at that point. Also, immediately after he was caught, police authorities did not give him the option to 'surrender'. He was promised a government job instead, and he probably helped the police with all his heart hoping the police officers too would keep their word.

'The person who helped the police most in this state to fight the Maoists has been going through a long, long wait,' the officer said. These were all off-the-record chats.

Suman has since been writing poems, posting some of them on his Facebook wall. He wants to get them published some day. As we ate sandwiches and drank coffee at the food court milling about with tired shoppers, Suman read out to me and his police officer friend the poem he had written:

> *Shobar priyo mor gram beesh baish grihey ghera mor jonmobhumi,*
> *sundor monushyer boshobash*
> *Krishi tomar royechhe shombol taito kaukey thakitey hoyna upash*
> *Gram ogo gram amar tomar prapyo shokoler uchhosthan*
> *Jai jekhaney choley ami bhulibey ki korey tomarey poraan*
> *Probhu jonmer jonyo bechhe dilo tomar koley amarey*
> *Dhonno ami hoyechhi boro tomar sneho peye barey barey*
> (My village of twenty odd homes and beautiful people, that's my motherland/People here work in the fields and do not have to starve/You, my village will remain at the highest pedestal/ Wherever I go, my heart will never forget you/God has chosen to send me to you/I have been grateful for the love and affection you showered on me)

This is not Suman's story alone. Scores of boys and young men who are part of this war have had similar experiences. In backward areas where jobs are few and a raging war leaves behind its scars even when it is over, whichever side one chooses may turn out to be uncertain and lonely.

It wasn't hard for Suman to transform himself from Saontha to Subir to Sukanta, one alias to another while he was leading the life of a Maoist. But of all the roles he has played so far, the most difficult has been the struggle to live the life of Suman— his own life.

2

Sunil Mahato

'Tell me Sir, will it help if I complete school?' a dark boy with deep, intelligent eyes asked impatiently. He never smiled. Sunil had come all the way from his village ten kilometres away to ask only this question, but it must have been an hour before he could actually broach the subject. He was too shy to plead for a job, but then, the situation was desperate for him.

Sunil was studying in class seven at a government-run school. The officer pleaded with him to stay in school and not drop out. 'I'll see to it that you get a job once you complete class ten. So don't give up studies, go to school every day,' he urged.

The teenager and the officer were talking at a police station that they visited from time to time in extreme secrecy. It was in one of the towns of West Midnapore, far from the villages. If Sunil had stepped into his local police station, it would not have remained a secret. I was allowed to talk to the boy for some time here. But first, the officer discussed with Sunil the progress he had been making in his studies, whether he was facing any problem at school, if anyone had been threatening him, and so on. The main concern for the boy however, was how soon and whether he would get a government job.

There are many boys like him in regular contact with the police. They share a symbiotic relationship—the boys inform the police about what's going on inside the villages; they bring inputs on whether Maoists are making fresh inroads into villages and the forests surrounding them and if anything out of the ordinary is taking place. In return, these boys hope that they may, in the process, find a secure government job. Despite their dependence on each other, the police clearly enjoy an upper hand, simply because there are many boys like Sunil who report to the police, but to each of these boys, it is a matter of their life and death.

The boys and their families are grateful that the police didn't arrest them despite their involvement in the Maoist movement. One became an informer in the hope of being pardoned by the State (this worked unofficially in the sense that cases were not slapped against them).

Sunil had been working and living in the group led by none other than CPI (Maoist) politburo member Koteswar Rao (alias Kishanji), and was part of the operation at Silda's Eastern Frontier Rifles camp on February 15, 2010 in which twenty-four jawans had been killed.[1] Once he was arrested, Sunil desperately pleaded to be 'pardoned'. He wanted to go back home, but wasn't confident that choosing the surrender scheme implemented by the government would be a good idea. He didn't want to be identified and stamped as someone who had tricked his comrades; it would also pose a threat to his life and that of his family members. Even as a teenager, Sunil realized this, and preferred to stay in anonymity though it meant giving up a lot of money.

'Maoists do not take kindly to traitors. Therefore, even if some boys have been arrested, they haven't officially surrendered. Instead, they live in their homes and act as our informers,' admitted the officer.

According to MHA figures, in 2015, ninety-two out of the 168 civilians killed in Maoist attacks in the country, were police informers.[2] In 2014, ninety-one out of the 222 civilians killed were police informers. In 2013, the figure was 113 out of the 282 civilians, while in 2012, 134 police informers (out of 301 civilians) were killed. On an average, 200 police informers died every year between 2008 and 2011 as well—170 in 2008, 211 in 2009, 323 in 2010 and 218 in 2011. Therefore, Sunil's perception that he was safer because he had not 'surrendered' before the police is rather misplaced.[1]

Working as a police informer is also a compulsion. There was no other way the police would let the detained go free. 'If they surrender, their former colleagues would notice them. So, while we have some who opt for the surrender scheme, others agree to help us informally. There are other informal ways to give them security and protection and as much money as we can,' the officer said. The money however, varies from Rs 100-200 every time they meet someone from the police, sometimes even less.

Sunil for instance, had fled the Maoist camp somewhere in West Midnapore. 'Running away is no big deal. All one needs is an excuse—one might go out to take a bath in the pond or leave the camp to fetch a newspaper. It may be anything... I had been planning to run away for a long time, and then, one day I managed to,' he said.

After Sunil was back home, he realized he would have to leave or else he would get sucked into the rebellion all over again. A relative took him to an undergarments factory in Howrah district—Kolkata's twin city by the banks of the Hooghly—hoping there might be some work there. But there were no jobs for the twelve year old. 'So I returned to my village. The comrade dadas kept persuading me repeatedly to join them again,' he said. 'But I couldn't go back. The images of the Silda camp keep coming back to me even now when I try to sleep.'

Not just Sunil, many others like him were rattled by the killing spree. That itself became reason enough for them to quit.

'Bikash and the other seniors in the group took me to the Silda operation to instill more confidence in me. I had been with them only for some months at that point. The plan was on for months and I used to accompany my seniors during visits to the Eastern Frontier Rifles camp area to understand the jawans' schedule—at what time they changed duties, at what time they cooked, the position of sentries and so on. Since there was a public toilet adjacent to the camp, we used to go and pretend to urinate there, but would actually have our eyes fixed on the camp.'

The gameplan was finalized, and the group zeroed in on the time of attack. 'I cannot forget that day for the rest of my life. We went in a group of fifteen to sixteen comrades to attack the camp. Suchitra (Mahato) and some others were leading from the front.'[3]

Sunil was part of the few towards the rear, closer to their vehicles. His primary role was to provide backup support to the team, in case something went terribly wrong for the rebels. The Maoists who, at that point enjoyed a clear upper hand in West Bengal thanks to the leadership of Kishanji, would have taken someone like Sunil to such a major operation just to make him feel important. The seniors thought it would make him courageous and proud and give him an experience he could brag about within the inner circle.

Instead, Sunil became a bundle of nerves. It took him just one moment to realize he didn't belong there. 'The moment the firing started, my head started spinning. I cannot explain what was happening inside me. My body went numb and it was as if I could no longer fathom anymore what was happening. I felt like vomiting. I could barely stand.'

Five Maoists and twenty-four EFR jawans were killed in this incident—it was one of the biggest and most gruesome attacks in West Bengal by the Maoists. All the injured and dead Maoists were taken away in vehicles by their comrades. While the bodies were being carried away—and Sunil helped in this work—he did not remember anything about this episode except as an unreal blur.

'I wanted to go home.'

* * *

Why are children made part of the war the Maoists and the State are fighting against each other? Why are they used by police and the rebels alike, to extract information? There is no clear answer. The only conclusion one may draw is that it is convenient for both parties to use children. Not only are they easy to mould into fearless killers, their presence draws least suspicion. They can be used conveniently as couriers, police informers or spies, and would be too scared and too meek to protest. Once they are part of it, the bloodshed they witness or cause leave them suffering from the trauma of the war forever.

Behind the sharp police tactics and intelligently planned 'rehabilitation' packages, there is tumult in the lives of these young ones. Underneath the surrenders, there are tales of separation from family and friends, helplessness and lack of choice.

In the middle of this uncertain future, the children have not only lost their childhood, many have also been killed or injured, and displaced from their homes forever.

3

Toofan Sahu

'*Aj kal kya kar rahe ho?*' I asked him over the phone. (What are you doing these days?)

'*Kuchh nahin…gaon mein ghumta rahta hai, khet mein ghumta rahta hai…*' he tells me. (Nothing much…I keep hanging around in the village, in the fields…)

Both of us were terrible in Hindi, but he spoke mostly Odiya and my knowledge of the language is rudimentary. So we managed with a bit of Odiya, Hindi and Bengali. Once in a while, we had to take resort to interpreters.

Here then is the story of Toofan Sahu (alias Bangra), now 22 years old.

* * *

Toofan sported the hairstyle of a 1980s film-star—he was likely to remind you of Mithun Chakravarty in *Disco Dancer*. He wore bellbottoms and filmi, oversize, dramatic jackets with frills, buttons and multiple pockets. Only, he was reed-thin, with high cheekbones, sunken eyes and a lovely bashful smile. Looking at him, you would never imagine he could as much as hurt a fly.

How does a person driven to violence and bloodshed continue to look so pure? How did Toofan manage to hide so much loathing, suffering and pain? Do cruelty and suffering not reflect on the contours of the face? Were the violent acts these young men committed justified because their purpose and vision were pure?

There are no answers, only fear that your own vision may have tricked you, that you had not been able to sense his suffering. These thoughts flitted through my mind as I sat in front of a quiet and withdrawn Toofan. He had travelled all the way from Ganjam district to Rayagada town. It is a beautiful town, 400 kilometres from Bhubaneswar, cradled by mountains on all sides. He had come to meet the police superintendent, Rajesh Pandit, who had, in fact, arrested him during his previous posting as Ganjam SP.

The boy shuffled his feet and spoke without looking up from the durries spread on the floor of an office at the Rayagada district headquarters. It was difficult to get Toofan to speak even a few words at first. But once in a while, when he talked through an interpreter, a police constable he had known for a while, he was more vocal. Perhaps at that point he felt he was not really talking to me, but blurting out his innermost thoughts to someone else. Once he was well into the story of his life, Toofan was charged with emotion. He looked up from the durries and began to talk directly to me, even while speaking in Odiya. Our eyes met, and from this moment onwards he spoke to me as if he had known me for years.

Some readers might find it difficult to believe that Toofan would speak the truth in the presence of a policeman (or, to a policeman). How could he tell me anything *against* the police if he is speaking to me through a police constable? In defence, I must say two things here. First, Toofan's story as I narrate here, is based on several conversations with him. Only once—the first time I spoke to him at the Raygada office—were portions of the conversation translated to me by a police constable. Subsequently, it was only Toofan and I talking (in a mix of Hindi, Bengali and Odiya). On other occasions, his uncle acted as the interpreter when he was at home among his friends and family members. Second, a police constable comes from more or less the same socio-economic background as a Maoist soldier. Those who have witnessed their interaction will know that there is sympathy and understanding between the two on account of the similarity in their upbringing and constraints in life. Also, there is no tension or bad blood as long as the police constables figure out that the higher-ups in the police are taking a 'sympathetic' view of the surrendered/arrested Maoist. That had been the case with Toofan Sahu.

* * *

Toofan was born in Gangapur village of Odisha's Ganjam district. The son of a poor farmer, he dropped out of school while in class seven. After a couple of years, his parents thought of setting up a shop for him. He had an older sister and a younger brother. Shops in remote, sleepy hill villages usually stock everything from rice and vegetables to washing powder, lentils, sugar, salt, batteries—so people from far and near dropped by to pick up all necessary provisions at Toofan's shop.

Days went by. Nothing adventurous or untoward happened. The drudgery, poverty and monotony of the hard, uneventful life engulfed the boy with a strange sorrow. Everyone Toofan knew was poor—engaged in manual labour or working in their own fields—with little hope for a brighter future. He desperately wished that there could be a magical door which he could open and walk into a life different from the one he was leading for so long.

But even if that was too outlandish for a poor villager to even dream of, a certain strand of that wishful thinking did descend on him one day in the form of Maoist leader Sabyasachi Panda and some of his associates. They were at his door and they needed a favour. Panda and his men were travelling within the thick forested and mountainous terrain of Ganjam villages, and they needed to charge their phones and laptops somewhere. Toofan's shop provided the solution. The boy was also, in a way, grateful that these men had walked into his life.

* * *

There are stories of both praise and notoriety associated with the name Sabyasachi Panda. He has been described as a Robin Hood character who looted riches from exploitative landlords and distributed money and jewellery among the poor. At other times, he has been seen as a notorious, ruthless, power-obsessed leader having tumultuous relations with both higher-ups and lower-rung soldiers in the Maoist hierarchy. Panda and his men had a strong presence in Ganjam, Gajapati, Kandhamal and Rayagada areas of Odisha during his heyday.

Panda was known to always carry approximately Rs 2 lakh in his bag and was always clad in olive-green shirts and six-pocket cargo trousers. His dislike for branded clothes was well known. But Panda enjoyed milk, chocolates, basmati rice, and used Dabur toothpaste and Sunlight washing soap, those close to him would reveal. When he was in forest hideouts, he would use a 'three-section' separate tent during the monsoons, enjoying his music on a laptop—listening to English songs and folk Koya songs, reading books and watching films.

Panda's association with the poor went back a long way. He was said to have left home after a fight with his father, a Left leader. In 1991, Sabyasachi Panda, Dandapani Mohanty, Budha Gomango and Tirupati Gomango joined CPI (M-L) Liberation. Around this time the PW was gaining strength in the Malkangiri area and other areas bordering Andhra Pradesh. Panda was in constant touch with this group. In 1996, Panda, along with some others including Budha Gomango formed the Chasi Mulia Samiti which was later renamed as the Kui Labenga Sangha (Kui Youth Association)—the organization stood for rights of tribals to jal, jangal and jameen. The organization took land forcibly from sahukars and distributed it among poor tribals. He soon converted his Kui Labenga Sangha into the Bansadhara Anchalika Committee (BAC) of PWG. Then, he became the state committee member of Andhra Orissa Border Special Zonal Committee (AOBSZC). He also had a new alias, Sarat.

In 2004, the PWG and MCC merged, to form the CPI (Maoist). The BAC had become an Area Committee in 2002. It participated in the Koraput armory raid in February 2004, when 1000 weapons were looted from the Reserve Office of Koraput District Police.[1] It became a full-fledged Divisional Committee of AOBSZC from 2005. Meanwhile, the Orissa State Organizing Committee (OSOC) of CPI (Maoist) was formed in 2006 and Sabyasachi Panda, alias Sarat, became the secretary and took on the name Sunil.

Apparently when MCC and PWG merged in 2004, and the OSOC was formed in 2006, the Central Committee had decided to send Balakrishna as the OSOC secretary to Odisha, but somehow this did not work out. Then, the party sent Girish (overlooking Panda in the process) to take charge as OSOC secretary. Girish was subsequently arrested in Jharkhand in 2007. Since then, Panda was practically the party head in Odisha despite not holding the official position, and he continued to bear deep grudges against the leaders from Andhra Pradesh because he felt he was constantly under the scanner and was being controlled by the party leaders from that state.

He had planned and executed some of the most audacious attacks in Odisha. On March 24, 2006, over 200 rebels had attacked a sub-jail and a police station in Gajapati district, freeing the prisoners and killing three policemen. The officer-in-charge and the jailor were taken hostage and freed after some days.[2] In February 2008, Panda was allegedly behind the Nayagarh armoury attack, which left fifteen dead. A huge amount of weapons were looted from the arms depot at the local police training school, the district armoury and the local police station.[3] In August 2008, he is said to have been behind the killing of VHP leader Lakshmananda Saraswati and five accomplices that led to Hindu-Christian riots in Kandhamal district, which left forty dead. And in March 2012, he was behind the abduction of two Italian tourists from the jungles of Ganjam-Kandhamal. They were held hostage for nearly a month.[4]

After these episodes, Panda's clashes with the top leaders from Andhra-Orissa Border (AOB) became well known. The differences of opinion were over the killing of Saraswati and over the abduction of the two Italians for which Panda apparently did not get clearances from the higher-ups in the party. The top Maoist leaders were upset about the fact that these two episodes had had a negative impact on people and had made the Maoists less popular. On June 1, 2012, he shot off a scathing letter to the CPI (Maoist) supremo Ganapathy, Vijay Dada (Narayan Sanyal) and Sumit Dada (Amitabha Bagchi).

Panda actually wrote two letters—one to senior party colleagues, and the other written for the general comrades in the party, addressed as 'for coms in jail and out'. Written under the alias Suman, the letters listed some of the core issues that frustrate footsoldiers, things that he asked his party to ponder and analyze. While Panda himself had often been questioned by his seniors and his junior colleagues, many points he raised had been corroborated by those who were no longer working with the CPI (Maoist). In his letters, Panda mentioned these clashes with Central Committee member Manoj (or Modem Balakrishnan, alias Bhaskar) and BR (Nambala Keshava Rao, alias Basavraj, in charge of the Maoists' Central Military Commission). Panda was expelled from the party shortly after he wrote these two letters. The letter written to the top leaders was particularly caustic. Many senior leaders of the CPI (Maoist) were left red-faced by this entire episode.

Following his expulsion, Panda formed his own group, the Odisha Maovadi Party (OMP), along with senior leader Pradeep Manjhi, who became the OMP's deputy commandant. The party had an armed strength of around forty men and women and worked in the Ganjam, Gajapati and Rayagada area. The OMP was later renamed CPI (Marxist-Leninist-Maoist).

After many rumours over the possibility of Panda's 'surrender', Panda was arrested in July 2014. The 'arrest' however, was considered to be a 'surrender' in reality, a backroom negotiation that even the police were tightlipped about.

* * *

Against the backdrop of this larger picture of the Maoist movement in Odisha and in India, Toofan Sahu may have appeared to be an inconsequential player in the periphery, too small and minuscule to make much of a difference either for better or for worse.

But his story was born from his meeting with a larger than life figure—Sabyasachi Panda.

Toofan himself believed that he was playing an important role in the Maoist war against the state to help the poor and backward. He had heard many stories about Panda and already looked up to him as a person who could liberate the poor. He offered his tiny ramshackle shop as a place for the exchange of messages and parcels for the Maoist squads led by Panda. This turned out to be the first step for him to becoming a full-fledged courier. It is not exactly clear whether Toofan did this work wholeheartedly or whether there was any pressure on him. He was supportive of the movement for sure, but whether he was actually keen on becoming an integral part of it remains uncertain. Toofan would just smile shyly when asked this question.

Someone would leave a packet behind with the boy and codes for it to be picked up by someone else. Most of the time, however, it would be just some information he had to pass on. 'It was mostly fun, but I knew who they were and what the work was all about. Slowly but surely, I was sucked into the thick of things,' he says.

Soon, inevitably, his responsibilities increased and the association turned into thick friendship. Toofan was barely sixteen then. His shop was in a quiet area in one corner of the village and no one had any clue what was going on there.

For Toofan, the job was also fun and gave him some much needed independence and confidence. From a quiet, shy person trapped in the confines of the shop and in a sedentary life, Toofan was converting surreptitiously into a confident man. Soon, he had other duties. He zipped across the forests, mountains, roads and waterfalls to reach railway stations and welcomed comrades from Chhattisgarh, Jharkhand or West Bengal. These comrades would come down for meetings in Odisha and Toofan was asked to arrange for vehicles, food, homes and hotels for their stay. He would arrange for clothes, shoes, water, food packets, vehicles to pick up and drop the comrades, directing them through roads where they would have to leave vehicles and walk, and ensuring they reached safely. Some comrades were kept at hotels. These would mostly be arranged in small towns and cities, but the quality of hotels and rooms depended on a comrade's designation. Sometimes, someone would grumble if there was no television in a hotel room, sometimes they would say the food was bad. Toofan took it all in his stride. 'It was part of the job. Sometimes I was scolded, but I never felt bad,' he said. 'For arranging meetings and conferences a lot of things were involved and there would be some chaos. I didn't mind all this.' It was hard work, and there was no money he earned from doing it. He was happy to get food and clothes to wear, and move from one place to another in cars and two-wheelers, though most of the time it would be on foot or on a bicycle.

Slowly but surely Panda had inspired and taken Toofan completely in his thrall. Soon, the teenager was an integral part of Panda's team, one of his most trusted aides and his courier. Within months, he was part of the innermost circle.

* * *

All this meant that he could no longer return home or to the shop. It would be too risky.

What did he get in turn? 'An exciting time and friendship,' Toofan said. It was fun to have boys and girls his age in the same squad, to work and live with, roaming about the forests, chatting in their free time and leading the life of danger and uncertainty. It was a stark contrast to the uneventful and static life back home.

Toofan fell in love with one of the girls in the squad, though he asked me not to disclose her name especially since they were no longer in touch. The hardship, the fear of being caught by the police or being killed in an encounter were no longer important considerations. Instead Toofan began to wonder how his dreams with the girl could be fulfilled in the confines of the squad. He was also frustrated about the fact that his love wasn't wholeheartedly reciprocated. She liked Toofan, it seemed, but she probably also liked someone else. This was as much as the shy boy would reveal. In any case, this part of the story does not play any role in how things turned out later.

It was actually a male friend, Ravi, who was central to this story. Toofan said he didn't know the person's real name. 'It was the name everyone used for him at the squad.' They were friends and had worked together for a couple of years. And then, one day, Ravi was dead.

According to Toofan, one of the operations planned by their group went bust. The police caught some of their colleagues involved in the operation. A senior leader from Andhra Pradesh, who was supervising the entire team, zeroed in on Ravi as the traitor. 'All the juniors in the camp were aware that Ravi had left the camp to get some medicines. But the seniors did not believe him,' Toofan narrated. 'Actually, Ravi had indeed gone to get some medicines that day. But these senior leaders kept alleging that his exit from the camp was mysterious and that he was the one who had leaked the information about the operation. I protested, because I knew my friend very well and even knew that he had gone to buy medicines. But no one believed us,' Toofan said.

Next thing he knew, Ravi was dead. No one got to know how he was killed or who killed him, but it was obvious, Toofan said. He paused, sipping some tea and fighting hard to stop his tears.

He recalled how the murmurs started following this shocking turn of events. Those in their teens and twenties were the ones who were the most shattered because they were the junior-most and therefore felt the most threatened. While many of these young men and women may have been junior to Ravi in the party hierarchy, they were scared and shocked that this could have happened to any of them. Toofan was perhaps the most horrified because he was friendly with Ravi. They would all huddle together and discuss among themselves the need to protest this terrible injustice. There were endless discussions; everyone knew about Ravi's innocence. 'We were all so upset—numb with shock and grief. It scared us. What if the same thing happened to us some day? We wanted to leave. We even asked Sabyasachi Panda to protest this rash decision to eliminate Ravi without giving him a chance to explain,' Toofan said. 'But strangely, he kept quiet on this matter.'

One of Panda's letters, written to CPI (Maoist) supremo Ganapathy, Vijay Dada (Narayan Sanyal) and Sumit Dada (Amitabha Bagchi) mentions Ravi's death: '*Annihilation of Ravi and then after* [sic]: In this period Ravi along with one militia com went for local ayurvedic medicine for one com. They were send [sic] by local commander. Com Manoj had arrested both of them before village people and killed Ravi after interrogation, kept another militia person in custody for one month. Ravi had become enemy agent through Sushant. His dead body has not been handover [sic] to his family. CCMs [Central Committee members] had done it without informing or discussing with local coms and even without informing me, done it secretly. Though the punishment is not questionable, the method is against our party constitution, that has created some problem.'

Panda mentions in the letter that Ravi had become an 'enemy agent' and that the punishment was 'not questionable'—certainly a stance different from Toofan's. It is clear from the letter that Panda felt Ravi was indeed a traitor. What he questioned was the method of killing and the kind of punishment. Panda also seemed to be upset about the fact that he was not informed about it—a leadership issue where he felt he should have been given more importance in the decision.

It would be difficult to draw a conclusion on whether Ravi had indeed been a traitor. What is more important is that Toofan and some others in the group believed Ravi was innocent, and the fact that he had indeed been killed by a senior Maoist leader based on the suspicion that he was leaking information. The episode left the younger members of the team afraid and angry with the way senior Maoists would not even bat an eyelid at killing a junior on the basis of suspicion. The ramifications were far reaching.

'In my mind, that was the end of my association with the movement. I knew I had to find a way to come out of that world, even if the other world that I had earlier rejected wasn't worth returning to. My dream was shattered, I felt betrayed, dejected,' he said.

* * *

There was one more surprise in store for me in Toofan Sahu's narrative. Despite his shyness, Toofan told me a secret. Why he blurted this out continues to baffle me. Among all the things that he was most shocked and upset about as a Maoist soldier, was the fact that a senior Maoist leader was living in a tent at their hideout with three women who were officially his guards. Toofan urged me to not disclose the name of this well-known leader.

While the tents of junior cadres were very basic set-ups, this senior leader's tent was covered on all sides, with more guards outside. No one could enter this tent easily except these three women. There were rumours and murmurs about this unusual living arrangement. In the world of adults, this would be easily acceptable if none of the four adults had any problem with it.

But for the young man and his other friends of the same age group in the camp, who hadn't seen much of the world, this appeared shocking.

* * *

The Maoists in Odisha were going through several rough phases at that point. There were differences between the local Odisha cadre and the Andhra Pradesh cadre (the latter were mostly senior leaders). There were undercurrents of tension and even open fights between the two groups on issues as varied as whom the party should target/kill, to everyday issues like food and which soap they should use.

Panda's letter mentioned many of these things. He talked about how Maoists beat up people, broke and burnt their houses. Many people had been killed only on the basis of allegations. Panda cited cases since 2000 where he had witnessed 'so many unnecessary annihilations' in Odisha. He added that he was against killing those with Dalit or tribal background, even if the person turned out to be an 'informer'. This was perhaps out of fear of becoming unpopular with the masses. According to him, it was better to expose the traitor before the 'people' as a first option, than to beat him up. He also 'confessed' to instances where action was taken on the basis of unconfirmed information. He also went on to say that action against cruel landlords who repress people should be taken at a 'later stage'— perhaps indicating that cruel landlords should also be given a chance first or exposed before the people initially.

Socialist Unity Centre of India (SUCI) leader Biswanath Madhi was killed by AOB leaders for political rivalry and it wasn't clear if he was actually an informer.[5] In another case a Centre for Indian Trade Unions (CITU) leader Thamaso Munda from the Odisha-Jharkhand border was killed in the trade union office. Panda regretted that this was done even though the Maoists did not have strong base in trade unions (and had perhaps lost an opportunity to improve the party's trade union support because of this episode).

Panda added sarcastically that the Maoists can kill anybody without being answerable to the people. This would have a negative impact on the trade union workers, and though he had raised the issue before the central committee through a central committee member, he hadn't got a reply.

Biju Janta Dal MLA Jagabandhu Majhi, who was wheelchair bound, had been killed in 2011 by Maoist rebels from Chhattisgarh, according to Panda.[6] He said that Majhi had initially been threatened and he had reported it to Panda, but suddenly he was killed. According to Panda, his colleagues had said that Majhi was corrupt, to which Panda said in his letter that all MLAs, MPs and officers are corrupt, so their property could be looted and distributed among the poor, instead of simply killing them.

In the Maoist organizations too there was politics, backstabbing, cruelty—oddly not unlike the world that Toofan had rejected. Toofan tried to analyze this deep disappointment: 'Despite ideologues at the top, the ground level is milling with rogues who swindle money, kill and loot to serve personal interests that have nothing to do with ideology. I saw it from close quarters.

'A lot of things were suddenly going wrong around that time. There were daily fights about plans being executed. Panda was angry about something going wrong, or his instructions not being followed. There were groups within groups, and it was frustrating. I started feeling out of place in all this,' he said. Toofan was frustrated that those at the top cared so little for the young people who did all the hard work. 'They never stood up for us. We expected that Sabyasachi Panda, who was a local person and our leader would stand by us in the trying times. But he chose to remain mum.

'There were killings and bloodshed, kidnappings and mayhem all the time. Yet I felt nothing about its implications till the time one amongst us became the target; till it hit us at an individual level. I started wondering what if this happens to me? What if some day someone alleged that I was a traitor? Would they kill me similarly, without batting an eyelid?'

Not just Toofan, many girls and boys in the squad also felt that way. They too had a similar urge to leave and return home. Yet, this possibility was fraught with danger because it wouldn't be possible to evade the police once they went back.

* * *

It wasn't easy for Toofan to surrender even after he had detached himself from the movement. He felt like an outsider but kept working like a machine, without emotions and waiting for something miraculous all over again. 'I knew I couldn't deceive them but I was desperately looking for an opportunity to come out.'

At this point, Toofan's and Suman's stories become eerily similar. They had both detached themselves from the Maoist movement and were looking for an opportunity to escape the camp. Yet, neither had the courage nor the inclination to be traitors and to surrender themselves to the police. They were too proud to 'surrender'. Just like Suman, Toofan too was waiting to be caught. And perhaps because of that, he became somewhat lax.

It was March 1, 2012. He set out on a two-wheeler, vrooming through a bustling town in Odisha, in order to receive some comrades (his other Maoist friends were in a car). Unknown to him, police officers were following the tower movement of his mobile phone which had recently been changed. Riding on his two-wheeler, and humming a song, Toofan was tense about just one thing: those whom he was going to receive should arrive safely and they should be able to identify him. Maoists use signs to identify their visitors. Toofan tried to recall the time, place and the exact sign language that would help the visitors identify him as the messenger who had come to meet them and take them to their destination. *Yes, things were going smoothly so far.*

His mind was filled with these thoughts when, suddenly, like a scene straight out of a Bollywood movie, a jeep came from

behind, overtook him and collided head on with his bike. For
a fraction of a second, Toofan thought it might be an accident.
A couple of men came out of the jeep and held him in an iron
grip. The game was over, he was told. Now, there was no escape.
He was face to face with two cops.

Toofan said he was relieved that the end had finally come.
It would lead him to yet another door and onto another life.
What would this new life be like? It appeared exciting initially.
To begin with, the police officer who had arrested him, Rajesh
Pandit, treated him well. He was the 'big' officer. He had heard
so many stories of police torture against the Maoist cadres who
had been arrested, that Toofan could not believe his luck. How
could this police officer treat him so well?

Pandit asked Toofan to 'surrender'. While Pandit himself
did not admit all this because he did not want to disclose these
details, sources confirmed that this is often the case. In fact, a
majority of the 'surrenders' are in reality 'arrests'. Officers give
the arrested rebels the option of surrendering so that their lives
are 'better' than staying behind bars for years serving sentences
for crimes like murder and for carrying and using arms.

Toofan agreed. He felt that this had also spared him the
torture that normal 'arrests' in the hands of police involve. He
also got a bonus: the government offered him money under its
surrender and rehabilitation scheme 'to rebuild his life'. Toofan
did not get the money immediately—Rs 1,50,000 was deposited
by the government in a joint account in the name of Toofan
Sahu and the Ganjam police superintendent.

When I met him for the first time, in 2013, Toofan was
hoping to get a government job. At the time, he depended on
small sums given to him by senior police officers from their
'source fund'. Sometimes this would be Rs 500, sometimes as
little as a hundred rupee note. For Toofan, even this was good
enough, and he would reach an office whenever he was called
by an officer.

His shop had long been shut. His sister was now married and

his father Ishwar Sahu had passed away (Toofan's uncle said it was due to old age and that he had been very upset about the way life changed so drastically after the boy left his family behind). His brother and Toofan now work in the fields, earning between Rs 125-150 daily. There are days when no work is available.

'Why did you not get a government job?' I asked Toofan months later. 'It's not so easy,' he replied. But he was still waiting. Toofan may not have been as pushy as Suman, but he was quietly hopeful. Finally a job offer did come, but it was for a private company, and he would have to move as far as Mumbai. Toofan was a bit baffled about the prospect of moving to a distant, enormous city so far from home. The Ganjam SP had offered him the job. He didn't take it and decided to stay back. He did not want to leave his family behind. He was happy to be at home, chatting with friends and neighbours, doing work in the fields when it was available. In this backward region of Odisha, no work was available on a regular basis close to his home, and home was where Toofan wanted to be. He was just one of the many in the list of surrendered Maoists whom the state had promised to guide to a better future.

Toofan was happiest to dwell in his inner world. Threats from his former colleagues were neither immediate nor enormous, considering the Maoist groups in Odisha had been going through a downswing. There had been infighting and Panda himself was arrested in 2014, after more than two years of talks (since the time he rebelled and shot off that letter to his party leaders) that he was likely to surrender.

Under the circumstances, Toofan felt that it was unlikely he could be killed out of revenge because he had turned against his former colleagues. 'But the threat is there for sure,' he admitted. 'What can I do? I will die if I have to.'

A few months from the time we last spoke, Toofan would finally be free to withdraw the money deposited in the bank in his name. He was planning to start a small business with the money. And no, it would definitely not be a shop this time.

4

Asiram Kashyap (alias Vikram)

September 2013. The cacophony of rickshaws, cars and people on the roads of Raipur could hardly pierce through the thick brick and glass walls of the Chhattisgarh government office building. The afternoon air was oppressively hot outside, but the office complex was sprawling and full of trees, and the chirping of birds could be heard somewhere in the distance. Inside, the corridors were semi-dark and empty, the only sound coming from the hum of air-conditioning machines and the low buzz of people working in different rooms.

I was led into the office of a senior officer by a short, young man in a white full-sleeved shirt and blue denims. I began to chat with the officer, who had loads of data at his fingertips. In fact, there was a man at the computer sitting in one corner of his office-chamber who took out one printout after another, to indicate the nature and intensity of 'Maoist violence' throughout Chhattisgarh over the years.

He told me how successful the government had been over the past few years in 'tackling the Maoist problem', and how worried the Maoist top brass currently was about the loss of its senior leaders in the recent past. Many top leaders had either been killed or arrested, and many junior level cadres (some leaders too) had surrendered to the government. The departure of such a huge number of their soldiers had led to the formation of the Buniyadi Communist Training School in the depths of the Abujhmarh forests some years ago, where some of the best in the business were trained to be the top leaders of tomorrow. The huge vacuum urgently needed to be filled up, the officer told me.

There had been some newspaper reports on this, but I asked him for more information on the nature of the training there, when the shy young man who had led me to the room appeared again, a file in hand.

'Ask him!' the officer told me, smiling. '*He* was trained at the Buniyadi Communist Training School!' The young man didn't look sure whether to smile at this or feel ashamed about his past. He smiled nonetheless, politely, his eyes fixed on the floor. 'As a Maoist cadre, he was often visiting your hometown, Kolkata, to reach computer chips hidden in mobile phones to their comrades in that area,' the officer told me. 'Though most of the time he would hand it over to his colleagues at Howrah station and take the next train back to Chhattisgarh.'

Really? So what was he doing here? At a state government office? These thoughts rushed to my mind immediately. But I already knew the answer. I realized that this young man had surrendered and was now employed in this office. Later, Asiram Kashyap (alias Vikram) told me the story of his life. Most of the time the demure young man looked at the clean, whitewashed walls of the office chamber where we sat and chatted.

* * *

Asiram was born in Chhattisgarh's Kohkawada village of Bijapur. According to the 2011 Census of India, Kohkawada had fifteen families with a population of seventy-one (forty-one male and 30 female). Only one man in the entire village is literate, which makes the literacy rate slightly more than one per cent. The literacy rate of women here is zero. The literacy rate in Chhatisgarh is 80.27 per cent (male) and 60.24 per cent (female).[1] The data is indicative of how backward the village is. Till now, Asiram told me, there were no television sets nor a mobile phone network in his village. 'One has to walk a kilometre and a half to get the first vibes of a mobile tower. The village is administered by a sarpanch (the head of a village), an elected representative of the village. The entire village population is scheduled tribe.'

Asiram's father, Hidma, passed away when the boy was about eight or nine months old. Asiram has two elder sisters. His father's elder brother, Gagaru, then married his mother, Chitiwai. Gagaru became Asiram's bade pitaji (elder father). Chitiwai and Gagaru subsequently had two sons, who were now fourteen and ten years old.

The three older children—Asiram and his two sisters—were sent off to hostels far from their home adjoining Abujhmarh, the forested plateau that borders Chhattisgarh and Maharashtra. They were not exceptions. 'From Abujhmarh and surrounding areas, many people send their children off to Narayanpur, or to ashrams, schools and hostels run by government and non-government organizations elsewhere, so that they do not have to give away their children to Maoist squads,' the twenty-year-old told me. 'The Maoists come calling in villages, usually asking the male child to be 'given away' to squads. People cannot afford to turn them down out of fear.'

Many of his neighbours studied in the same school and lived in the same hostel. But, going far from home didn't mean the Maoists did not have access to the boys any more. Messages were repeatedly sent to Asiram even at his hostel asking him to join the movement. 'I could see how the poor suffered and I wanted to be part of the Maoist movement. I wanted to bring about justice and couldn't be selfish and continue with my studies when there was so much poverty and injustice all around,' Asiram said. 'But it is also true that I was so young at that time that in reality it was the plays, songs and dances that got me attracted to the movement. I thought it would be fun too,' he said. He was referring to local folk songs and dances that are part of small skits and plays telling stories of how the poor are being exploited by the government, rich landlords and corporate houses. These songs and skits are used by Maoists as a tool to appeal to villagers, especially the children.

Eventually, he did respond to the Maoists' call, though most of his friends continued to study at the hostel. Asiram was just 'eleven or twelve years old' when he joined 'the party'. He got lessons on Karl Marx, Vladimir Lenin, Mao Tse Tung, governance in India and gradually realized how the poor were being deprived of their rights and why his village continued to remain so backward. Asiram was sure he had chosen the right path. His personal life—his parents were saddened he had joined the Maoists—did not perturb him. He was named Vikram by the party and was trained in arms. While he worked mostly as a courier, he would carry a .303 revolver most of the time.

After working in different squads of Abujhmarh, Asiram was handpicked for a specialized six-month training course at the Buniyadi Communist Training School. He was among the first batches to be trained in 2008. Some of the brightest boys and girls who had passed classes eight to ten were handpicked and put through this exhaustive advanced course to prepare future leaders. Classes were taken by top cadres and the main objective was, more than anything else, to prepare a 'new educated leadership'. But Asiram was taken out of the classes midway due to some urgent work. He went back to Buniyadi school in 2009. This time, he completed the course.

The blueprint for the training was devised after many top Maoist leaders were killed and arrested, leading to a huge vacuum at the top. The course, incorporating training in arms and theoretical back-up, was aimed at creating the next generation of leaders of the CPI (Maoist). The party's supreme commander, Ganapathy, himself regularly checked up on it.

* * *

At the school, Asiram, along with thirty-nine other boys—all aged between fourteen and twenty-two—were up by four in the

morning. They got ready for roll call at 5.30 a.m. and started
physical training drills sharp at 6 a.m. After an hour and a half of
PT drills, it was time for breakfast—either freshly made chapattis
or some left over food from the previous day, usually rice soaked
in water. The food was prepared by villagers who also offered
protection to these boys and their teachers in the forests. The
villagers informed them of police movement in and around the
area. But the location was well chosen—a place where police or
civil administration had never even ventured before.

After breakfast, the boys and their teachers were deeply
engrossed in charcha (debate and discussions) on Marx, Mao,
Lenin, military affairs, Constitutions of different countries,
Communist teachings, leadership, mathematics, politics,
Constitution of the CPI (Maoist), Jail Code of India, police
system in different countries, civil administration, laws,
languages, arts, communication systems (from operating
computers, sending e-mails, using chips to transfer various data/
information) and so on. The main thrust of the training was on
leading teams; there was in-depth military, as well as ethical,
intellectual and academic knowledge. They also learned how
to build unity among people, how to woo villagers into the
movement, collect information and spread their intelligence
network. 'We studied ways to spread the Naxalites' network in
urban areas. This was a relatively new area which the organization
had been focusing on. While there had been some success, more
needed to be done,' said Asiram.

After breakfast, there was an interactive session that went
on till 11.30 in the morning. Lunch was served between 11.30
and 12 noon. There was a break for everyone between 12 noon
and 2 p.m. 'This is usually utilized by informal discussions, or
personal reading,' he said. After another session that included
discussions, it was time for sports between 5 and 6 p.m. when
the students and teachers played volley ball, kho-kho, kabaddi
and so on. Dinner was served between 8 and 9 p.m. and the
camp lights went off at 10 p.m.

Asiram's area of expertise was that of a courier. He was deft at passing information and bags from one place to another, from one squad to another, from one city to the next one. For bigger assignments, he would travel in trains and pass on money or computer chips to people in places such as Patna, Bhubaneswar and Kolkata, taking trains mostly from the Raipur railway station. Usually he would take a train, reach the destination, hand over the parcel, hang around in the city for the rest of the day and take the next train back to Raipur. He remembered how he once carried Rs 25 lakh in a backpack from Raipur to Kolkata, handed it over to Sadanala Ramakrishna and his men (who were later arrested in central Kolkata in February 2012 for the manufacture, of ammunition, spares and repairing of arms). Ramakrishna, a mechanical engineer and senior CPI (Maoist) leader and his team apparently purchased hardware such as pipes and motors and made them into weapons and ammunition parts. They worked from a flat in Kolkata purchased under a fake name. Money was also sent to Mumbai through Kolkata for purchasing raw materials.[2] 'I got off the train, handed the money over, and left Howrah station. Through the day I went to different places in Kolkata—I saw Dharamtalla which was milling with people, and also Victoria Memorial…and in the evening I was back in Howrah station and took the train back to Raipur.'

Despite the hard work, his leader Prabhakara [an aide to CPI (Maoist) general secretary Ganapathy] often scolded him and alleged that he had 'spent too much money' during his trips, Asiram told me. 'Prices of things, especially food, are higher in cities. I hadn't overspent. I had been submitting bills for all expenses, but he kept harping on the fact that I hadn't curtailed my expenses.' This made Asiram angry and upset, but he stuck around for some more time. But when the news of his stepfather and grandfather's death reached him, he decided to call it quits.

'I hadn't met my family for more than six years. Badey pita-ji had passed away in 2012, but I wasn't informed by my comrades and leaders about his death. This made me very bitter. What kind of a job was I doing where my leaders would hide the news of my father's death from me because I might leave the camp and visit my family for a few days!'

The shy smile that had so far been playing on his face vanished in an instant. 'My grandfather, a sarpanch, was alleged to be a mukbir [police informer] by the Maoists. They went to his house and he was stabbed with a sickle in front of other villagers. He was killed by those that I had been working with all along,' he mumbled under his breath. 'I find it hard to accept this.'

Asiram didn't hide the fact that he was also extremely overworked. Finally, he decided to flee the camp. 'I wrote a letter addressed to my leader Prabhakara, telling him I was quitting.' But he did not disclose this before stepping out, lest he was stopped or killed by his colleagues as punishment. 'I said I was going out to take a bath,' Asiram said. This was a common pretext for those who run away from squads. Asiram and another boy left the camp and walked for hours through the forest to reach a bus stop. It was a distance of approximately 90 kilometres from where his squad was based, to his village home in Kohkawada. The road was dotted with police outposts and dangerous for the two young men. A huge distance had to be covered on foot before a bus route was even available.

It turned out that another boy from the squad who had gathered the information about the two boys' escape had passed on the message to a police chowki at Kanker. 'We were stopped on the way by the police. They began to interrogate us. Initially I tried to bluff them by claiming that my name was Hemant Kumar Kashyap.' But after a while, Asiram decided to give in. He laughed now, recalling how surprised he was to find that the police did not beat him up even after he conceded he was a Maoist. 'I decided to surrender and told them I would help them'.

Was he driven by fear that led him to surrender rather than

face arrest? Going by the way the state had unleashed terror on villagers in the name of Salwa Judum, it wasn't difficult to guess that Asiram might have been overpowered by fear.

* * *

The circumstances under which a large number of 'surrenders' have taken place, is especially significant in this light. Since it is difficult to ascertain the exact moment of the change of heart— whether it took place *before* or *after* one came into the clutches of the police—it is not always possible to say which argument in the mind of the Maoist had *led* to the surrender. In fact, that should not be a consideration either.

Asiram, Suman, Toofan and several others have in reality been caught by the police first. They had either walked into a trap or were picked up during a raid. It was only after the rebels were with the police that they were given the option to choose to surrender. In reality, this was not much of a choice at all, between a miserable time of facing arrest and imprisonment or the relatively easier option of a job and family life through surrender.

As a policy, all state governments gave tacit support to officers to make this offer to arrested Naxals. All police superintendents admitted this in private conversation, but would not go on record on this. This is not a 'policy' on record. In fact, it would be more appropriate to call this a strategy of the State—a strategy that the officers of the police force and the civil administration, ministers and other policymakers have discussed and decided amongst themselves, but which has not been officially framed as a document or policy. The simple reason behind such a strategy is that it is more of a success for the police to get someone to 'surrender'. An arrest means that a Maoist cadre has come under the police net but has not given up her/his ideological war and still wants to continue to fight against the State even in prison. But a Maoist cadre's 'surrender' means that she/he has given up that fight against the State. This is the reason why the police officers coax, cajole, sweet talk and even pressurize the arrested cadres to accept the 'surrender package' offered by the State. The package has been made more and more 'attractive' over the years, in terms of the amount of money on offer and other 'benefits'.

In any case, Asiram didn't admit to me that fear had anything to do with his decision to surrender. After all, he told me, he had written his resignation letter at the camp and had fled the squad.

A few months after his surrender in mid-2013, he had been working in a state department under the Chhattisgarh government. The details of Asiram's job profile are not disclosed here for his safety. He draws a monthly salary of Rs 19,000 and lives in the quarters that the state government has provided. When I met Asiram, he told me about his plans to bring his mother to his quarters in Raipur. 'I was ready to do any job and bring my family to the city and live a peaceful life.'

His sisters were now married, but his mother continued to live in their Kohkawada village with her two sons. Whenever I spoke to Asiram over the phone subsequently, he told me that his mother didn't want to come down to Raipur to stay with him. 'She wants to stay in the village and look after the little land that we have, where they grow maize and lentils. She has lived there all her life and doesn't want to leave that and come down,' Asiram said. 'But I keep worrying every single waking moment that they [Maoists] will come and kill her. They have already threatened her and asked her to disclose my whereabouts. My mother is a courageous woman, so she has admonished them. But I don't know how long this can go on. It is, after all, a real threat.'

He also told me about an eighteen-year-old woman his mother had chosen for him to marry. She is from Gidam— where Asiram's family was originally based—and works at a government-run anganwadi centre. Does his past put him in a disadvantageous position as a groom, I asked Asiram. After all, his life was under threat. Would a girl want to marry him with this knowledge? He told me then that he had known his would-be bride since childhood. 'We were in the same class,' he told me over the phone. 'She will come and stay here with me at Raipur after we are married.'

Asiram may be one of the few surrendered Maoists who do not have pending cases against them. For most surrendered Naxals, the cases are pending, and they must appear before the court during hearings. Despite the so-called freedom, they continue to live in a veritable jail, unable to move out of the accommodations offered to them, or to move freely without security cover of the police.

So far, Asiram has been happy to do a simple job, earn a salary and is looking forward to marriage to a childhood friend. Yes, there was the fear of his own life and that of his mother and brothers back in the village, but Asiram feels it is the price that needed to be paid for the little happiness and peace he now has in his life. From the outside, Asiram became happy and contented after his surrender.

* * *

In fact, there is a common thread that ties the stories of Suman, Toofan and Asiram together. It is about the induction of children in this armed war. By now, it is a known fact that children are an integral part of this armed war. Suman was fifteen years old, Toofan was sixteen and Asiram twelve years old when they joined the Maoists in their armed war against the state. Champa, from Odisha's Koraput district, a surrendered girl I met in Rayagada, told me she was inducted into a Maoist dalam when she was sixteen. Another girl, Rajani Mutha Majhi, whom I also met in Odisha's Rayagada, said she had left her home and joined a Maoist squad as a ten year old. This element hardly figures in narratives and treatises on the Maoist war. And somehow, by way of glorifying the sacrifices of people who give up their life and liberty to fight the government, this aspect of the war is never condemned or criticized as bitterly and wholeheartedly as it should be.

Not that the young would have been spared in the war had the Maoists not recruited them. The armed forces are equally brutal in their treatment of children—they don't bat an eyelid when it comes to shooting, beating up children or subjecting them to threats at gunpoint in order to extract information. Villagers (including children) are asked by the armed forces to check the bodies of slain jawans, as they fear landmines might be attached to the body. If there are bombs, the armed forces do not care if children die in the process of checking for them.

Children as young as seven or eight years or even younger are inducted into the Chetna Natya Manch (CNM), the cultural wing of the CPI (Maoist). Maoist ideologue, Varvara Rao, had told me: 'Why blame Naxalites if children become part of the armed movement? A doctor's child may be surrounded by medicines and lawyer's child may be surrounded by law books.' The analogy is not as shocking as it sounds. In fact Rao's statement is well meaning in the sense that he feels adults ensure that their children are not harmed by the guns, and therefore they are kept engaged in the songs, dance and theatre as part of Maoists' groups.

During a long chat that I had with Rao as we rode from S.N. Banerjee Road to the Kolkata Airport in a cab on one of his visits to Kolkata, he told me: 'Children get naturally drawn to the same profession as their parents. The same goes for children of Naxals. They are surrounded by their parents who work with arms and ammunition, so the children too may be seen with arms.'

True, but perhaps that is not the only truth. Many young boys and girls I spoke to, who are either in their teens, twenties or thirties now, told me that they had been inducted into the Naxal movement when they were between eight and fourteen years old. They had left their village homes forever, leaving behind parents and siblings unwillingly. At such a young age, children do not want to 'willingly' leave home, their parents, siblings and friends. Delicate, yet sharp and intelligent, young boys and girls can be easily moulded and trained in body and mind. Moreover, they don't know any reality beyond the ones into which they are initiated.

I managed to get hold of two photographs of a boy, barely seven or eight years old, holding a gun. The pictures had been taken from a video shot inside a camp by a Maoist cadre. The boys, girls, women and men are seen moving from one part of the forest to another with their clothes, utensils and tents. The boy has his possessions tied in a gamchha while he playfully aims the gun at the person shooting the video. This boy—unkempt, with large and beautiful eyes and a fabulous smile on his tiny round face—is said to have once pulled a trigger and killed a cop but there is no confirmation on this. Neither is it known whether he was afraid of the bloodshed or whether he was thrilled to see the power of the gun he was carrying.

This boy vanished from Jangalmahal—the forested areas of Purulia, Bankura and West Midnapore districts of West Bengal—at the time the Maoist movement began to fall apart in the region. He apparently travelled to a different city, worked in a factory close to Mumbai for some time, and then joined the Maoists again when things cooled down a bit.

The children's experiences are the same everywhere. They are forced into a war that puts them at enormous risks and even kills them.

Rajani Mutha Majhi, a sixteen-year-old now, recalled how the Naxals would keep visiting her village Chandrapur in the Koraput-Rayagada area and there would be 'songs, dance, music and plays. I loved it.' The Koraput-Rayagada region is stunning—the red earth, brown mountains and green forests make it one of the most picturesque parts of the country. But there is poverty too. 'They (the Naxals) would sometimes live in our homes. One day, I was asked to accompany them to their squad,' Rajani recalled. 'I followed them, much against my family's wishes, but there was a sort of pressure on us, so my parents could not even object,' she said. 'No one knew what would happen if we said "no", so my parents let me leave, unwillingly.'

She went to the camp, ate, cooked, participated in plays that had many songs and dances, and eventually was given arms training. After the initial novelty wore off, Rajani started feeling miserable. 'I missed my family so terribly. No one harmed me at the camp. But I did not like that life. I loved the songs and dance and plays, but couldn't live without my parents.'

Her family constantly missed her too and her father and brother kept sending messages to the Maoist group to send her back home. 'I would lie on the mat and sleep. But I would weep even in my sleep, I missed home so desperately.' Finally, Rajani got back home, but as there were cases pending against her, the girl 'surrendered' before the police. The narrative here is disjointed because her surrender too is possibly an arrest in reality, which neither the police nor Rajani herself were keen on revealing.

Another girl, Champa, told me she was inducted into a Maoist group when she was sixteen. Champa, from Odisha's Koraput district had lost both parents as a child and was being brought up by her maternal uncle. She had nothing to look forward to in her life. She was almost relieved when groups of men and women visited her village, singing songs and acting out plays that spoke of social injustice and how the poor should unite to fight an armed war against the exploitative rich.

Champa joined them and it was fun because she didn't have to go hungry anymore and she made new friends. If she was almost non-existent earlier, at the camp she felt important as she was now part of a social cause and was being treated as a human being. She also felt empowered with a .303 rifle. On relatively lighter days, she would massage her hair with oil and tie it into a plait, chatting and giggling with the other girls and older women. But mostly, she would move from one part of the forest to another in the dead of the night. It was dangerous but fun until a bullet fired from the gun of a policeman got wedged into the flesh of her left arm. She was on sentry duty when a police team swooped in on their camp and started firing. As the bullet lodged in her flesh, Champa lay reeling in pain and soon lost consciousness. When she awoke, she was in a hospital in police custody and subsequently underwent three operations.

The police gave her the option to surrender instead of facing arrest. She chose to surrender, hoping her life would change if she got some money and a job.

A portion of Champa's arm is now only a huge lump of flesh that makes it difficult for her to wear even a simple salwar kameez. She presses and squeezes the flesh to allow the sleeves of her clothes to make way through the arm, but giggles all the same at this 'funny' thing that's happened to her. Now, she stitches clothes and runs a tailoring shop.

* * *

When children as young as six or seven become part of the bal sangams/sangathans, they spend happy times singing songs, dancing, and learning in schools run by the Maoists. But they have to grow up quickly, and the lessons are then about political tenets of Marx, Lenin and Mao. Soon, the children assume the roles of couriers and informers and then the next step is to train in non-lethal weapons like lathis.

Once the children are around twelve years old, they join other sections—either they are promoted to become part of Chetna Natya Manch (CNM) or street theatre troupes, or they are in jan militia and small groups. The children are given weapons training with rifles and trained in different kinds of explosives used in landmines. There is no fixed age for this. Some are twelve or thirteen when they train in arms and explosives.

It's not easy to lead a normal life in the villages, keeping oneself completely detached from these things. The pleas from Maoists asking villagers to allow their children to join the organization's children's wings are persistent. And once they become part of squads, leaves are not allowed easily. This is the usual process of recruitment in Chhattisgarh, Jharkhand, Odisha and Bihar. In West Bengal, however, the recruits have mostly been slightly older—teenagers—though some younger boys were also recruited during the Lalgarh agitation.

There are schools run by the CPI (Maoist) where Maoism is taught up to class four. Over the past few years, the party has been focusing on mobile schools that tour villages in the interiors of Chhattisgarh and Jharkhand. These mobile schools have teachers who train children through crash courses in temporary camps. The teachers belong to the Maoists' 'local organizational' (LO) and 'local guerilla' (LG) squads. There are usually four to five members from these LG and LO squads who form the mobile schools.

Human Rights Watch, an international rights organization, observed in its September 2008 report, 'Dangerous Duty: Children and the Chhattisgasrh Conflict'[3], that children have been caught in the crossfire between Maoists and the security forces, schools have been bombed and children have been robbed of their childhood. The report is based on research conducted by Human Rights Watch in Khammam and Warangal districts of Andhra Pradesh, and Bijapur, Dantewada, and Bastar districts of Chhattisgarh between November 2007 and February 2008. It states:

'Children in jan militias and dalams participate in armed exchanges with government security forces. Children in bal sangams and CNMs do not directly participate in hostilities, but are nevertheless open to attacks by government security forces during anti-Naxalite combing operations. Children recruited into dalams may not be permitted to leave, and may face severe reprisals, including the killing of family members, if they surrender to the police.'

The researchers spoke to several children and this is what they had to say:

I joined the military dalam when I was thirteen or fourteen years old. I was studying in an ashram school, eighth standard— when Naxalites came to my hostel. I didn't want to go. They said I could study until the 10th, but I should go with them… We got weapons training, learnt about landmines and a little karate… [Finally] I had an opportunity to run away… One year after I ran away, both my younger brothers (age eight and twelve) were killed [by the Naxalites in retaliation]. They beat my mother and broke her arm. They burned our house and took all our things.

—Former child dalam member, December 2007.

The police asked me also to become an SPO [special police officer] but I refused because I did not want to become an SPO and commit heinous crimes. I did not want to shoot and kill people… They do not ask anyone how old they are. Even fourteen-year-olds can become SPOs if the police want them to become SPOs.

—Poosam Kanya (pseudonym), former resident of Errabore camp, December 2007.

Officially, the Naxals do not admit they induct youngsters into their dalams, but there is evidence (apart from actual confirmation by those who are/were in the groups) to show that this is a reality. Hundreds of youngsters less than eighteen years of age have laid down their lives in the war. The Maoists' document, *Balidaano* lists such youngsters, showers praise on them for laying down their lives and hopes they will inspire many others. While the ones mentioned are over eighteen years old, the number of years they have spent with the party and their experiences indicate that they had been inducted into the groups as children.

* * *

If the acts of children are glorified by the CPI (Maoist) and if Maoists have been catching them young, so too does the State. The Chhattisgarh government has been working for years to inculcate their point of view, their side of the story, among the children. Who better to start with than those who have lost their parents in the war?

Astha Gurukul is a children's home in Dantewada district, set up by the Chhattisgarh government where education and stay is offered to children orphaned by Maoist violence. There were 271 children (141 boys and 130 girls) aged between five and sixteen years at the time of my visit. The home was started by the Chhattisgarh government in 2007 with 80 children.

Children here are up very early—between 5.30 and 6 a.m. They have to be ready to leave for school at 7 a.m. One batch of 104 children go to Kendriya Vidyalaya. At 8.45 a.m., the next batch of 85 children are sent to Gayatri Vidyapith, a private English medium school and, at 10.15 a.m., the rest go to Shishu Mandir, a Hindi medium school under the State board. The state government has tied up with these schools so that the children staying at Astha Gurukul—which is more of a hostel that offers accommodation, food and evening tuitions—can attend them. The hostel building is three-storied with a number of small dormitory rooms. Each of these rooms has four single beds. There are common toilets on each floor. The boys' and girls' dormitories are on separate floors.

When I reached the hostel, the last batch of children was preparing to leave for school. But five-year-old Nahid Khan didn't want to go to school. He claimed to have a pain in his stomach, and hearing this made me smile (do children everywhere find this one perfect excuse to bunk school?). It was a pretext all right, for he happily munched on the poha which we ate around 10.30 a.m. (while chatting with the teachers and helpers and the warden), and ran around the shadowy, narrow corridors of the dormitories where only streaks of light seeped in. He smiled mischievously whenever he met my eyes and we could see Nahid appearing and disappearing with peals of laughter as the warden and I criss-crossed the length and breadth of the hostel to find a relatively 'clean' toilet that I could use. Most of the toilets were dirty with excreta lying about along with leftovers of the rice and vegetables the children had eaten for breakfast that morning. These toilets were also used for bathing, and the warden was visibly embarrassed. 'Most of the children here come from extremely poor homes, and it takes a lot of time to teach them hygiene,' she told me.

Sometimes we found the doors to a room or two ajar and some adolescents lying on the beds chatting. On being questioned by the warden some replied that they were ill, at which the warden said she would arrange for a visit to the doctor.

Meanwhile, I spoke to a small batch of students who were ready for their school in pretty red-and-white uniforms, their well-oiled hair tied in ponytails or plaits. Most of them wanted to be either collectors or policemen, a few, predictably, doctors or engineers.

The most riveting story was that of Nahid Khan, who had a mischievous smile permanently embedded in his small, dark eyes. Nahid wore a striped half-sleeved shirt and brown shorts. He was only four or five years old. I could barely bring myself to ask him what his story was. Who had he lost in the violence? His father? Or mother? Or both? I asked him other things like 'What games do you play? Will you teach me how to play marbles?', 'Do you like to go to school?', 'Who all are your friends?', 'Why didn't you go to school today?', 'What is your favourite song?' and so on.

Nahid answered some of them, dismissed others with giggles, and headed for the dining table, where he picked up a plate of poha and began to eat busily. He quickly finished his share and left. When he was playing somewhere around in the garden, I asked the teachers about him. One told me that the boy had lost his father in 'Naxal violence'. After a while, when Nahid was back, I asked him who was there back home. 'My father is no more. Papa guzar gaye,' he answered matter-of-factly. He knew why he was at the children's home and that everyone around him had either lost one or both parents in some violent episode involving the Maoists.

'My home is in Namaram village. My father used to work as a mason. One day, he boarded the thela (handcart) of his friend, a banana seller. After a while, two policemen asked for a ride in the thela as they wanted to be dropped off somewhere,' Nahid told me. There was no hint of fear or discomfort as he recalled an event that would make anyone shudder. 'There was a booby trap and a powerful blast took them all away.' he spoke without a pause and did not dwell on the horror of it all. Perhaps he had narrated this to many strangers many times before.

'After the death of my father, my mother Qureshia put me in this home. She works at a place close to this school. My brother Shahid also lives in this home. My sister, Muskaan, is in class 2.' Muskaan stayed with their mother, said Nahid. Did he like going to school? Of course! Why? 'Because I like playing baati,' Nahid quickly reasoned. Baati is a game played with marbles, he explained to me. He also loved maths, he was quick to tell me. I asked Nahid what he wanted to be when he grew up.

'A policeman,' he proudly announced, without even waiting for a moment to ponder.

'Why?'

'Because policemen kill bad people.'

Who are the bad people?

'The Naxals'.

* * *

For children living in the battlefield where the Maoists and the State are fighting this protracted war, the most important thing is to choose a villain and side with the other.

Without considering the ethics of wooing the children in this game of war, the State, its armed forces, and the Maoists have all taken in children in their bid to get more support. Whether it is the mobile school run by the Maoists or the Astha Gurukul, the situation is bizarrely similar to Satyajit Ray's film *Hirak Raja'r Deshey* where the tyrant brainwashes his subjects so they can parrot his favourite lines and surrender themselves to him.

Part II

THE MEN

~

'The Chhattisgarh Police gave Kasru a job which requires him to carry firearms. His job entails visits to the forest in search of hideouts where his former Maoist colleagues are likely to be. His former foes—the police—may have ceased to be his foes, but his earlier comrades have now turned into his greatest enemies. His job now is to hound them out and hand them over to the police. His life is pretty much the same in that it could end any moment in a chance encounter with a Maoist. His peace of mind is lost forever.'

Kasru after his surrender

5

Naveen Nureti

Travelling down south from Raipur, through Kanker and Pharasgaon, right down to Kondagaon, I come to a crossroads. There is a sharp turn north towards Narayanpur. The straight road goes towards Dantewada. How lucky for me that, at this crossroads, I have only to decide whether I should stop here for lunch! For many Maoist cadres who have travelled along this same path, it must have been a much tougher decision regarding the course their lives should take.

It is a five-hour drive from Raipur to here, well past lunchtime, and quite hot and humid. At Kondagaon bus terminus, I settled down to eat a quick lunch along with the driver of the vehicle I was traveling in, at a tiny eatery where only egg curry and rice were available. It looked similar to the egg curry available at roadside dhabas throughout a large part of India, with thick red gravy achieved with the help of a generous use of red chilli powder. I sat on a wobbly wooden bench and ate out of a steel plate placed on an equally unsteady table. My eyes were blinded by the smoke billowing out of an earthen chullah and from the curry that I could eat only in small portions.

All around, there were men sitting and downing bottle after bottle of beer in the heat. Though the prospect of drinking alone inside a semi-dark roadside dhaba under the spell of a thick envelope of blinding smoke was genuinely appealing, there was work to be done. Moreover, it would be quite unbecoming of a woman travelling alone in unfamiliar terrain. So I paid my bill and scooted, deciding to be adventurous another day.

There was a cacophony of people boarding long-distance buses just by the side of a market, where everything from marigold garlands to bananas, sweets with flies buzzing over them to cheap rexine bags and brightly coloured polyester sarees were being sold.

From Kondagaon, the road takes a sharp turn north-west towards Narayanpur.

Carved out of Bastar district in 2007, Narayanpur is now a separate district surrounded by Kondagaon, Dantewada, Kanker, Bastar and Bijapur. The main tribes living in 366 villages of the district are Gond, Maria, Muria and Halba.

At Narayanpur town, which is a really small town, I met Naveen Nureti—also known as Kamlu Ram Nureti—who used to be a middle-level Maoist leader. He was one of the nineteen Divisional Committee (DVC, zilla party committee) members in Marh-Uttar Bastar division in 2013. He was a short, dark and lean man with small, deep, intelligent eyes. He had a thin moustache, and smiled a lot. We ended up talking for hours at the guest house where I was staying for the night.

Naveen was born in Kohkameta village of Narayanpur district (then Bastar) of Chhattisgarh, and he was a bright 22-year-old when he joined the Maoists way back in 1995. He used to live with his parents in the village and recalled how, as a little boy, he had seen the village zamindar hire poor villagers to cultivate his land, but sacked them from time to time without paying them.

The people of Kohkameta village were poor and lacked basic facilities like clinics, hospitals, schools, or even ration shops. The landowners and government officials made matters worse. Rich landlords deprived them of their pay and the government employees who worked in the local offices (especially the forest officials) stole the poor villagers' chickens or goats, or lifted the grains and vegetables that they somehow managed to grow within their limited means, leaving them angry and bitter. There was sharp class and caste divide, too, as untouchability was also a major problem.

Naveen, young and intelligent, did not want to remain resigned to his fate like most others in his village. Their silence came from fear of being beaten up, of being ostracized and being denied work and pay. How would they survive if they protested?

But, no matter what risks it involved, Naveen decided to speak up. He, along with some fellow villagers raised their voice against the zamindar—but they faced the heat from the entire moneyed class in the village. Their anger kept simmering and was just waiting to explode.

Around that time, a Maoist commander from Andhra Pradesh—Ringanna—came to Naveen's village along with a dozen associates and organized the villagers into a movement against the landlords. Backed by Ringanna and his men, the villagers of Kohkameta found the confidence they never had earlier.

So, finally, how were the rich made to realize the value of the poor? The so-called lower caste villagers vowed that they would not remove carcasses of buffaloes and cows belonging to the rich, upper-caste families. It was then that their worth was finally acknowledged, though not openly. 'We told them, "Cut open your arms, let us see if blood flows out of your body, or milk,"' Naveen recalled, enthusiastic to narrate the events of those heady days of struggle and subsequent success.

As Naveen fearlessly led fellow villagers, demanding equal pay and equal rights, Ringanna and his men noticed his leadership qualities and asked him to join the Dandakaranya Adivasi Kisaan Mazdoor Sangathan (DAKMS). 'When I first joined, I would simply play with the kids—we used to bathe them in the ponds, clean them with soap, give them biscuits to eat. We had to teach them about basic hygiene,' Naveen said.

Soon, he was part of the Dandakaranya farmer and labour

wings of the party. Several schools—called ashrams—were opened in the Marh region to teach children from classes one to eight. In addition, they formed community farming—pooling in with small plots of land and yielding crops, raised awareness on the rights of the poor and counselled against alcoholism.

'In those days, foreign journalists would visit forests and villages in the area to shoot photographs of nude women. Some tribal people are so poor they do not even have clothes to wear; for some others, it is a part of their culture. But the foreign journalists who went in—with the help of some local people who made money by giving access to these journalists—neither respected the culture nor sympathized with the poor. They took photographs for all the wrong reasons. That's why we decided not to allow them entry in the area,' Naveen said. 'There was a major social change quietly taking place.'

Naveen was also part of a civil organization that met teachers, students, retired government and non-government employees and made speeches on Independence Day and Republic Day, talking about the futility of the country's independence ('"Yeh azaadi jhoothi hai", we would say very often during our speeches,' he recalled).

Then, in 1999, he got arrested for this apparently undemocratic work or perhaps due to his association with the Naxal cadres. Naveen was eventually let out on bail after seventeen days in prison. 'The police were still after me. I was on the run, hiding in various places, returning home after long intervals. But this was turning out to be very inconvenient. At one point Gautam—my leader—said it was no longer safe for me to stay at home. It was then, in 2002, that I left home permanently and joined a dalam.'

In 2004 March, Naveen became an Area Committee commander of Nellar region, then an Area Committee secretary in 2011, and a DVC member in 2012. He was consistently taking on more important roles.

He married a comrade, Nagabatti and the couple had three children—Hemlata, Hemlal, and Maheswari. The children, too, became members of the party's children's wing and studied in schools run by the Maoists.

The children easily blended into the organization, like their father Naveen who had all along been so deeply involved and dedicated. Naveen was in the party's organizational wing— so his role was mostly non-military. He was involved in decision-making, in organizing camps and in setting policies or implementing them. However, almost all members have to take basic training in arms. Naveen had started training and operating firearms since 2002 and almost always carried an Insas rifle. Guns are a basic necessity for the cadres as they have to move around in the forests and need to protect themselves from sudden attacks from the police or wild animals.

'Using weapons was no big deal for people like us who were born in remote, backward villages. Our home was by the side of lush green forests. At home we had weapons like *bharmar* to kill wild boars, wolves, bears and other wild animals. The bharmar is a weapon that was used by tribal leader Mangal Pandey…' Naveen explained. 'It wasn't difficult for me to move on to Insas. It was more for self-defence as I had to run around a lot from one hideout to another, sometimes in groups, and often alone.'

But after a few years, Naveen began to worry about the way policies were rapidly changing in the party. He explained it to me quickly and clearly—I realized he must have pondered, considered and justified to himself and to people close to him about these reasons a thousand times.

'I was most worried about the incessant killings,' Naveen said. Just a few months after he surrendered, Maoists attacked a convoy of Congress leaders in Chhattisgarh's Sukma, killing eighteen persons including former state minister Mahendra Karma (the man behind the infamous Salwa Judum initiative), Chhattisgarh Congress chief Nand Kumar Patel and injuring former union minister VC Shukla (who died later). The dead included mostly Congress leaders and workers, apart from police personnel.[1] This incident took place on 25 May 2013, while Naveen had surrendered on 23 February that year.

Survivors said that the Maoists sang and danced around the bullet-ridden body of Karma, even as they spared others who were not their targets.[2] Karma had long been the target of the Naxalites because of the way he planned and spearheaded the Salwa Judum—unleashing terror on villagers in the name of consolidating them and fighting the Maoists.

Naveen was glad he had not been a part of this and many other gruesome attacks that followed. 'Incessant killings, targeting political leaders, police jawans and even civilian deaths were being seen as collateral damage by those at the helm. But I had strong objections,' he said. 'It is difficult to fathom how human beings can get such joy out of killing other humans. It is true that this is an armed war but we have to be careful about the use of arms,' Naveen added.

Some of the issues he posed before the organization were:

- Let us decide whom we should kill and whom we should not. And let's also make sure why we are killing them.
- The war is against the moneyed people who are exploiting the poor. So why are the poor killing the poor? The policemen dying in Maoist ambushes are after all poor soldiers, while the senior members of both Maoists and the police are not engaged directly in the clash. Is this the war we wanted to fight?
- What is to be prioritized in development? Is it water, agriculture or education?

Naveen's argument against targeting ordinary policemen was discussed at various levels of the Maoist hierarchy. In Sabyasachi Panda's letter, there was a similar argument, in which Panda said that the Naxals often killed ordinary policemen who were themselves tribals and had sympathy for 'our movement'.

'We had a lot of *charcha*—discussions—on these issues. But there is no respect for the opinions of the local people. The dominant voice is that of the Andhra cadres, and the policies are framed by them. There is no respect for the feelings of the local people of Chhattisgarh,' Naveen said.

This rift, between the cadres from Andhra Pradesh and the local people of the state in which the movement was on, has often been discussed. According to Naveen, 'The cadres from Andhra—who form the top leadership—take the major decisions and I dare say that it was under their instructions that so many of my relatives were killed. They don't know how to trust the local people despite working with them on such an important social issue,' Naveen said.

Naveen was angry and frustrated that some of his relatives were killed by Maoists like himself. 'There were allegations that they had leaked information to the police, and the Maoists did not spare them,' he said. Like Asiram Kashyap's grandfather, who had been charged with *mukbiri* (leaking information), six relatives of Naveen Nureti lost their lives for a similar reason. All six were accused of mukbiri and killed. His father's elder brother Aituram Nureti, cousin (Aituram's son) Kamal Ram Nureti, three uncles (one from his mother's side and two from his father's side) and another distant cousin were all killed by the Maoists on allegations of mukbiri.

As we discussed several ethical issues, sitting in picturesque Narayanpur with dusk beginning to descend, Naveen said he was most perturbed by the deaths of his relatives.

It was difficult to ascertain if the 'traitors' were truly guilty, and the leaders were not willing to take the slightest risks. If anyone is suspected of mukbiri, then the leaders do not bat an eyelid to kill the person, whether she/he is a member of the party or an ordinary villager. That is the dictum in this ruthless job.

Yet, it was not uncommon that in many cases the allegations were baseless and often the result of unsubstantiated suspicion or simply a personal rivalry. Often, these were random killings for other reasons and mukbiri was only the pretext. 'Every move of the locals is questioned by the Andhra cadres. They were always suspicious of us. I was terribly upset over this. I had begun to work for the organization since, to me, it was a social cause. But while we were talking of development, the means to achieve that had turned out to be only killings.'

He was also sarcastic about the way pictures of Maoist camps were portrayed in the media and in books. Naveen alleged that the camp milieu would become completely different when there were visitors. 'When representatives of human rights organizations, or journalists visited us, things looked very different. It was a big sham because, in reality, they (the senior leaders who hailed from Andhra Pradesh) looked down upon the local people—the Mariyas. There was an inherent organizational duplicity. It was all very friendly and congenial when visitors came, but when these people left, we got back to being cynical about each other.'

Frustrated with it all, Naveen called the Narayanpur police superintendent's number—it was easily accessible because the police had distributed it widely in posters all over the area for Maoists to call if they were keen on surrendering. Naveen had asked his wife, son and younger daughter to reach his village home at Kohkameta while he and his elder daughter made their way through the forest to surrender.

The sub-inspector who was handling the calls, on the number advertised all over Narayanpur, reached Jagdalpur following a discussion with Naveen. The father-daughter duo reached Jagdalpur and made sure none of Naveen's teammates suspected that he had made his escape from the camp. Finally Naveen surrendered on 23 February 2013. Next, Naveen made sure his wife and two remaining children reached Narayanpur too. At the time of his surrender, Hemlata was fifteen years old, Hemlal was thirteen and Maheswari was eight.

The family has been staying at Narayanpur under police protection since. 'We all wanted to start afresh. When we were part of the organization, even my little girl was picked up by the police in Delhi during an agitation. Somehow, some important people with connections helped us in getting her released. We now want to leave all that behind,' Naveen told me.

The then district police superintendent, Amit Kamble, who has been instrumental in several key surrenders said, 'We've really worked hard on surrenders these past few years. We had issued posters in Hindi and in Gondi to make sure Maoists moving through these areas would take a good look and think about their future.'

The following year, there was a high-profile surrender—in Andhra Pradesh, though the cadre was based in Chhattisgarh. In January 2014, Gumudavelli Venkatakrishna Prasad, spokesperson and member of the Dandakarnya Special Zonal Committee (DKSZC), surrendered before the Andhra Pradesh police.[3] Prasad, better known as Gudsa Usendi—the name given to all those who hold the position of the Dandakaranya spokesperson—belonged to the Mariya tribe and worked in Chhattisgarh's Abujhmarh region.

A graduate who hailed from Andhra's Warangal district, Prasad surrendered along with his Maoist wife. Many feel that after the May 2013 attack on Congress leaders in the Darbha valley, Prasad changed his hardliner position. He is said to have surrendered because he was against the killings—though there is another view that he had been ailing for some time. It is even said that he took permission from the top leadership after expressing his wish to surrender.

In recent times, scores of foot-soldiers have surrendered. They said that the killings were the most frustrating and depressing part of this job. It is somewhat ironic that this should be the case for a party that originates from the 'revolutionary political line of annihilating the class enemy'. How can soldiers of a declared armed war against the State back out from the battlefield because the violence is too much to handle?

In *A Few Words About Guerrilla Action*, Charu Mazumdar mentions how to form 'guerrilla units' in complete secrecy, where he advises the comrades to whisper into the poor peasant's ears, 'Don't you think it is a good thing to finish off such and such jotedar?' Mazumdar also talks about the use of choppers, spears, javelins and sickles. He talks about gradually increasing the frequency of attacks and a time 'when the battle cry will be: "He who has not dipped his hand in the blood of class enemies can hardly be called a communist".'[4] But this extreme position of the Naxalites has been getting less popular within the party over the years.

Former Naxal leader Ashim Chatterjee, during an interview at his home in the northern fringes of Kolkata, said that the CPI (Maoist) leaders today do not fight a political/ideological fight with the CPM and other political parties, whom they are opposed to. 'It is more of the killing spree, murders at individual levels. This has been so in West Bengal and even outside. The Maoists would have been relevant if their differences with mainstream political parties had been political. It is due to its detachment from the people and the class struggle that the movement is failing. Its dependence on the party's squads, instead of getting involved in the people's struggle is what ruined it completely. This has been more so in West Bengal, where the movement originated.'

In Chatterjee's opinion, it was impossible for the movement to progress against this backdrop.

The Maoist cadres are much better equipped today with professional training, armed with the newest technology, sophisticated firearms and latest information. They are very different from those who were inspired by Mao-Tse Tung and became part of the Naxalbari movement.

Their appeal to the middle class and large scale support from urban students in elite colleges has been on the wane. What are the reasons?

In March 2010, Kanu Sanyal, who inspired hundreds of youths during the Naxalbari uprising along with Charu Mazumdar, was found hanging in his house at Naxalbari's Sephtulajote village in West Bengal.[5] Sanyal had continued to work with peasants till the very end. In 1967, he along with Mazumdar, broke away from the CPM's Darjeeling district unit when the party's United Front government was in power in West Bengal.

Over the years, Sanyal had turned totally bitter about the CPI (Maoist)'s endless killing spree.[6] Sanyal could not approve of the policy of targeting individuals. In fact, he did not even approve of the word 'Maoist'. While he believed that the way to freedom lay in armed movement alone, he felt it should be an armed movement that would not target individuals and never indulge in a killing spree.

'That (*khatam* line) was the line Charu Mazumdar and his followers adopted in the late 1960s and 70s. And it was one of the prime reasons that distanced people from the movement, making it a failure,' Sanyal had said in the interview. 'If one really follows Mao's thoughts, one should aim to unite people to launch an armed struggle against the State rather than kill individuals. Mao had advocated power being distributed among common people,' Sanyal had said before his death.

It is not clear what prompted Sanyal to kill himself, but it is generally agreed that one of the original proponents of Naxalite ideology had himself grown bitter about the changes in the movement in recent days.

* * *

To test the claims of Naveen, and others like him, that there is not much of difference in the lives of the Maoist foot-soldiers and that of ordinary policemen, I visited the home of Snehalata in 2013.

Her home was a two-roomed flat on the first floor of the CRPF's quarters in Bhubaneswar. The green paint from the walls was peeling off and the rooms were filled with children's exercise books, clothes and stationery along with a framed photograph of her husband Tek Chand, a head constable in the Central Reserve Police Force (CRPF) who died in 2010 in an attack by Maoists.

Snehalata smiles a lot. She was probably accustomed to greeting and politely smiling at all the sahibs who visited her home (or whom she visited in their offices) since Tek Chand's death.

The demure woman from Odisha's Kalahandi brought out her treasure trove—albums filled with photographs of herself, her deceased husband and the couple's four children. There were piles of photographs and albums. 'Look! I was in Srinagar, where my husband was posted for two years,' she said, showing me pictures of the two in each other's arms, dressed in Kashmiri clothes. It was the kind of picture one would probably hide from strangers or from one's own children. But Snehalata showed this beautiful picture, of herself and her husband in a tight embrace, so unselfconsciously before her children it appeared that the children were also wrapped in the warmth of this love between their parents.

His absence loomed large in the room. 'I've also been to Hyderabad and Assam, we used to travel together a lot,' Snehalata said, showing me pictures of herself, her husband and the children—Sagarika, now fifteen years old, fourteen-year-old Priyanka, eight-year-old Rahul and Sanved, who was a little over two years old.

She was pregnant with the fourth child when Tek Chand was shot dead by the Maoists at a busy marketplace. The shooting happened at Hanumantpur village under the Chandrapur block of Rayagada district of Odisha on December 30, 2010.

'He was on a two-wheeler. The Maoists know which ones the policemen use. He was easily identified,' Snehalata said.

'He must have been in touch with a few who acted as informers too.'

Around noon, a group of armed Maoists began to fire indiscriminately at Tek Chand and another policeman. The duo was doing routine surveillance at a busy marketplace of Hanumantpur, about 25 km from the closest CRPF camp at Dangasorada. Tek Chand, who had a strong intelligence network in the remote village areas of Rayagada, was known to the Maoists and it wasn't difficult to kill him while he was on duty. As soon as the firing began, it created panic, and people started fleeing the area. Within moments, the entire marketplace became deserted as Tek Chand and another jawan, Ramesh Kandhapani from the Orissa State Armed Police (OSAP) slumped to the ground. Tek Chand died instantly while Ramesh was seriously injured.

More than two years after this horrific incident, when I met her, Snehalata was composed. She knew she could not let her sorrow engulf her. Her children doted on their mother and were working hard in school, they told me. Some day, they planned to go back to Kalahandi—the district in Odisha that has long been synonymous with poverty and starvation deaths. While the Centre and the state have focused on a huge increase in rice cultivation in the area apart from setting up educational institutions, the Kalahandi-Balangir-Koraput region of Odisha still remains one of the most backward and poverty-stricken areas of the country, with reports of people there dying of malnutrition still coming in.

At Kalahandi, the family has a small ancestral home and little land where they want to settle down. As of now, Snehalata and the four children were staying in a two-roomed pigeonhole quarter at a CRPF campus in Bhubaneswar. 'Life has been very unkind to us. He (Tek Chand) knew many Maoists, and wasn't their personal enemy. It was simply a job he was doing. I don't know what they gained by killing my husband. It took away what was most precious to us,' she said. But there weren't any tears in her eyes.

* * *

In the past few years, a lot has changed in Naveen's life. Have all the worries of the past given way to a perfect present? Naveen himself is not so sure anymore.

He had surrendered in early 2013, but had to wait till the end of 2014 (for nearly two years) to get the job of a constable. (This is specified in the surrender policy of the Central government: a surrendered person would be trained for 36 months and get monthly stipend of Rs 4,000. However, the training period may be either less or more depending on a particular state and its policy, and there are often 'procedural delays' in getting appointment letters. Also, a surrendered person may not be clearly informed about this clause of the policy.) It was evident that the frustration about not getting a secure job had saddened Naveen. He was inducted in the Chhattisgarh state police force in 2014 as a constable and drew a salary of Rs 18,500 a month.

One of the disadvantages of surrender has been that the lives of all his family members were affected by this decision—his wife and children, his two brothers, his mother and stepmother (Naveen's father married twice and passed away a few years ago; Naveen says he has 'two mothers'), were all at Narayanpur now. 'We had to leave our land and home at Kohkameta forever. We have land and our small house but we can neither go back nor sell it off,' he said.

While Naveen, his wife and three children lived at the police quarter offered by the government, his brothers, mother and stepmother had to rent an accommodation at Narayanpur. 'Had they stayed back in the village, they would have been killed for sure. I couldn't risk it,' he said.

His problems were manifold. Back home, they would be able to grow some crops that would be enough to feed them even if the yield was not enough to bring some extra money. But here, they all had to toil hard to feed so many mouths.

The sum assured by the government is handed over after three years of surrender, but Naveen has so far received only Rs 1.5 lakh from the government apart from the job and accommodation for his family. According to a poster issued by the Chhattisgarh government, a DVC member is supposed to get Rs 8 lakh as compensation, but Naveen says that he has little hope of getting the full amount. "Utni ummeed nahin hai," he says. It's been over three and a half years that he has surrendered.

His children were going to an English medium school for which the fees were borne by the government. Still, there were other expenses for his three teenage children—from food to clothes—that could not possibly be fathomed by the government. Naveen kept harping about these gaps as we talked over the phone several months after we had met at Narayanpur.

Families of scores of people 'affected by Maoist violence' are finding it tough to find their feet in Narayanpur, says Naveen. These people—hundreds of them—have come down to this small town from surrounding areas. Some are families of surrendered Maoists while others have lost their dear ones to 'Maoist violence'. 'They are all trying to get ration cards, Aadhar cards and so on, without which it is difficult to make ends meet or to find work,' said Naveen. 'As a result of this difficulty, some surrendered Maoists are even going back to their village homes, risking their lives.'

For Naveen, going back to his Kohkameta home was impossible. 'Already I put my own life and the lives of my family members at risk. If I go back, I may be killed right away,' he said. Naveen had no security cover now, which exposed him to the risk of attacks by his former Maoist colleagues. To add to his woes, there was pressure from local people asking his brother, who had found a job in a local school, to leave the area. Jobs are few and contenders many.

Those like Naveen figure nowhere in India's growth story. But they also have aspirations, they too wish to benefit from the burgeoning wealth that they can see all around them.

At some point, Naveen and others like him who have suffered on account of poverty, have managed to move away from the actual, physical space where that hardship existed—from remote villages where the state machinery never entered nor cared about those who lived in them. Yet, policymaking in our country does not take into consideration these aspirations.

The surrender policy, in fact, has been designed mainly to the advantage of the government. Because the Maoists are causing large-scale damage to public properties, garnering public support to oppose factories by multinational companies designed to displace them and attacking and killing police personnel that need millions of rupees to raise and train, it is necessary to rein in rebels to prevent the enormous financial losses. But the result has been policies that can, at best, only curtail this loss as much as possible. In terms of perspective, the policies were never designed to make the surrendered rebels happy or to make them truly understand that taking up arms was never a good idea in the first place.

Appealing to the Naxals to give up arms has not turned out to be an 'inclusive' policy in that sense.

In Chhattisgarh alone, 37 Maoists surrendered in 2012, the number was 39 in 2013. The following year has been a year of the biggest 'achievement' for the Chhattisgarh government in recent times—the number of surrendered Maoists shot up to a whopping 421, and till August 18, 2015, already 114 Naxals had surrendered.

Perhaps the policymakers were so obsessed with increasing the numbers of the surrendered Naxals that they did not take into consideration the various ways in which the quality of the lives of those who surrendered could be improved.

When I met most of the surrendered Maoists for the first time, they had surrendered a few months earlier and were hopeful about the future. They looked forward to jobs and a happy and peaceful family life. But when they found that they had to wait for two to three years to get employed, most of them were frustrated about the delay. Strange that this should be the case, because the rehabilitation policy of the Central government (which has been adopted by different state governments through notifications) mentions that the surrendered Maoists would be trained for 36 months and paid a stipend before they are provided with jobs. In case they get jobs before these 36 months are over, the stipend would be discontinued. It is difficult to understand why these terms and conditions are not clearly explained to the surrendered Maoists.

(In recent times, several aspects of the surrender policy have been changed in Chhattisgarh—housing for the surrendered Maoists, compensation for ammunition [earlier it was only for weapons], offer of a government job within six months of surrender if the person's behaviour is considered to be good, and so on.)[7]

Also, while the Central policy mentions that the Maoists would be trained in a 'trade/vocation of their liking or befitting their aptitude', the fact is that most of these women and men have not had a choice at all. This is evident from talking to them because many say they were not keen on handling arms any more as it is the use of firearms and the loss of lives that had frustrated them the most when they were Maoists.

Many government officers say that the Maoists cannot be employed in other departments of the government because then these women and men would need to be provided additional security. It is for their own safety that many are offered jobs in the police, and that some of them handle arms and thus ensure their own safety, said an officer.

But Naveen and many others like him are going into forests to catch their former comrades not as a matter of choice, but purely out of compulsion.

6

Khagen Mahato

'I am not an intelligent or educated person, Didi, I hope you don't mind... I mean... I cannot tell you anything about Naxalism... Maoism...' Khagen Mahato was visibly embarrassed and apologized before I started interviewing him. He blushed, thinking perhaps that the interview would be pointless if he couldn't explain the larger political and historical context of the Maoist movement. He hadn't figured out the context or purpose of the interview, nor his role—if at all there was any in it. The sense of anonymity, of being trivial has been a reality all through his life.

He also requested me to change his name, and so I have.

I assured him that I was keen to learn only about his experiences. Khagen was part of the agitation in Lalgarh that had started in 2008, and had been charged in several murder cases and under the Arms Act. The cases were pending and he had to appear in court from time to time. He had surrendered before the police in 2011, after the Trinamool Congress came to power in West Bengal. Now, he had been recruited and trained as a home guard and worked with the state police in one of the district police lines.

Immediately after the formation of the new government under the Trinamool Congress, a number of leaders from the Maoist-backed frontal organization in West Midnapore district, the People's Committee Against Police Atrocities (PCPA), began to join the ruling party. Among the first few were Manoj Mahato, Shyamal Mahato and Laso Hembram. Prabir Garai, who was later to marry surrendered Maoist Suchitra Mahato, also made a similar move from being a PCPA to a Trinamool Congress functionary. Grassroots supporters and workers also joined the Trinamool Congress.

Manoj Mahato, a PCPA leader charged with sedition, murder, arson and so on, joined the Trinamool Congress. Twenty-five cases were slapped against him by the former Left Front government.[1] He was a prominent leader of the Lalgarh movement and led the PCPA from the front along with the organization's convenor, Chhatradhar Mahato. But Chhatradhar Mahato refused to bend before the Trinamool Congress government and continues to languish in jail. The way Trinamool Congress took a tough stand against the Maoists and those who were part of their frontal organizations was one of the main reasons cited by leaders and grassroots workers for joining the Trinamool Congress.

While the PCPA leaders had several cases against them, their switch to the ruling Trinamool Congress helped them evade arrest, and, according to the Opposition CPM, this was 'proof enough' of the long-alleged nexus between the Trinamool and the Maoists.[2]

Manoj Mahato, Asit Mahato—both spokespersons of the PCPA, a Maoist-backed arm—Laso Hembram, Tulurani Mahato, Dilip Mahato, other former PCPA members, joined the Trinamool Congress at various times after the Trinamool Congress formed the state government in West Bengal in 2011. According to the police, some of them joined the Trinamool Congress to evade the police and stay relevant to local politics.[3]

In fact, Manoj Mahato was awarded a contract by the panchayat to build houses for the poor under a government scheme. Shyamal Mahato, acquitted of the severe cases and with some minor cases pending, has campaigned for the Trinamool Congress for the panchayat elections.[4]

Khagen and I were chatting by the side of a huge pond. Throughout the evening, frogs croaked and crickets buzzed incessantly. In the numbing atmosphere of the frogs' and crickets' songs and a low-powered bulb's light glowing in the distance, Khagen had the perfect ambience to begin his story.

Khagen was tall and well built, dark complexioned, and in his late 30s or early 40s. We talked for hours, during which time only I had tea. He did not want tea or even water, he just chewed paan masala. Cops kept a watch over him from a distance, though they had agreed not to listen to the conversation. However, we still talked in subdued voices, making doubly sure that no one was listening to us.

Looking at Khagen while he recalled his heyday in Lalgarh, when young men like him were part of an armed movement, it wasn't difficult to visualize him riding around in a two-wheeler, exuding power. The new-found power and freedom completely changed the lives of many ordinary villagers in the tiny forested sleepy hamlets of Purulia, Bankura and West Midnapore. From the time the Lalgarh agitation took shape, the poor and insecure villagers bullied by the Left parties' political bigwigs (chiefly those from the CPM that had ruled West Bengal uninterrupted for three and a half decades) were desperate to find ways to free themselves from their dictatorial oppression.

Khagen was one such soul happy to be able to show off his power to the oppressors, thanks to the quiet entry of the Maoists in his village. The Maoists became an invisible (and invincible) power that challenged the powerful Left, and helped snowball a growing agitation in which the opposition Trinamool Congress was a key player.

Politically, the Trinamool Congress was growing in popularity every passing day around this time. After three decades of Left Front rule in West Bengal, here was the most powerful challenge that the ruling party in the state found hard to handle. It is alleged that the Maoists and Trinamool Congress had agreed to help each other to oust the Left from power. But the Trinamool Congress functionaries have always vehemently denied this.

If Maoist leader Kishanji (who was killed by security forces in 2011) was to be believed, there had indeed been an informal tie-up between the Maoists and the Trinamool prior to the Assembly elections vis-à-vis Nandigram. According to Kishanji, 'when Nandigram villagers rose against the State's land-grab move, we took on the CPM's armed brigade. This time, Trinamool supplied us the ammunition. We kept up the resistance along with Trinamool ranks for months after the Nandigram carnage. During the final assault in November, we ran out of stocks and had to beat a retreat. The CPM men had captured 300 of the local militia and literally treated them as slaves, like war prisoners, with their hands tied behind.'[5]

This close working relationship in Nandigram is said to have continued and spread to Lalgarh subsequently. Trinamool Congress leaders, however, have never admitted to this liaison. This is what *Frontline* reported in July 2009:

> Trinamool Congress leader and Railways Minister Mamata Banerjee found herself in an uncomfortable situation when Kishanji proclaimed that she should break her silence over the Centre sending security forces to Lalgarh and called on her to choose a side. In February this year, Mamata Banerjee went to Lalgarh to express her party's solidarity with the tribal movement there. She not only shared the dais with Chhatradhar Mahato, but also acknowledged him as her 'former party colleague'. 'I am all for his cause even though he has left my party,' she said then…The CPI (Maoist) also supported the Trinamool in its opposition to the proposed chemical hub at Nayachar in the same district.[6]

Those like Khagen Mahato—who had always had a tough time making ends meet in a backward region of a poor village of Bengal—soon became a part of the enormous tide that eventually swept away the ruling party from power.

Khagen's role was more personal than political in nature.

Khagen told me, 'Frankly speaking, Didi, I entered the scene in Lalgarh because of personal reasons, not political.'

A personal crisis—especially when it is a common (or combined) predicament of several people—is a major societal concern and can lead to political movements. But perhaps Khagen meant that the larger political movement became a means for him to resolve his personal crisis.

Recruitment in the CPI (Maoist) was mostly random. The war had escalated thanks to the use of sophisticated arms and intelligence, yet it was difficult to find dedicated and strong people who could be a part of this war, and especially those who would continue to stay on. A large part of those recruited comprised the poor with no other source of survival and for whom this was the only reality.

* * *

Khagen Mahato's story began in a sleepy village of West Midnapore. (The name of the village and other details about him are changed, on his insistence, since he didn't want to be identified by his former colleagues.) Now he was a police home guard, but his job was primarily gardening. He watered and nurtured plants and insisted that even if he was in the police force, he wanted to do a job that did not involve handling arms.

No one in the different state police forces I have spoken to—from junior to senior level officers—has offered a satisfactory answer as to why the surrendered Maoists are always offered jobs in the police force and why they are trained in arms for it. They are offered 'rehabilitation' packages, but the irony remains that the armed Maoists turn almost overnight into armed state police personnel. Perhaps it is a bureaucratic practice that no one wants to disturb by considering an option to offer them jobs in any other department of the government.

'Since the police force is directly involved in arrests and surrenders, it is easier to offer them jobs in the police force rather than involving other departments in this exercise,' said a senior officer in West Bengal.

But do surrendered Maoists themselves *wish* to take up jobs in the police force? No one has ever actually *asked* the surrendered Maoists.

Luckily, for Khagen and many others like him, not much work is available for home guards on a regular basis in villages and small towns. Therefore, some do the job of gardeners, some carry files in offices and others are teachers in schools (in kindergarten classes) though they are officially 'home guards'. But the irony—as many surrendered Maoists admit—is the fact that they have to work with the same police force that had once beaten up and maimed them or their dear ones. Home guards in West Bengal are not given arms on duty, but use lathis when they are deployed for maintaining law and order. However, they are trained in arms as they may need to use them if there is such a need. None of the surrendered Maoists I have spoken to, however, were keen on becoming a part of the police force that was their primary enemy and target as Maoists.

The other reason for offering former Maoists jobs in the police force is also to 'use their expertise'. Mostly, it is a case of fighting fire with fire. A large number of the surrendered Maoists are in reality helping the police obtain information on their former colleagues, assisting in planning and strategizing to arrest more members of different squads or helping them surrender. The State usually leaves no stone unturned to make use of each and every surrendered Maoist to extract information or to continue to make them work as informers for as long as they are alive or useful.

Khagen's father worked with the Indian Railways. Khagen and his brother were both unemployed around the time the Lalgarh agitation started brewing. 'It was always a hand to mouth situation at home for the four of us—even if we were better off than many in our village,' Khagen said. The seasonal paddy and vegetables they grew in their small plot of land brought some extra money, but life was still tough.

'I had dropped out of school after class eight and was desperately looking for a job for several years. By 2008, I had appeared in most police recruitment examinations meant for constables but I wasn't selected anywhere. It was frustrating to see some neighbours and acquaintances finding work in the police force by paying bribes to political leaders,' he said. 'Frankly, we were poor and I couldn't risk paying bribe as I didn't trust the political leaders. How could I risk losing the money?'

Khagen talked about how local leaders of the Jharkhand Party and the CPM would take bribes and do everything from getting local people jobs to ensuring their names got included in the Below Poverty Line (BPL) list. Once someone got their name in the BPL list (even if she/he were not poor enough to qualify), there would be government grants under various schemes like Indira Awas Yojana to build homes or for getting cheap subsidized ration from the government. Therefore, there are always many contenders, and it was an unfair competition between the poor and those who had cash to spare (as bribes).

Around this time, his younger brother was in a relationship with the daughter of a CPM local committee member. 'The girl's father was against this match, so he lodged a complaint of abduction against my brother. The girl admitted to the affair but things did not cool down,' Khagen said. 'There were constant threats of—'*merey debo, ketey felbo*' (will kill you, chop you to pieces)—to every member of our family in different ways by CPM men. Ask anybody around—this used to be a typical threat the CPM used for people who were not their supporters.'

Finally, Khagen decided that offence should be his best defence. Things were fast changing in the political scenario of West Bengal around that time—the Trinamool Congress was launching movements against the Left Front government in an aggressive way (the Singur agitation had already happened in 2006-2008, and in Nandigram 14 villagers were killed in police firing on March 14, 2007.) The movements continued in a very violent form marked by armed clashes between the people's formation, Bhumi Ucched Pratirodh Committee—BUPC—and the CPM.

The buzz doing the rounds was that the opposing political force in West Bengal had got into an 'understanding' with the Maoists—an unofficial tie that was meant to be kept secret. This was the case with all the major movements opposing the state government at that point, especially in Lalgarh and Nandigram.

'I knew that I had to show off my strength if I had to fight the CPM's constant bullying. And I could do so by getting the support of the powerful people. It struck me that I could do this by meeting Maoist leaders, since at that time they were the most powerful, and they were fighting against CPM's atrocities. So I met some Maoist leaders through one or two friends. In this way, I was able to ward off the threats in no time,' Khagen said, chuckling.

But what was the import of these meetings? Khagen said he only wanted some people 'to know' he was meeting the Maoists and had their support. 'I wanted to brag about my association with the Maoists, and I was happily doing it. But I had no idea that a simple association with them and being in touch with them would make me a Maoist too.' He laughs now at his own 'foolishness'.

Soon, he did become a Maoist. First, he became part of the PCPA. Then he became a part of the CPI (Maoist)'s inner circle in West Midnapore.

'Initially I met them (the Maoist or PCPA leaders) once or twice a week, but then it became a regular affair.' He was in touch with Sashadhar Mahato—one of the senior leaders who was later killed in a police encounter in Jamboni on March 10, 2011.[7] His bullet riddled body was identified later.

Khagen admitted that no one forced him to take up arms. 'In fact, I was myself keen on carrying arms. At that time, people in my village and some neighbouring villages too knew about my contacts with the Maoists, especially the CPM men. It was no longer safe for me to move around unarmed—so I asked Sashadhar to provide me with firearms for my own safety.'

Khagen became a block president of the PCPA and quickly rose further up in the hierarchy. 'Honestly, Didi, initially it *was* a lot of fun. It is fun to be part of a group that wields so much power. All along—because I never had been part of either the CPM or the Jharkhand Party which were the most powerful political parties in our area till then—we always cowered before them. But now, for the first time, I felt in my veins the thrill of power.'

However, the fun element fizzled out quickly for people like him, who were more accustomed to a quiet village life. Now, the sound of guns rattled the sleepy villages. People were afraid to move in the dark, murders were the order of the day, blood splattered on the roads was not an unusual sight.

'I was soon feeling uncomfortable about certain things,' he said and paused. He pondered for a while and said, '...*mrityu* [death].'

'The nature of the battle we were fighting wasn't very clear to me then. Yes, it is true we were fighting the CPM's long tenure of misrule, but I ask myself repeatedly if this could not be fought differently. After all, if it was one political party in power being replaced by another one, what were the Maoists doing in it?' Khagen asked. 'Political parties are ousted through elections, so what does armed killing have to do with it?' he wondered aloud. 'But as I said, I don't know much about Maoism, Naxalism. I don't know the larger picture, nor what it means.'

Khagen's questions are simple, but there are no straightforward answers. There had always been rumours of a pre-election, under-the-wraps alliance between the CPI (Maoist) and the Trinamool Congress before the May 2011 Assembly elections. But the Maoists' association with mainstream political parties is nothing new. Nearly a decade earlier, the Maoists were said to have supplied arms to the ruling Left in West Midnapore to fight the Trinamool-BJP (Bharatiya Janata Party) combine.

In an interview, the CPI (Maoist) politburo member in charge of West Bengal, Bihar and Jharkhand, Koteswar Rao (alias Kishanji) had said: 'Yes, we joined the CPM ranks to fight the Trinamool-BJP offensive in Keshpur. That was in May 2000, when the Trinamool chief announced that Keshpur would be CPM's graveyard. Armed men were setting the huts of poor villagers on fire. We sided with the poor. I distinctly remember that I collected 5,000 cartridges from the CPM party office. CPM leader Sushanta Ghosh would have been nowhere, had we not been with them. But the CPM atrocities in Chhoto Angaria, Suchpur, Nanoor, did not go unnoticed by us. It was only when CPM came to grips with the situation in 2001 and began targeting our men that we struck back. Finally, when Nandigram villagers rose against the state's land grab move, we took on the CPM's armed brigade.'[8]

In these few sentences, Kishanji made clear how mainstream political parties and Maoists have a symbiotic relationship. Each helps the other survive, and perhaps thrive too.

For those like Khagen, who view things without that knowledge, it could be confusing. The survival strategy for ordinary villagers is, therefore, to identify the most powerful, and to side with that 'party' (party here is not used in the sense of a political party though it does not exclude it either).

Khagen spent a good three years—from 2008 to 2011—exuding power. But during this period, he was going through a 'deep emotional crisis which was not exactly madness,' he said. 'It was my conscience that was troubling me'.

The 2011 elections were just around the corner. 'I don't know if there really had been any tie-up between the Maoists and the Trinamool Congress at the top, but at the grassroots level we would discuss with Trinamool Congress men how the (then) existing government ought to go and how the state would progress if the Trinamool came to power. You could say we were fighting to bring them to power.'

Dynamics between the political parties and the Maoists are forever changing, so villagers and Maoist foot-soldiers best survive if they are constantly gauging the situation on the ground.

According to Khagen, he was most perturbed by the killings of people whom he had known for many years either in his own village or those in neighbouring areas. 'There was someone called Panchanan, he was close to the Jharkhand Party workers, and possibly even close to the CPM leadership. He would keep an eye on me and my PCPA colleagues. We realized he could be informing the police and the CPM about us. So it was decided that he had to be finished off,' Khagen recalled.

These killings, he said, were pretty common. If there was a suspicion that a villager was spying on them, the decision usually was to eliminate her/him. 'Another murder had hugely upset me. There was one man, Mrigen [name changed], who always cosied up to whoever was in power—his CPM and Jharkhand Party proximity was well known,' Khagen said. Mrigen's wife had even thrown an open challenge that despite their best efforts, the Maoists or the PCPA would not be able to harm her husband. 'Probably she had no clue how ruthless we were. We had to prove ourselves. So, when I heard him speaking over the phone, informing someone about the amassing of arms in our village, I informed my group. It was decided that Mrigen would be killed.'

In retrospect, Khagen regretted telling his group about these people. 'Once something was decided by the leadership, there was no backing out.' He had since spent many sleepless nights wondering how much Mrigen's children and wife suffered as he was pulled out of his home in front of them and bullets pumped into his body. 'I clenched my jaw and looked the other way as he pleaded for his life and asked forgiveness. And then, everything was quiet.'

Who pulled the trigger? Did you? I asked Khagen. This was no interrogation room, no courtroom trial, no official statements were being recorded. Only a deathly silence in the backdrop and the incessant songs of frogs and crickets. No words came from him. Finally, Khagen murmured: '*Ami bolte parbo na, Didi... kichhu mone korben na...*' (I cannot say it... please don't mind.)

'In any case, there isn't much of a difference between pulling the trigger to kill a man and to participate in a killing. The agony, the shrieks keep haunting me still. It happened like as though in a dream, I cannot believe it happened for real.

'At that time, my wife was pregnant. You can imagine the feeling I had. I thought of myself as a rogue, a devil.'

Many CPM leaders and ordinary villagers suspected to be leaking information were killed, their houses were looted and chaos was the order of the day.

Khagen also told me, embarrassed, that one of his relatives had once been stopped on the road by the side of the jungle and forced to hand over his cell phone to a young man. Khagen knew the area so well that he promptly figured out who was on 'sentry duty' at that point. When he pressed his colleague, it led to heated arguments, but finally his colleague took out forty mobile phones that he had amassed through looting people on that road. 'He had been snatching mobile phones for a long time—either for his personal use, or he may have planned to sell them off when convenient for him.'

Petty crimes unrelated to the 'movement' were not uncommon. It was this 'personal' component of the Maoist movement that Khagen was increasingly perturbed about. He admitted that his own involvement was to serve his personal interest and there were many others who used their association with the powerful Maoists to take personal revenge or to loot people even when there was no need to.

But didn't it happen because the people were poor and genuinely deprived for years? I asked. Khagen laughed. 'Perhaps we can blame the fact that the leadership should have been more careful while recruiting their soldiers or at least managed and disciplined them. But the way I see it, there was quite a bit of chaos for sure.'

What he was not sure about, though, was the way forward. Would he continue to be a Maoist all his life? His wife did not want it. Neither did he. His wife was from a neighbouring village and had no links with the movement.

'Just before the 2011 Assembly elections, I fled because I had been stamped as a Maoist and there were chances of an arrest. I left my home and my village and went off to a place called Dungri, in Odisha. I started working in a Telco factory,' Khagen said. 'But soon I realized that staying away meant I could never come back home.'

The tide turned soon enough. The CPM was ousted from power in the Assembly elections of 2011 and the Trinamool Congress formed the new government in West Bengal. Khagen now felt a little less afraid and knew that there were chances he would be treated less harshly than in a CPM regime. 'I thought that if there had been a stamp on me, I had to pay for it to rid myself of it.' So he immediately got in touch with a Trinamool Congress leader and was 'advised' to surrender. He and six other colleagues surrendered on the same day. One of them was Kishanji's bodyguard, Jagannath Soren.

Eventually, the newly formed Trinamool Congress government's repeated attempts to sit at the talks table with the Maoists led to a dead end. The Maoists' new enemy was now the Trinamool Congress—and some of its leaders were killed after the new government was formed. The manner of killing was the same as that of the assassinations of CPM leaders a few months earlier.

This is how the situation changed in a matter of a few months:

2011
- May 20: Mamata Banerjee sworn in as new CM.[9]
- July: Team led by Sujato Bhadro [from the Association

for Protection of Democratic Rights (APDR)], a human rights organization based in Kolkata, formed to mediate talks with Maoists.[10]

- August: Announcement of new surrender and rehabilitation package for Maoists.[11]
- September: Jharkhand Mukti Morcha leader Babu Bose killed by Maoists.[12]
- October: CM gives seven-day ultimatum to Maoists to lay down arms and join peace talks, calls the Maoists 'supari killers'.[13]
- October-November: Talks fail between intermediaries and government, Maoists attack Trinamool men and the Chief Minister announces intensification of joint operations against the Maoists.[14]
- November: Asit Mahato, main accused behind Jnaneswari incident, arrested.[15]
- November: Maoist couple Jagori Baske and husband Rajaram surrenders at Writers' Buildings.[16]
- November 24: Maoist politburo leader Kishanji killed in Burishole forest.[17]

2012

- February: Yudhishtir Mahato, Maoist squad leader, killed in Jamtal forest in police encounter.[18]
- March: Sadanala Ramkrishna, Maoist central technical committee member and four Maoist leaders arrested from College Street.[19]
- March: Suchitra Mahato surrenders at Writers' Buildings.[20]
- May: Kishanji's bodyguard Jagannath Soren and six others surrender.[21]
- July: Bikram (alias Arnab Dam), a state committee member, arrested from Purulia's Biramdi station.[22]
- September: Abishek Mukhopadhyay (alias Aranya), top Maoist leader, arrested from Kolkata's Tallah.[23]

During 2011-2013 after his surrender and before his recruitment as a home guard, when Khagen was living in different police quarters of south Bengal waiting for the government to decide on the surrender scheme compensation (funds, jobs and stay) packages, he was heaving a sigh of relief that he had chosen to surrender.

Had he stayed outside, he could have been imprisoned or killed because by then the dynamics between the Maoists and the Trinamool Congress had changed already.

PCPA spokesperson, Chhatradhar Mahato, continues to be in prison (though he was arrested during the Left Front regime). While some expected that Mahato, who had been at the same rally as Chief Minister Mamata Banerjee during the Lalgarh agitation, would have been treated more leniently, that did not happen. Banerjee took a visibly firm stand against the Maoists after she became chief minister.

Since then, her government has made every attempt to wipe out the Maoists from the state. In fact, in April 2016, two top Maoist leaders from Bengal, Bikash and Tara, were arrested by Kolkata Police's Special Task Force. The duo had been on the run and hadn't managed to conduct any major operation in the past few years.[24]

It is assumed that unless Banerjee's government finds a strong opposition or comes under flak on some important issue in the state, the situation is likely to remain the same on the Maoist front. There have been several attempts made by the Maoists to make their presence felt in Bengal, since 2011, though none had much of an impact.

In August 2015, the CPI (Maoist) in a review report, said the organization had committed 'mistakes' during the Lalgarh movement by killing people and covertly removing the bodies. The party said that it had wrongly believed that the Trinamool Congress would withdraw joint forces from Jangalmahal after coming to power.[25] This is being seen as a desperate bid by the organization to win back the people of Lalgarh, who are wary since the murders that took place in Jangalmahal during the agitation in the period 2008-11. 'We had the belief that if the CPM is defeated, then the joint forces will be withdrawn and all political prisoners released, but we were wrong.' While the ruling Trinamool termed this as 'propaganda', the CPM said the Maoists were 'spilling the beans'.

The few reported 'movements' of Maoists through the forested areas of Jangalmahal in the past few years are in fact, seen as 'minor' incidents.

In July 2015, two Maoist cadres were arrested from Purulia for pasting posters in favour of the party. Khori Hansda and Mutru Hansda were arrested from Balarampur of Purulia.[26] In August 2015 again, two Maoist supporters were arrested on charges of extortion in Balarampur of Purulia district. The duo from Belpahari of West Midnapore district was extorting money from shopkeepers, who reported the matter to police.[27]

In September 2015, the Criminal Investigation Department (CID) of West Bengal recovered a bag full of explosives—including low intensity landmines—from the Howrah-Secunderabad Falaknuma Express at Howrah Station. It was suspected that the bag was sent from Secunderabad and was on its way to the Maoists' den in Bengal.[28]

While the Maoists continue to move in and out of West Bengal—they stay mostly in adjoining Jharkhand and move further into Chhattisgarh for longer periods—they have not been able to stage a major comeback till now.

Given this backdrop, former Maoists like Khagen realize all the more these days that surrendering before the government was certainly the best thing to do.

* * *

If there is one trick villagers must learn in order to survive in rural Bengal, it is the ability to gauge the state's political climate and ingratiate themselves with the strongest political party.

Else, one might get caught in a political storm involving armed clashes. In the areas where Maoists are a force to reckon with, this becomes a rather complex situation.

Not everybody can scrape through unhurt. But there are hundreds like Khagen, who have flitted, floated and moved from one group to another and managed to save their skins. In the armed war for clinching political turf (and money and muscle power), there is need for people like him or for those like Alok Chandra Mahato. Khagen and Alok were political opponents during the armed clashes between the Maoist-PCPA combine and the CPM.

A quick peek at a small part of Alok's life will help us understand this better.

When I met Alok in early 2015, one of his uncles, a CPM local committee member, was lodged in Midnapore Central Jail and another uncle had been found murdered in the forest some distance from his home, a few years earlier. Alok was never a member of the CPM, but used to follow his uncle, Manik (who was in prison) like a shadow. In fact, he was such a known face in the area due to his closeness to the local CPM leaders that people assumed he had official membership. He didn't.

But the CPM needed a well-equipped armed gang as they had been unofficially running nothing short of an underground army for several years. Men like Alok were engaged in the party's underground 'work'. Alok did not bat an eyelid while admitting that he was an armed CPM cadre—part of the *harmad bahini*— that unleashed a reign of terror in Jangalmahal for many years. I met him at Lalgarh, though he continued to travel all over West Midnapore on work.

From the time the Lalgarh agitation began to brew in the state, the CPM had been on the backfoot, its leaders forced to flee their homes, or they were kidnapped and killed. In all these phases, the *harmad bahini* played a key role—these were groups of arms-toting local youths that countered the armed Maoists, PCPA and the Trinamool men. Their aim: to keep the CPM in power and to keep their foothold in the localities where these battles were being fought.

The short, dark, bald man, who had a perpetual smiling, amused expression on his face would hardly pass for a *harmad*, a dacoit. But Alok himself admitted that he was part of such groups. 'When so much of arms are coming in, one will become a hot-blooded fellow, madam!' he told me, offering what seemed to him a logical explanation for taking up arms. He smiled, chewing paan, or maybe it was paan masala.

'The arms would come in from Keshpur and Belda of West Midnapore, different parts of East Midnapore, and so on,' he added. 'We used them to fight Maoists and the PCPA people. It was a fight for the turf and the fierce battle went on for months. We had to use our guns to get our people back home. But in the end, we lost the battle and the CPM lost the control over the area.'

Alok, who was once part of many 'actions', remembers how he was caught off-guard one day at the Lakshmanpur forest of West Midnapore while riding a two-wheeler on his way home to fetch a physician's prescription for his newborn. 'The situation was very tense around those times in 2009-2010. The Maoists were very powerful and those like us who were close to the CPM were perpetually trembling in fear.'

He remembers being stopped by the Maoists mid-way and there being no way for escape. 'I was all alone and they were in huge numbers. All of them—Master, Saontha (Suman, whose story has been narrated in chapter I), and many others—were sitting on chairs at the edge of the main road with a table placed in front. It seemed they were checking some accounts. A Trinamool Congress leader, who stood close by, identified me as the nephew of a local CPM leader. I knew I couldn't return alive from there,' he recalled.

But Alok did manage to escape! He addressed the Maoist leaders—some of them local boys he knew since childhood, most of whom were younger than him—as 'Sir'. They wanted to know how much money had gone into the CPM's coffers from public funds such as the local panchayat and other sources, and the names of those who had swindled this money. Possibly, Alok said, in this way the young men were shortlisting names of people whose homes they would attack.

'When I said I had no idea, they started beating me up with lathis. I grimaced and cried but did not protest. That's the only way I could survive, else they would surely have killed me that day,' he said. Finally he was let off under the condition that he would return to his village and send ten persons to join the group attacking the police camp at Koima that day. 'And they did attack the camp later in the day though I never went back,' Alok smiled.

Nothing remains now of the power that Alok and his uncle had flaunted once. Alok had to keep a low profile, become anonymous, even invisible. He did manage to survive it all. Then came the biggest surprise. Alok took out an identity card and showed me that he had recently been recruited as a 'civic police volunteer' by the Mamata Banerjee government.

Conversions are essential in these parts of the country where survival is dependent on political leanings. The state government had cleared in April 2013 a plan to create a pool of 1,30,000 civic police for West Bengal, who are requisitioned for various occasions like elections, festivals, disaster management and so on.[29] They are trained for ten days and get a pay of Rs 141 per day, with twenty days of assured work every month. The job— under the District Intelligence Branch—involves enrollment from the police station level.

He smiled and told me that he did 'odd jobs for the police' (a euphemism for acting as a police informer) once in a while and had nothing to do with political party activities any more.

Khagen and Alok—once arch rivals who were fighting each other—are examples of how common villagers have been recruited and converted into armed soldiers for the execution of bigger political gameplans. Representing different political entities and fighting for the largest slice of the turf, they have fought in a fierce battlefield where allegiance and submission to the most powerful force is the key to survival.

* * *

After his surrender, in this so-called 'new life', Khagen soon began training in arms along with thirty-one other surrendered Maoists in Durgapur, an industrial town in Burdwan district.

He was trained for a month and a half before he was formally recruited as a home guard. He also got an initial 'pay' of Rs 50,000. The entire sum was spent in paying all his past debts. Now, as a home guard, he earns a salary of Rs 338 per day. His younger brother works as a driver and the financial condition at his home is much better, there being four sources of income—his father's pension, his brother's and his salary, and some extra money that comes from selling the produce from their land back in the village.

Khagen was looking forward to the principal and interest of Rs 3 lakh that the government had promised him against his surrender. He hoped to start a business with the money. The only regret was that he had to stay away from home most of the time due to the job and he missed his wife, two-year-old daughter and four-year-old son.

Khagen knows that this is the best bet for him. But while he no longer needs to be afraid of facing arrest, he continues to fear his former Maoist colleagues. If he goes out without 'police protection', anywhere, he might be killed, Khagen says. Therefore, even for short visits home, he needs a police escort.

If there is any *real* regret, it is this compromise on his freedom. Khagen felt he was living in a prison in any case, despite surrendering. And mostly, he missed out on those gloriously free days—enjoying the might of the gun, vehicles and money and belonging to the most powerful group. Khagen never thought those days would abruptly come to an end. So now, he is jittery about how short-lived the present might be.

'I don't know, Didi… Who can say what may be the policy of those who come to power in the state in the future? What if they take out their anger on us because we surrendered before this government? What if I have to languish in jail despite giving up all these years? Everything happens for political reasons after all.'

A senior police officer in West Bengal said that it would be unreasonable to expect that those like Khagen would be able to get back to a completely normal life. 'But after all, they have been offered money and a job by the government, they didn't have to go to jail and they are earning a salary.'

Khagen and others had committed crimes during the Lalgarh agitation, people were murdered, looted and kidnapped. 'With several cases pending against them, this is the only way to keep them disciplined. They used to wield a lot of power, had money to spend, used guns and kept people under threat and control. Now that has become a thing of the past, life has become boring, but that is our only way to keep them under control. Surely you don't expect that we give them all the money they want, plus all the freedom they wish for, do you?' the officer asked, his left eyebrow arched up sarcastically.

* * *

There are many Khagen-like figures in the Naxal movement, who have either joined the 'people's movement' to serve their personal interests, or found that this path was a way to survive the odds. This association was just another way of making money by looting and embezzling funds from a huge amount of cash that came from threatening businessmen and government officials. The movement also gave them ample ammunition to exude power and authority.

These soldiers were and still continue to be used by mainstream political parties in their battle to wrest power and political control over a certain area. There is no end to the corruption, political manoeuvres, money laundering, looting, stealing and other activities that are, in reality, criminal in nature.

7

Lachchu and Kasru

Sometimes, it may be possible to put everything at risk and fight an armed war for years. It may not matter if one's partner, parents and children are pining at home or struggling to make ends meet. It is, after all, not a question of individual happiness but a larger war of the *people* to attain equal footing in an unfair and cruel world.

But then, a sudden bout of inexplicable sorrow may come like a wave and change the course of one's life. Perhaps it arises from not feeling equal, or not being treated with love and respect as an *individual?*

Such were the feelings that Kasru and his nephew Lachchu went through when they stayed and worked as Maoist foot-soldiers in Dandakaranya for nearly seven years.

I met Kasru and Lachchu at Narayanpur, the same place where I had met Naveen. Kasru, 33 years old, was a short, dark, quiet man. He was so meek and withdrawn that, in a crowd, it was as if he ceased to exist.

On the other hand, Lachchu, his nephew—just three years younger than him—was jovial and smiled a lot. He also emitted a full throated laughter. When the two were together, Lachchu did most of the talking.

Yet Kasru, when given an opportunity to speak, could clearly say what was on his mind. This happened many times as we spoke on the phone after our first meeting in 2013. He couldn't assert himself nor shout for attention when he was among many, but when he was talking to just one person, Kasru had very strong opinions and well thought-out arguments. He was proud of who he was, and knew what he wanted.

Kasru's story began in a tiny peaceful village under the Orchha tehsil of Chhattisgarh. It is the village Irakbhatti, located in the depths of the hilly, forested area of Marh (or Abujhmarh) of Dandakaranya.

Around 1999-2000, Lalchand, a young Maoist area commander from Andhra Pradesh, would visit different villages of Orchha tehsil. He was a visitor to Irakbhatti village too, where Kasru and his three brothers lived. Lalchand's speeches, songs, dances and the way he spoke about equality for all people moved the young Kasru to tears.

Kasru had lost his parents and a brother at a young age. He got no opportunity to study in a school because he had to work in the fields to sustain his family. There was hardly any presence of the civil administration in the area where he lived and it lacked basic facilities. So, very early in life, Kasru and his brothers had to toil in the fields for survival—they grew crops over a portion of their land.

According to the Census of 2011, Irakbhatti in Orchha tehsil of Chhattisgarh's Narayanpur district had 43 households with a village population of 225 people (130 males and 95 females). The literacy rate was 47.4 per cent—lower than the Chhattisgarh average of 70.29 per cent. A majority in the village—97.33 per cent are from Scheduled Tribe and the remaining 2.67 per cent are from Scheduled Caste.[1]

Mesmerized by Lalchand's speeches, Kasru began to associate himself gradually with the Jantana Sarkar or People's Government from 2002 onwards. He remained at home, but visited the Maoist squads from time to time.

Maoists run a parallel administrative network in Dandakaranya, the hilly, forested stretch in Chhattisgarh that spreads over 60,000 sq.km, also covering parts of Maharashtra, Odisha, Madhya Pradesh and Andhra Pradesh.

Home to scores of tribes like Gond, Muria, Halba, Abuj Maria, large swathes of the forest and hills have remained inaccessible to the administration for years and beyond the touch of so-called development. It is the original homeland of the Gonds. For decades, the people of Dandakaranya have been neglected by the government, though the area is rich in mineral reserves like iron ore, bauxite, tin, granite, marble, limestone and so on.

In June 1980, three dalams (guerilla squads) of the CPI (ML) [People's War] of five members each entered the Dandakaranya from Telengana and a major war against the State began to spread from this belt. From a few select areas, it spread to more than 2,500 villages involving lakhs of people.

Soon, there were organizations in Dandakaranya such as Dandakaranya Adivasi Kisan Mazdoor Sangh (DAKMS), Krantikari Adivasi Mahila Sangh (KAMS), Krantikari Adivasi Bal Sangh (KABS), and people's militia such as Gram Raksha Dal (GRD), Area Raksha Dal (ARD) and so on, that united to fight the State.

The system of parallel administration—known as the Jantana Sarkar—is a direct challenge to and defiance of the state's administration. Each Jantana Sarkar is elected by a group of villages. There are ten divisions of Jantana Sarkars in Dandakaranya, each division comprising three area committees. A group of Jantana Sarkars are supervised under an area committee. Every Jantana Sarkar has departments like agriculture, defence, education, health and so on.

With the help of the Maoist forces, the people of Dandakaranya built tanks, set up rice mills, crops were cultivated, cattle was reared and several initiatives were taken to protect the forest ('forest protection committees' and 'environment protection committees' were set up in Gadchiroli), drinking water wells were dug, education was imparted (through 'vidya committees') and health centres were set up among other things.

Over the years, there have been many changes in the administration and functioning of the Maoists, their policies and practices. This not only includes the transition from the Naxalbari days through the PWG and MCC right down to the present CPI (Maoist), but also various changes in the administration of the Jantana Sarkar and the recruitment process as well.

During the 1980s, the Maoist cadres took up local problems and issues—such as cruelty at the hands of feudal lords and forest officers. Dalams or groups were formed that roamed the forests and gave firearms in the hands of the people. Indigenous arms traditionally used by tribals were also used.

In the mid-1980s, sangams, or groups were formed and only the hardcore supporters became part of the more organized, armed groups. This was also an indication of the kind of increase in support that the CPI (Maoist) got from the people. The number of supporters grew so much that there were various tiers in the support—it took years and lots of hard work to reach the core group. Even those who were not members of the dalams could be sangam members and work actively for the Maoists—especially in providing support to dalams in villages, bringing food for them or helping in passing on their information.

There have been further changes in the recruitment procedure in recent times. There was more focus on the Jantana Sarkar after the merging of the PW and MCC. Now, there is greater stress on the local organizational squads (LOS) and local guerilla squads (LGS) instead of dalams. New tactics, better technology, more firepower—all this has made the organization increasingly more formidable.

In recent times however, there has been a barrage of systematic and prolonged government action on the CPI (Maoist) in which enormous firepower and money has been pumped in to tackle the 'threat'. As a result, the Maoist strategy, apart from its focus on alternative governance, also had to focus on military power. This shift to military tactics from social welfare has been a point of disagreement between various individuals and groups within the party. It has also made the job extremely difficult and risky.

Against this backdrop, Kasru and Lachchu spent nearly seven years working as grassroots workers, managing administrative affairs of the Jantana Sarkar.

Kasru, to begin with, had meant to work from home. Only, it wasn't possible as he was being hounded by the police for a case in which, he tells me, he 'really wasn't involved'. Therefore, in order to escape the police, he had to go underground in 2006.

'It was a compulsion. Returning home was tough because there was fear of arrest,' said Kasru, as we talked at Narayanpur town just about four months after he had surrendered.

'Initially, after my first association with the Naxals began, for many years, I kept visiting the squads, did some work and came back home. Since I was an ordinary Naxal worker and mostly looked after administrative matters, there was no major threat for me,' he said. 'But once my name got involved in this particular case, I had to leave home for a while.'

Lachchu and Kasru left home together in 2006. Lachhu was by then married, but Kasru was still single. When the threat of arrest receded (there was no proof against him and the case was put on the backburner), Kasru kept going home from time to time. In 2007, he got married.

For the next seven years that he worked from within the secret forest hideouts, Kasru took up many responsibilities as an area committee member. Those years were difficult as he had to straddle two worlds—manage home and continue with the tough job. 'Unlike many other comrades, I could not leave my home and family behind forever. I constantly went back and ensured they were doing fine,' he said. 'My family is most dear to me. I had to carry out my responsibilities towards my brothers, nephews and my wife. From the core of my heart, I was never comfortable with the idea of leaving my family behind and devoting my entire time to work. So, no matter what the risk, I always went back home from time to time. I did this throughout, till my surrender,' he said.

It is, however, difficult to manage home, since a Maoist cadre's work is no 'regular job' and one does not earn a salary. 'I barely managed to survive with whatever little money I got, there was never much money to send home.' His brother and nephews continued to toil in the fields to make ends meet.

'In any case, those like us who worked at the lowest level of the party have to work very hard and make do with very little money,' Kasru said. He added that in their platoon, which had 15-20 people, the annual allotment was Rs 1.5 lakh—'and that included almost everything from food, civil clothes, soaps, hair oil, and other things essential for survival. Some basic materials needed for preparing booby traps also had to be funded through this money.'

Kasru used to work in the *rakshan vibhag* (defence department) of the Jantana Sarkar. He would meet the people in the villages of Marh, talk to the militia and find out about their stock of arms and ammunition. The type of arms and ammunition ranged from the indigenous *teer dhanuk* (bows and arrows) to *gola barud* (explosives). He would prepare the reports and submit it to the higher authorities and go back and replenish the supplies. While the villagers had traditional arms like bows and arrows, these were also supplied by the Naxals. When there were agitations or some 'action' against police, the militia would often use the bows and arrows, and so a constant supply was needed. Explosives and guns were used by the jan militia and this too was supplied to the villagers by the Naxalites.

Kasru would note down all these meticulously, submit it to the higher authorities, get the supplies and submit reports again.

But life is full of ironies. Even though his job revolved around arms and ammunition, it never struck Kasru that he would get a higher compensation package if he surrendered with arms. The surrender-cum-rehabilitation package in Chhattisgarh for those who surrender with arms ranges anything between Rs 30,000 (for 12-bore) to Rs 4.5 lakh (for Light Machine Gun). However, since Kasru did not have any arms or ammunition at the time of surrender, he got Rs 15,000 from the Chhattisgarh government immediately after surrender, another Rs 50,000 to build a house, and a job of a constable that pays him Rs 18,500 per month. He also has Rs 1.5 lakh as fixed deposit in the bank given to him by the government.

Kasru doesn't mind. Yes, he feels that his life would have been easier had he got a better compensation package. But mostly, he doesn't dwell on such thoughts.

Lachchu meanwhile, looked after the finance department— he was a Jantana Sarkar *upadhakshya*. He was in charge of the day-to-day running of the Jantana Sarkar and sometimes looked after levies collected from tendu leaves, bamboo, tractors, trucks, shops and so on.

In the Raoghat area (Marh/north Bastar division in CPI-Maoist communiques), where Lachchu primarily worked between 2011 and 2013 (comprising 50-60 villages), he would look after administrative matters and allotment of funds under different heads. The money collected from various sources always had to be handed over to higher divisions, Lachchu said.

Raoghat has been on the boil over the construction of the Dallirajhara-Raoghat-Jagdalpur Railway line for improved connectivity, mining and transportation of iron ore deposits in the region, for which a memorandum of understanding (MoU) had been signed on December 11, 2007.[2]

There were, however, allegations and fear that the project will not only displace hundreds of tribals, but also tamper with the eco-system. While the Central government undertaking, Steel Authority of India Limited (SAIL) and the National Mining

Development Corporation (NMDC) are in charge, there were fears that the mines were in reality meant to be given away to private companies on the lines of the Bailadilla mines in Dantewada district (gopetition.com, August 2, 2007).[3]

The day the MoU was signed for the progress of the railway line (May 9, 2015) also saw the signing of another MoU in the presence of Prime Minister Narendra Modi and Chhattisgarh Chief Minister Raman Singh between Ministry of Steel, Chhattisgarh government, SAIL and NMDC for an 'Ultra Mega Steel Plan' (UMSP) of three million tonne capacity in Bastar.[4]

The Raoghat area has been a Maoist bastion for years, and the local people's organizations along with Maoists have held a series of protests against land acquisition, deforestation and rehabilitation of tribals.

Despite the protests over displacing the tribals and tampering with the bio-diversity of the rich forest area, the Chhattisgarh government has taken a tough stand with heavy contingents of CRPF, BSF and Chhattisgarh Armed Police (CAP) deployment.

Lachchu was well aware of this, though he did not understand the full import of the agitation. 'We would tell the tribals living in the area to not part with the land for the projects coming up in the area. But beyond that, I know very little of what is going on. My job was more about looking after the smooth functioning of the organization and allotment of funds for our work.'

Lachchu was one of the many from the Raoghat area to have surrendered before the government. Deployment of more police personnel and a government keen to implement a major project involving several thousand crores also meant that those like Lachchu would have a tough time escaping the police net.

'The police were on a major drive to either arrest the Maoists or to get them to surrender. A number of plans were in place for the surrender of Maoists working in the area. Kasru and I were approached by a former colleague. He got in touch with us and we were told about the various benefits of giving up arms and living a peaceful life,' Lachchu said.

Lachchu and Kasru were among the huge number of Maoists who have surrendered in the past few years (the figure was 39 in 2013 and shot up to 421 in 2014). A large part of the surrender has been from Raoghat and from elsewhere in Narayanpur district.

'Already we had spent so many years away from home. Moreover, greater police action meant greater threat to our lives. So we decided to respond to the call for surrender,' said Lachchu.

'There were other reasons too,' Kasru added, a bit shyly.

* * *

Lachchu and Kasru admitted they had both surrendered 'for selfish reasons'. 'I couldn't wait and be arrested by the police, lose my life in an encounter or be finished off by my comrades based on the suspicion that I was leaking information. After all, these are the only possible outcomes for a Maoist soldier,' Kasru said.

Instead, both Kasru and Lachchu gave in to the demands of their family and prioritized home and domestic life ahead of the life of a soldier. Here too, the personal became far more central to their decision-making than the larger battle they were fighting against the State.

'I couldn't help it. I had two children at home. What would have happened to my family back home if I died? I had no time to spend with my children, I used to miss them terribly. What can be so wrong if I feel responsible towards my family?' Lachchu said.

For Kasru too, family responsibility was a huge demand. 'My nephew (brother's son)—who used to take the main family responsibility due to my absence—had been arrested. How would our entire family survive in such a situation? This thought drove me mad. Sooner or later, I would have been in the police net. Under the circumstances, I decided that surrender would be the best option before it got too late.'

So, now, after their surrender, they were able to look at their past critically and neutrally. They were able to figure out what it was that made them withdraw from the movement slowly but surely.

'We had joined the movement to bring about equality in this world. But there are clear disparities between senior and junior cadres even when it comes to something as basic as food. We ate not like family members, but as juniors and seniors at work,' Kasru said.

'DVC (divisional committee) camp meetings are held for almost twenty days at a stretch and for those meetings, there is often mutton or chicken preparations on the menu. This meeting is meant for senior ranking teams of 25 cadres. Perhaps that is the reason behind the better quality of food,' he said matter-of-factly.

The glaring difference was evident at other meetings where senior and junior cadres participate together. These are more like study camps for 20 to 25 participants. Here, Lachchu said, the seniors got 'better' food, which was also cooked separately.

'Even if one points this out, the colleagues ask us to hush it up. "Make some allowances for the elders", we were told. But the difference was for everyone to see,' Kasru said. 'For the seniors, there were endless cups of tea with milk and sugar, but for us, the lower level cadres, there would be tea without milk only once or twice daily. The food for guards and junior soldiers was cooked separately during meetings when senior cadres from Andhra Pradesh visited.'

This apparently trivial act continued to hurt Lachchu and Kasru like it did many other juniors in the party. Why should the seniors—especially the visitors from Andhra Pradesh—get better food and treatment? They discussed this among their friends within the group. 'But no one protested at this disparity. The visitors from Andhra were senior in position, and we were too small to protest. The hierarchy was clearly defined and you had to be unusually bold to raise a question like this,' one of them said. Being in the same family, Lachchu and Kasru would often discuss amongst themselves these differences.

The same applied to clothes and undergarments, they told me. 'We got three briefs, three vests a year, and never got more even if required. But such rules never applied to the seniors. They got as many as they asked for. Some even smoked bidi and cigarettes, but such practices are unthinkable for the juniors.

'What's more, there is a disparity in attitude. It is as if they are important, as if they exist on a higher plane… and we are small inconsequential things. That hurt terribly,' Kasru said.

All this made Lachchu and Kasru deeply disenchanted with the movement. 'I couldn't help turn pessimistic. It soon turned into just another job for me—not the work I had taken up as a dreamer who had set out to change the world in my limited way. Therefore, it did not seem worthwhile to take so much risk or to sacrifice my family in the process,' said Kasru. 'In the end, probably we are all selfish people interested only in our own individual happiness.'

They were also disappointed, they said, to see that some women were close to SZC members and were used as guards. 'They (the women) laughed and joked with the senior leaders. But the same behaviour from male cadres wasn't tolerated. Isn't that disparity? How can women and men not be treated equally? Why should the senior leaders give preference to women cadres over the male ones? What is the reason?' they questioned.

It was not difficult to understand what Lachchu and Kasru were hinting at.

Lachchu also recalled that 'many people—including our own comrades—were bullied, tortured and forced to "confess" that they had leaked information. As a result of this system, those who joined the party as soldiers automatically put to risk the lives of their relatives back home. Too many people had been killed mercilessly.'

In reality all of them were not traitors, said Kasru. 'Many innocents were being killed and villagers were angry and upset with Maoists over these random, ruthless killings.'

The last thing Lachchu and Kasru would have wanted was

to be considered traitors. 'Had we protested against what we did not like, we could have been killed. And others would have been told that we had leaked some information. So we realized that surrender was the best option.'

Naveen Nureti (whose story has been narrated earlier) got in touch with Lachchu and Kasru. He had written letters to the duo, appealing to them to surrender. 'After much pondering, we responded and surrendered on June 26, 2013.'

Over the past few years, the Chhattisgarh government has gone on a massive publicity drive appealing to Maoists to surrender. One of the points emphasized by the Chhattisgarh Police is this disparity allegedly practiced by the CPI (Maoist). Therefore, the posters ask local people of Chhattisgarh not to be duped by the 'outsiders', or the Maoist cadres from Andhra Pradesh.

In one such poster, Sampat alias Sutte, a surrendered Maoist, makes an appeal to the people of Bastar. The poster is in Hindi and, in the name of Sutte, says:

Our Bastar has for decades been an abode of peace. People in Bastar have been living here happily for years amidst the forests and rivers. But, for a while now, some outsiders have been ruining the peace of this place through violence. The Naxals from Andhra Pradesh have had to flee from their own area because of the action taken against them and they have chosen Bastar as their new address. Not only did they want to hide in the forests in Bastar, it was also easy for them to take advantage of the innocence of the people in the region.

Till now, the crude Naxals of Andhra have not allowed our innocent brothers to come out of the clutches of their lies. The Andhra people have themselves reduced to dust the revolutionary dreams that they had shown. The ideology with which they had inspired the villagers into Naxalism have been shunned by the Naxal leaders now. These outsiders are threatening the local people, trampling them under their shoes and killing the innocent villagers is their favourite pastime. It is strange that they are making us kill our own people. But brothers, the time has come for us to work towards the progress of the area and shun the violence. Come out my brothers and see how the villagers outside the influence of the Maoists have progressed. The children are happy here, there is health and education, they have an urge to do well and to progress. I have come here and realized that true revolution is all about progress (*vikaas*)—we can help those lagging behind and realize their dreams.

I appeal to my colleagues who are still indulging in the violent activities, to give up arms and embrace progress.

He then appeals to certain colleagues, like Niti didi, Kosa bhai, Raiju bhai, Pawan, Aitu (Vilas), Rasul, Hemlal and Nasik, to get in touch with him and to give the police and administration a chance. 'Not only will you be able to improve your life through this, but also the lives of all villagers here. If you can do this for Bastar today, Bastar will be forever grateful to you.'

There are scores of similar posters in Hindi and Gondi languages appealing to those who are continuing to fight this war.

* * *

The sorrow that overtook Lachchu and Kasru for not getting the food and clothing that their seniors got was washed away by the happiness of their reunion with their family after their surrender. But every new turn in life is filled with impossible challenges for those who are too small for this enormous war.

'How are you doing these days? Are you happy with your new life?' I asked Kasru a year and a half after we had met in Chhattisgarh, which had been almost immediately after his surrender.

'*Khush nahi hai, Medaam!*' he tells me, his voice quivering, his words crying for support, seeking succour.

Yes, at the core of every happiness there may be a shadow of incompleteness. But when the bliss of reuniting with one's family is overshadowed by an emptiness, then perhaps there is something wrong with the way things have unfolded for Kasru.

What was it?

'We were asked to give up arms. But surrender does not really mean giving up arms…' he stuttered, unsure if he should utter the obvious.

Kasru, a constable with the Chhattisgarh Police, now earned a monthly salary of Rs 18,500. He got a government job in December 2014, nearly two years after his surrender. However, the dearth of money (though others like him have enriched themselves through surrender) did not upset him.

But Kasru was depressed because when he had decided to surrender, he had visualised a life that would be carefree and without any threat. Before his surrender the fact that his life could end any moment in a chance encounter with the police had scared him the most. As a reward for surrendering before the police, he hoped he would get some money, a home, a regular job and spend the rest of his life peacefully.

But that was not meant to be. The Chhattisgarh Police gave him a job which requires him to carry firearms. His job entails visits to the forest in search of hideouts where his former Maoist colleagues are likely to be. His former foes—the police—may have ceased to be his foes anymore, but his earlier comrades have now turned into his greatest enemies. His job now is to hound them out and hand them over to the police. His life is pretty much the same in that it could end any moment in a chance encounter with a Maoist. His peace of mind is lost forever.

There's no way Kasru can go back to his village no matter how unhappy he is with his present life. '*Wahan pe khatra hai* (there is danger for me back in my village),' he said. All surrendered Maoists fear that their former colleagues would be baying for their blood. Therefore, only his brother and a nephew work in the fields back in their village Irakbhatti. Kasru did not take the risk of going back.

Kasru felt that not only was it unethical—for him to have changed sides and to now have to target his former colleagues—but also a matter of enormous risk that he had to face.

His fears are not unfounded. In Chhattisgarh, on July 13, 2015, four assistant constables were abducted by the Maoists and their bodies were found a couple of days later riddled with bullets.

Jaidev Yadab, Raju Telam, Rama Majji and Mangal Sodi were abducted by Maoists when the four were returning after collecting their salary from the headquarters. The first two were abducted from a bus and the other two were in a two-wheeler that was stopped by the Maoists in the middle of the road. Two days later, their bodies were found on the Bijapur-Kutru Road.[5]

These four men were residents of Judumpara, one of the oldest camps set up by the Chhattisgarh government for those who left home following the Salwa Judum of 2005.

At different times in Chhattisgarh, the special police officers (SPOs), constables, assistant constables, former Maoists and inhabitants of Salwa Judum camps who were forced to work for the state, have all been targeted by the Maoists.

Earlier, in December 2014, a group of Maoists killed a surrendered former comrade who was working as a *gopaniya sainik* (secret agent) of the Chhattisgarh Police. Shivaji Korsa, who operated in west Bastar division and had surrendered in 2012, was shot at from a close range and his throat was slit near the Bijapur district headquarters where he and his friends were gearing up for a new year's party.[6]

With Shivaji Korsa's case fresh in his mind, Lachchu too feared he would be the next target of his former colleagues. 'Many of our former colleagues spread fabricated stories about us simply to give us a bad name. So we fear we may be targeted,' he said.

Lachchu's job of a *gopaniya sainik* gets him Rs 9,000 per month. He bought a two decimal plot at Narayanpur with Rs 30,000 and built a small house on it where he lives with his wife and their three children—two daughters and a son. He got Rs 10,000 as an immediate reward from the Chhattisgarh Police and the job. But behind the façade of a happy home filled with the laughter of his children and the heady smell of food cooking in the kitchen, there are sleepless nights filled with worry. Lachchu fears for his life and the safety of his family members because his work (getting 'secret' information on the movement of the Maoists) has now exposed him to the great risk of attack from his former colleagues.

Security for the surrendered Maoists hasn't been a major priority for the State, where such surrenders have become quite common. The huge number of surrenders in 2014 are said to have taken place after S.R.P Kalluri took over as the Inspector General (IG) of Bastar and gave this project a major push with publicity, increased pay, jobs and housing schemes.

R.K.Vij, Additional Director General of Chhattisgarh Police, whom I met at Raipur and spoke to several times over the phone later, said: 'Security is a major cause of concern. However, the Maoists can stage attacks anytime, anywhere. Recently, they have killed two of their comrades on the grounds that they were planning to surrender. It is a complex problem.'

Vij feels that the spate of surrenders in the past few years in Chhattisgarh is definitely indicative of the fact that 'the romance associated with the CPI (Maoist) that had long inspired youths from both rural and urban areas, is on the wane'. One of the main reasons behind this disenchantment is that the war has continued for many decades now but has not produced positive results, he says.

Despite Vij's views on the 'positive' ramifications of the Maoists' surrenders, the fact remains that those like Kasru and Lachchu, who were never 'high profile', have been unable to voice their concerns. These women and men from the grassroots, who were mostly engaged as foot-soldiers in the party and are now constables, face enormous threats from their former colleagues. But there is no system of security in place perhaps because the number of surrenders is so huge.

The poorest of the lot like Lachchu and Kasru (who were never significant players), have been forced to work with the police in the absence of an alternative. There are many more like them in Chhattisgarh, forced into lives and livelihoods over which they have had no control.

Take the case of Salwa Judum. For 30 months since June 2005, the Chhattisgarh government led a counter-insurgency operation against the Naxalites under the guise of a 'spontaneous people's movement' called Salwa Judum.[7] The government claimed that it was the people's reaction against the Maoists' collection of levies, destruction of roads, and so on, in which people from more than 200 villages had participated.

To begin with, the Salwa Judum was neither peaceful nor spontaneous. The Chhattisgarh government had placed arms in the hands of poor tribals and appointed them as Special Police Officers (SPOs). They were then trained in arms by the government to form a counter-insurgency army to fight armed Naxals. People were forcibly picked up and confined to 'Salwa Judum camps'. Those who did not go to the camps were considered to be Maoists. The state unleashed a reign of terror and there were hundreds of cases of looting, rape and other violent incidents. People were forced to attend meetings and live in camps, else they were faced with dire consequences—their homes were set on fire, they were beaten, their access to markets was snapped. Some villagers even 'disappeared'—a punishment for refusing to participate in the attack against Naxals. The Salwa Judum was led by Mahendra Karma, a Congressman.

'Salwa Judum leaders mostly consist of people aggrieved by Naxalite activities—contractors or middlemen, members of non-tribal and landed tribal communities, sarpanches (village officials), patels (village headmen), and priests. Salwa Judum members—ordinary tribal and non-tribal civilians, including children—carried out their leaders' instructions and conducted operations along with government security forces. They traveled from one village to another, particularly to villages they believed were Naxalite strongholds, conducting violent raids, combing them for Naxalites, evacuating villagers to government-run camps (also known as Salwa Judum camps, base camps or relief camps) and in some cases, beating, raping, and killing villagers' (quoted with permission from Human Rights Watch report, 14 July 2008).[8]

In 2007, a group of petitioners approached the Supreme Court to challenge the legality of the appointment of tribals as SPOs and highlight the violations committed.

In July 2011, the Supreme Court declared the deployment of tribal youths as SPOs—either as Koya commandos, Salwa Judum or any other force—in the fight against the Maoist insurgency as illegal and unconstitutional. The ruling, issued by Justice B. Sudershan Reddy and Justice S.S. Nijjar on the writ petition filed by social anthropologist Prof. Nandini Sundar and others, said: 'The State of Chhattisgarh shall forthwith make every effort to recall all firearms issued to any of the SPOs, whether current or former, along with any and all accoutrements and accessories issued to use such firearms.'[9]

But soon after the Supreme Court verdict in 2011, the Chhattisgarh government re-designated the SPOs as assistant constables (sahayak arakshaks) and increased their salary. They were also sent to schools to get basic education. Now, their salary has been increased to approximately Rs 15,000. Their work remains the same, just the designation has changed.

Mahendra Karma was subsequently killed by the Maoists during an attack on a Congress convoy in May 2013. His death will remain one of the most gruesome attacks by the Maoists—a massacre in which several Congress leaders and security forces were killed.

But even as Salwa Judum continued for 30 months, the same pattern of violence unleashed on poor tribal villagers continues even now in various forms.

A decade after the Salwa Judum, when the Chhattisgarh government led by Raman Singh, signed MoUs for the steel plant and the railway line in Bastar, a front similar to the Salwa Judum called the Vikas Sangharsh Samiti, led by late Mahendra Karma's son, Chhavindra began to fast emerge.[10]

At the Salwa Judum camp of Kasauli, in Dantewada district, which I visited, a strange silence pervaded. People living here hardly talked but when they did, it was evident how much they missed their homes and pined to go back to their villages. Yet they knew they couldn't, and that the camp where they were living could come under attack as well.

The Kasauli camp has 610 people in 311 homes, none of whom can return to their villages because the Maoists may take their anger out on them. In more ways than one, this home is like a prison—the gates are guarded and those who enter and leave the premises must register their names every time.

This fear *is* real. In July 2006, the Maoists had attacked a Salwa Judum camp at Errabore in Dantewada district, in which 33 tribals were killed. The Naxalites went on a rampage for over three hours in the camp and the Salwa Judum activists were outraged that the CRPF and the state police could not come to their rescue.[11]

Not only has the Chhattisgarh government taken to various means to crush the Maoist movement in the state, it has also, in various forms, forcibly pitted a large number of ordinary women and men against the rebels. This has put the lives of these poor and ordinary people at risk whether they are surrendered Maoists working as armed constables or those continuing to live in Salwa Judum camps. In the absence of adequate security, the lives of the family members of surrendered Maoists too, have come under threat.

Those like Lachchu and Kasru became beneficiaries of a 'surrender and rehabilitation' policy that did not even take into consideration an individual's wish to pursue a particular profession. It made the whole concept of a farewell to arms a complete sham.

In an odd way therefore, the Salwa Judum led by Mahendra Karma, the 'movement' led by his son Chhavindra in a newer avatar of the Salwa Judum, and the forcible use of surrendered Maoists in the police force are very similar.

'We are doing exactly the same work we were engaged in back in the Maoist squads. If surrender means farewell to arms and living a peaceful life with family members, that at least has not been the case with us,' said Kasru. Lachchu nodded in agreement, adding that there was nothing much they could do about it. They were getting paid ('and money is essential for survival'), and going back to their village was not an option.

For the duo, it has been a plunge from the frying pan into the fire.

Part III

THE WOMEN

~

'More and more women are becoming part of the "State versus Maoist" war—currently women are said to be approximately 60 per cent of the total Maoist force according to Maoist and home ministry sources. Little boys are often sent away to live in boarding schools where the parents consider the boys to be "safe". Therefore, back in the villages, it is mostly the girls who stay back…'

Suchitra Mahato worked as a Maoist for nearly ten years before her surrender. She rose in the ranks due to her courage and her mental and physical strength, becoming one of the most prominent Maoist leaders and remaining at the top for many years.

8

Suchitra Mahato

'*Shaala! Shunbi ami ke?*' (You devil! Want to hear my name?)
The blood was oozing steadily, so she stuffed the wound
with cloth and began to walk—slow, staggering steps at first.
Then she increased the pace and managed to walk on.

The cloth soaked up the blood and slowly, the flow reduced; it
only oozed a bit and fresh pieces of cloth pressed tightly against
the wound seemed to have stopped the bleeding for now. Two
bullets that had pierced her skin and flesh were still wedged in
her abdomen, so she desperately needed to get to a doctor. But
both her own identity and the fact that she had been injured
were such terrible secrets that Suchitra could not just walk into
any doctor's clinic or hospital. How many hospitals or health
centres were available in villages in any case?

She pulled her saree around her in such a way that the wounds
were not visible. Thankfully, it was winter and she could wrap
a shawl around as well.

Stepping onto the pucca road from the forest, she met a lone
cyclist. She asked him for a favour. Could he drop her to the
home of someone in the next village? He agreed but she was
sure he would be asking for something in return. It was a long
stretch of silent road and as the sun shone brightly in the winter
sky, Suchitra Mahato rode pillion on the bicycle of this stranger.
The pain had numbed most parts of her body, but she knew she
had to handle this man with equanimity.

'What can I give you? A poor woman like me can only arrange some money with difficulty. If you take the trouble to come to this side of the village a few days later, I'll see if I can give you some money,' Suchitra told the stranger.

'What will I do with money? You know what might be more useful,' he chuckled. He asked for her phone number but she told him she was too poor to own a mobile phone.

In some other situation, Suchitra would have probably slapped the man, or beaten him black and blue. But right now, the need of the hour was to save her own life.

'I thought that if he made another move, I would just scream out my name and show him my wound just to scare him away. *Shaala! Shunbi ami ke?* Fortunately, he stopped at that. So she let him go. It was the only time, Suchitra tells me, that she let a person who had misbehaved with her get away. 'In the end I probably forgave him because it was due to him that I am alive today.'

This was the story Suchitra told me. This was *her* version of how she had escaped from the forest when she was hit by two bullets on her belly during an encounter with the police, as she and CPI (Maoist) politburo leader Kishanji were running from one part of the forest to another. I had learnt from other sources that the man on the bicycle knew to whom he was offering the ride. Perhaps that is the reason why he did not make another move.

The name 'Suchitra Mahato' was widely associated with the killing of policemen and political party functionaries in West Bengal's Jangalmahal for ten years or so. It was bound to be treated with fear and awe.

It is said that Kishanji was killed in a major conspiracy and the death was in reality a fake encounter.[1] The buzz was that he was killed despite being 'caught alive' because his death would have been far more significant than an arrest. Suchitra had apparently betrayed Kishanji by leaving him in a forest he was unfamiliar with and some young boy had perhaps tipped off the police on being promised a huge sum of money.

Had Suchitra been trapped by the police? Had she in turn trapped Kishanji in collusion with the police and the ruling Trinamool Congress? Was it entirely a political gameplan executed to perfection where even some of the top police personnel were kept in the dark? None, apart from a few, can say for sure. All that the public saw was Suchitra standing by the side of West Bengal Chief Minister Mamata Banerjee in March 2012 as a 'surrendered Maoist'[2] and that she had married a Trinamool Congress functionary named Prabir Garai.

Garai, a veterinary doctor, was associated with the CPI (Maoist) frontal organization PCPA, when the Left Front was in power in West Bengal. With the change of guard in the state, Garai was given important charge of the Trinamool Congress in Jangalmahal and he also got married to Suchitra. She was earlier married to Sashadhar Mahato, a Maoist leader who had died in an encounter with a combined Central and state government force in March 2011. After his marriage to Suchitra, Prabir has since discontinued his 'practice' as a vet.

As we sat on a creaking charpai in her small room in Bankura, Suchitra caressed her long black tresses; she was preparing to shampoo them in the evening. But she eventually changed her mind and decided to put it off for later as she narrated stories of her work, her thoughts on life, and about people's attempts to tarnish her 'character'.

In the ten years she worked as a Maoist, she would go into small, sleepy hamlets inside dense forests, her long, black hair tied into a thick plait, a rifle slung over her shoulder. 'What kind of oil do you use for your hair? What is the secret? Please tell us!' the didis and mashis in the villages would gather around and ask her. 'Nothing, just the usual brands of oil,' she would say, blushing. Suchitra was popular with the villagers. She had a casual air about her—friendly and approachable.

Yet, Suchitra Mahato is a mystery. If you talk to her, you will perhaps never know which one of her various personae is real. Are they all real, or all fake? Perhaps it's a mix of both.

Sitting there, she laughed at and mocked potential death threats. 'I am told I will be killed because I got Kishanji killed.' There is a smirk playing on her lips. Does she admit it? No. Does she deny it? No.

But she was not afraid to die. 'I don't think I can be killed like this, all of a sudden without any hint of death coming. I know how Maoists kill their targets. I was also a Maoist, and we would always tell individuals the reason why they were being killed. Maoists—if they want to kill me—will first write a letter, telling me the reasons why they want to finish me off. And I haven't got any letter. If death will come, let it come and embrace me. I am not afraid to die.'

The next time I met her, she told me: 'I didn't kill Kishanji, nor got him killed. I even told that to the top officers in the state. They all know it. And even the Maoists know it. There was a young boy with us and we were all fleeing at the same time. So why should the Maoists kill me?

'Moreover, if I wanted to get him arrested, I would have ensured he was alive. Even *I* was hit by bullets. Why should I deliberately sustain bullet injuries to make this appear more authentic? Look at my wounds. I could have died. The bullets were wedged by the side of my kidney.'

She was now a little harassed about the security bandobast around her and the repeated reminders from the state government authorities that the Maoists were after her life. Ten home guards were guarding her and Prabir's Bankura home for months and the police had to spend Rs 2 lakh per month on this arrangement. She had also had to leave home and settle down elsewhere, at a place offered by the police which was less vulnerable to attacks.

What upset her, though, was the fact that people keep

gossiping about her. She was well aware of the accusations. 'Why do people keep saying all these things about Kishanji and me? Why am I accused of trapping men? Women are always seen as temptresses, as objects of lust and greed. As if, beyond this, she is nothing else. In the party (CPI-Maoist) too, people look at you with desire and lust and treat you as an object of sexuality. But thankfully, the party has strict rules on this. No one can get away with bad behaviour against a woman. He will definitely be punished.

'Women have to suffer right from childhood! I have seen a lot of women being tortured back in my village, including my mother. That made me want to fight back and protest from the time I was a child.'

* * *

Suchitra was born in a poor family in the Binpur area of Jhargram in West Midnapore. Her parents used to collect wood from the forests and sell it in the local market for a living. But that hardly fetched enough money to feed five people. They all had to struggle to survive.

After she left home and joined the Maoists, Suchitra quickly learned to change her fortune. She rose in the ranks due to her courage, her mental and physical strength, and became one of the most prominent Maoist leaders. She remained at the top for close to a decade.

She was involved in one of the most daring attacks West Bengal has seen—at Silda Eastern Frontier Rifles camp on 15 February 2010—where 24 jawans were killed by the rebels.[3] She is said to have plotted and led the attack.[4] In fact, she was one of the most prominent leaders to have organized the movement in Lalgarh since 2008 and played a key role in organizing the women there. Women from the village homes would cook meals, travel hours to feed the Maoist leaders and foot-soldiers and offered them shelter in their homes. Many joined the core movement and stayed in camps, took up arms and were part of operations—abducting, shooting and killing policemen and members of the ruling Left parties.

Suchitra was said to be involved in some of the major incidents of Maoist attacks on policemen in West Bengal for close to a decade. Way back on 26 February 2004, she was allegedly part of the team that had caused a landmine blast in Belpahari (in West Midnapore bordering Jharkhand) in which eight policemen were killed. A police jeep was blown to pieces and among those killed were a sub-inspector (SI) and an assistant sub-inspector (ASI).[5]

The same year, in mid-October, six jawans of the Eastern Frontier Rifles (EFR) were killed in West Midnapore's Ramgarh near the Jhitka forest in an attack by the Maoists.[6]

In October 2009, two policemen were killed and the officer-in-charge of Sankrail police station in West Midnapore was abducted and a bank was looted. Sub-inspector Diwakar Bhattacharya and ASI Swapan Ray were shot dead. The officer in charge (OC) Atindranath Dutta, was tied up and taken hostage while the entire state machinery went into a tizzy in a bid to get him back. Finally, the Maoists had the last laugh, with the OC freed after fifteen tribal women were released on bail by the Jhargram court.[7]

Then again, in October 2009, the Rajdhani Express was blocked in West Midnapore's Banstala halt by over 400 tribals owing allegiance to the PCPA, a game plan allegedly backed by the Maoists. The train was held up for several hours with passengers inside in a hostage-like situation. After the state and Central governments decided to send in troops to free the train and passengers, the tribals and Maoists retreated.[8] Suchitra's role here is not very clear, but it is suspected that she may have been a part of it, say police sources.

In December 2009 the Maoists attacked a sponge iron plant, set a dozen trucks on fire, killed four CPM workers and set some oil tankers ablaze on the national highway in West Midnapore. Suchitra was alleged to be part of this episode as well.[9]

Before I go into the details of how her life changed completely after Kishanji's death and her 'surrender', I want to first discuss here the role of women in this war in general and about Suchitra in particular.

How is she viewed by those she worked with? When I asked one of her former colleagues if he knew Suchitra, the man (who was in his late 30s), smiled mischievously. 'Yes, I know her, like a sister,' he said. Another former colleague too had a similar expression on his face when I mentioned her. There were many smirks and sneers. A senior IPS officer, who has worked in Jangalmahal for years, told me how she managed to rise in the Maoist ranks 'by being close to powerful men all the time'. The same perception exists among journalists covering the Maoist movement in Bengal.

Her female colleagues, on the other hand, were angry that she remained in a 'safe' and 'domineering' position by choosing an influential leader as a spouse/partner. The fact that she instantly moved from being a Maoist to becoming the wife of an influential Trinamool Congress leader at a time when there was a change of guard in West Bengal , is seen as the result of her clever manoeuvering power.

Female Maoists have surrendered—just like their male comrades—when their career was either over or they were frustrated with some aspect of the movement. Some had been 'intercepted' by the police, but their arrests were officially projected as 'surrenders'. Men too, have surrendered because they wanted to live peacefully with their partners and children, but the men were never branded by notoriety. It is deeply entrenched in our culture that a female soldier is never seen as a desexualized individual. On the contrary, she has always been viewed as possessing overwhelming sexual prowess—someone whose sexuality can be used or abused unless she is a mother and/or spouse of a senior leader.

Women are 'affected' on both sides of this war—as soldiers

and as ordinary village women who have not joined the war but are not outside the area of violence on account of that.

More and more women are becoming part of the State versus Maoist war—currently women are said to be approximately 60 per cent of the total Maoist force according to Maoist and home ministry sources. There are many reasons behind this.

In the states where Maoists routinely visit villages looking for young recruits, little boys are often sent away from homes to live in boarding schools or at relatives' places. If they live in places where Maoists have no influence, the parents consider the boys 'safe'.

Therefore, back in the villages, it is mostly the girls that stay back with their parents. This has resulted in Maoist groups recruiting a larger number of girls than boys in recent years.

In the squads, women are used to deceive cops—a woman is far less suspect than a male cadre. Women foot-soldiers are also used as shields when major operations are carried out, as they raise less suspicion.

To the government, women's involvement poses a greater threat because it means 'greater acceptability of the movement among communities', said an officer. Significantly, women have also played an important role in *making* top leaders surrender before the police. If the police get tip-offs about a top male cadre pondering surrender, they send feelers through the woman—his partner or spouse. 'There are always concerns over family life and children. And it has always been the women who influenced the male leaders to give up the life of a soldier because it threatens the family life,' the officer said.

At the outset—during the Naxalbari uprising—it was a movement for social and political equality for which the educated youth, both male and female, participated. It was idealism that swayed hundreds to give up their material comforts and fight the exploitative landlords and empower the poor for which men and women had fought together. But ironically, those who aspired for social equality had glossed over the relevance of gender inequality in the same war and women ended up as more or less invisible—made to do the cooking, or work as couriers and not easily allowed to rise up in the ranks.

In the Maoist microcosm of warfare, heroism remained in the masculine paradigm and the woman got the role she always had back home. There was no escape from the trappings of domesticity and her role in that sphere.

Those fighting the *class* war perhaps feel that it was a far more important issue than *gender*. Kishanji, 'who was looked up to as an elder brother figure by the women cadres', was approached several times with complaints of sexual violence from members of the teams he was leading. 'But at the end of the day, there would be attempts to somehow sort out the issues of sexual violence and gender discrimination, and not get bogged down by these things because we were all fighting the greater war against the police and the ruling establishment,' said a member of the team close to the deceased Naxal politburo leader.

Maoist soldiers—from foot-soldiers to senior cadres—understand that when women and men are fighting this war, 'there will be such problems', and that the real war is not about gender equality, but 'a much *bigger* social problem'. This is where the fight against gender discrimination stops, this is where it fails. Even the top leaders of this movement have not considered gender equality important enough to practise in their own set-up.

So a woman became an important leader by being a senior leader's wife rather than by fighting the war with valour and grit.

In her book, *Muscular Nationalism: Gender, Violence, and Empire in India and Ireland*[10] Sikata Banerjee looks at the role women played in the Naxalite movement and how the female revolutionary remained suspect because of her body. 'Although the basis of Naxalism and CPI-ML ideology was a critique of the postcolonial state in Bengal, with its implication in oppressive capitalist hierarchies, the gendered aspect of postcolonial modernity was ignored by the party,' she writes. She also points out that the female revolutionary remained suspect 'because her body had the potential to disrupt, through its expression of sexuality, the path of self-discipline embarked on by both women and their male comrades. Indeed, given the movement's dedication to the creation of the new man and its reliance on small squads of male revolutionaries, armed femininity required that female bodies occupy a space in the borderland between normative manhood and womanhood, erasing any consequence of the physical embodiment of being a woman.'

If we keep this at the back of our mind, it will not be difficult to see how female soldiers like Shobha Mandi, Suchitra Mahato, Nikita, Tara—'known' names in the Maoist movement in recent times—were embodiments of that sexuality, which either had to be repressed or considered as a potent threat to lead men astray. 'At all times, women revolutionaries had to guard their sexuality and emphasize their chastity and purity because it was believed that female sexuality would lead men astray,' Banerjee writes.

And interestingly, though not surprisingly, only motherhood could exonerate the 'unchaste woman'.

Suchitra's role, on the other hand, had been completely different, perhaps because she had not transformed herself into the role that is perceived to be 'natural'. She remained in her quiet shell, not posing before the camera with a child, not taking up motherhood as her new role that would erase her past life where her sexuality was central to her persona. What made this worse (and added further to the stereotyping) was that she never had a biological child.

After her mysterious surrender, Suchitra was not keen on joining the police force as a home guard when she was offered the job initially by the Mamata Banerjee government. 'It is the same police force we were fighting against for years. These cops got my brother arrested and beat him up so much that he is a bundle of nerves today. My husband—before we were married—was taken to jail, his wife who died some years ago had been imprisoned and tortured. So many people in our family were tortured by the police at different times that we were all against this job offered to me,' Suchitra said. 'But then, life has to go on, and for that money is needed.'

So she finally acceded after two long years. 'I need money for my treatment—I need thorough checkups from time to time even though I was operated on for the bullet injuries more than three years ago.' She also needed money to buy medicines after being detected with diabetes.

Her husband's family owns some land, but the produce is not enough to sustain all of them, Suchitra said. Money was also needed for the education of her step-son (her husband, Prabir Garai's son from his first marriage) who was studying at a school away from home.

She shared a deep bond with the boy. 'When I was staying with them during my recovery, he told his father [Prabir]—"Please do not let Mashi leave us". That's when his father and I got married,' Suchitra told me, smiling. From this part of Suchitra's narrative, I also got to know that she was staying at Prabir's place while recovering from her injuries. It also helped that Prabir was a veterinary doctor, and perhaps knew better than many others on how to heal injuries.

Suchitra and Prabir knew each other for years, because he was married to her neighbour. 'He was a jamai [son-in-law] in our village. I knew his son, too, and he called me Mashi [aunt].' Prabir's wife died and so did Sashadhar, Suchitra's first husband.

'We share a rare bond—my husband, the boy and I. We were united together through our grief. All three of us went through extreme suffering at that time and each helped bring the others' lives back on track.'

She told me more about this bond. 'I like to eat chicken, my husband loves goat meat, and our son loves both.' She told me that she wanted the teenager to grow into a young man who would be respectful towards women.

She was all praise for her husband's sense of humour and generosity. 'Even if my husband works for a political party, he is honest and generous. He does not "earn" anything from the party. If he has Rs 10 on him, he will give away Rs 20 to a person in need, he is such a kind man.' All the more reason for her to work and share his burden.

This Suchitra clashes with the story of the shrewd politician and the cunning Maoist woman who, in connivance with the political party in power, plotted against a CPI (Maoist) politburo member, leaving him alone in an unfamiliar forest to face the security forces and certain death.

* * *

Whatever the truth, Suchitra's life changed dramatically overnight. It had always been out of the ordinary for sure. But she would have preferred to live in anonymity, doing some ordinary work, earning a modest living. Now, she had to move around with four security personnel (her husband is guarded by two security men). 'It is impossible to do the job of a nurse or that of a school teacher, the kind of work I really would have preferred to do.'

'We may appear "free" but this is freedom with certain restrictions. There are cases pending against us, so where else can I go but do a job with the police? One cannot miss this irony in my life,' she said.

The police job came with little expectations from her. 'I don't expect that people here work for principles, the way we did in the party [CPI (Maoist)]. I will try not to be part of any injustice against innocent people, now that I am working with the West Bengal's police force. After all, that is what we fought for all these years. And if I see that I am being made part of any injustice, I shall put my foot down.

'I have worked for women's rights in the party. We worked to prevent beating of women, alcoholism and police torture on villagers. We have worked against state atrocities on villagers,' she said. 'I used to tell my mother as a teenager that I would marry someone who did not drink and beat me up. My mother wondered how such a miracle could happen.'

By her own admission, that miracle took place twice in Suchitra's life. 'I got respect and love from both my men. Life goes in a flash. The moment my first husband died, I realized I had so much to tell him. Much was left unsaid. Now that I am married to someone again, if we have a tiff, I remember my first husband and feel he would surely have treated me better. But then, when the anger subsides, I realize I love this man so much as well. He likes me to decide what clothes he should wear each day, and I find it a gesture full of warmth. People may have different perceptions about someone from outside but it does not matter. Inside, you know who you are and the kind of relationship you have with your husband.'

* * *

Suchitra did not believe in the signs of marriage like wearing *shakha-pola* bangles and *sindoor*. 'In the party, I learnt that these things do not have relevance. But my husband told me with a lot of love that his family believes in these customs, so I readily agreed to wear them.'

She told me that her mother still visited Suchitra's first husband Sashadhar Mahato's mother. 'Perhaps the old woman will not like it if I visit her along with my husband now. So I tell my mother that she should go and visit her. It is through my mother that I connect with the poor woman who lost her son in this deadly war.'

Suchitra Mahato has a wonderful spark about her. You cannot miss it, even if you harbour doubts about some elements in her version of what has happened in her life. Life has treated her harshly, but she has turned the misery on its head, mocked at life's cruelties and risen from the ashes every time.

She showed me her wound—scattered brown marks on the flesh of her belly. 'When you breathe, Didi, you feel the air rushing in, isn't it?' she asks me. I nod. '*I feel nothing inside. It's numb. I can't understand if I am breathing or not.*' Here is a veritable superhuman, who it seems, may have died at some point, and begun to breathe again; her existence is itself a mystery.

Looking at her, as we ate dates from a steel plate and she shared some of her recipes with me (how to cook fish in spicy, tamarind and mustard sauce; and how rice powder added to wheat flour enhances the taste of chapattis), and put away in her bag the packet of chocolate cookies that I had taken for her, I thought that a winner like her is extremely hard to come by.

When I met her the second time, she looked much thinner. 'It's because of all the housework I do and the medicines I have to take regularly,' Suchitra said, blushing. She had happily settled down in the new accommodation.

She had taken her mother, her two nieces (her brother's daughter and sister's daughter) and their pets (two birds and a dog) to the new home. The girls are both five-year-olds whom she plans to admit to a school. 'I don't have a daughter, so I thought of bringing up these two girls.' Her stepson and mother-in-law had moved to a different town and lived in a rented home near the boy's school. 'That arrangement is for his education, so he doesn't have to travel long distances every day to school. Now that he is in a higher class, there is fear of falling into bad company, so it is better to take a rented accommodation rather than sending him to hostel.'

She didn't want the children in her family to go through the same hardship that she had gone through as a child. One of the two girls had already suffered a lot. 'It's easier for me to bring her with me and to do whatever I can for her rather than spending money.'

In her village home (her husband, Prabir Garai's place) they were constructing a new pucca house by the side of the two-storied mud house where Suchitra and Prabir had been living for so long. For now, Prabir lived there alone.

'He comes down to this new accommodation sometimes. And he tells me that managing the home won't be difficult. But I know it is tough for him to live alone without anyone to even warm the food after a hard day's work.'

She told me I could write all that she had told me about herself. And she took me by surprise when I asked her if I could click a few photographs. 'I am really fond of photographs,' she said. 'But I don't like close-up shots.' I took a mix of close-up and long shots, and some selfies.

Life goes on. For now, they are all immersed in the happy chaos in her two-roomed flat with her mother, nieces and the pets. Yet another new life, yet another new beginning.

Suchitra will not give up on life. She has died and risen many, many times. She has mocked death and internalized the notion that there is no power greater than herself. She has suffered and seen people take sadistic pleasure from her pain.

And every time she has burst forth and sprung back into another new life.

9

Jagori Baske

Jagori Baske was very hassled. 'Can't I ever lead a quiet and peaceful life?' she asked. A couple of days ago, she found out that a journalist was inquiring about her son's school and about the car that dropped him there from home. Not only that, he even landed straight at her place which was located—apparently securely—inside a police housing quarters. This not only raised doubts about the efficacy of the security arrangements for the protection of a high-profile surrendered Maoist like her, but also didn't help her peace of mind. 'Why don't people leave us alone?'

She was wearing a fuschia and yellow cotton salwar-kameez, gold earrings, red and white (shakha-pola) bangles, an iron (loha) bangle, a vermilion dot on the forehead and sindur in the parting of her hair that was tied into a neat plait. Her dark skin glowed in the faint light and she still managed to smile at me while talking about the travesty she thought people were making of her life. There was a tattoo below the thumb of her left hand, perhaps from years ago.

She talked to me because, by now, she knew me. I had met her twice already. I had even met her son when he was six years old. Now he would soon be eight years old. Jagori's husband, Rajaram Soren (who used to be her fellow Maoist comrade and who surrendered to the Mamata Banerjee government along with her in November 2011)[1] was sitting by her side dressed in a loose purple shirt and dark trousers but Jagori did most of the talking.

'We had two sets of marriage rituals,' she told me, smiling at Rajaram. 'The first one was done like people in the cities practise, by signing documents. And the other was a social one by following Hindu rituals.' I had asked her about the signs of marriage that she so prominently displayed. She felt a bit guilty about it because 'it is not followed in the party'. At the back of her mind, she probably still belonged to the 'party' (the CPI-Maoist) or felt that she must at least offer an explanation for all the deviations from its path and tenets.

Jagori and Rajaram got married in a village surrounded by thick forests (another couple also got married along with them and a joint celebration followed) many moons ago. There were 300 guests and '*luchi, chholar daal, patha'r jhol*' (poories, Bengal gram daal and mutton curry) was on the menu. For the feast, meat of two goats was required, she said, highlighting the huge number of people that attended the wedding.

Later, Rajaram put sindoor in the parting of her hair and she wore the red, white and iron bangles during a social function attended by friends and relatives from both sides. Her parents however did not attend the wedding. She offered no reason about their absence in this important event in her life. Perhaps her parents were constantly under police surveillance in order to track her down, so they couldn't put her life at risk by attending her wedding, or perhaps she was not in touch with them at that point? One can only hazard a guess.

In Jagori's narrative of her life, there were bound to be gaping holes. According to her, she had spent only two years with the Maoists. But the truth is that she had left home when she was only sixteen, and was part of Maoist squads—chiefly in West Bengal's Purulia district—for nearly a decade.

Her name first emerged in 2005 in the murder of a CPM leader from Purulia—Rabindranath Kar and his wife Anandamoyee.[2] The leader and his wife were killed and burnt in their two-storied mud house. A portion of the house and walls of an adjoining hut still bear testimony to the horrific incident. Jagori is said to have led the team that carried out this operation. In the same year, she was suspected to have been part of a team that killed another political leader in the area, Mahendra Mahato.[3]

Jagori had become an expert in handling all kinds of arms, including the sophisticated ones, and it was no wonder that Gurucharan Kisku alias Marshal, a senior leader, took her under his wing. She participated in more than thirty incidents for close to a decade involving looting of arms, abduction and murder in Jangalmahal, primarily in the Purulia district. She was quick to rise in the ranks and was soon one of the top commanders in the Ayodhya squad. She inspired awe and terror—a woman in war fatigues who brandished rifles, knocked on doors in the dead of the night and did not twitch an eyebrow before killing a politician or a policeman. Jagori had become the talk of the town—a 'dreaded' Maoist about whom many legends and myths were created by imaginative villagers.

In subsequent major Maoist operations at Jangalmahal, her role is somewhat unclear. By 2007, Jagori had been married and had given birth to a son. It was around this time that she had fallen out with the Maoist leadership and had even been expelled from the party. For two years, she was out of action, living in different villages in the homes of friends and relatives. At that time, her son was so young that Jagori was not really much concerned about anything else other than the security of the child and herself.

She was eventually taken back into the party in 2009, but things were not the same as earlier. The leadership and the issues had changed, and the tribal leaders in the party were an alienated lot. There was deep disgruntlement as leaders from outside called the shots and prepared the agenda. The dissatisfaction among local leaders and the foot-soldiers was of the same nature as it was in Odisha, Jharkhand and Chhattisgarh. Her mentor Marshal had had a major fallout with the party, and was rumoured to be working for the police. By 2010, Jagori had bid farewell to the party for good, had snapped all ties and was living in a 'shelter' offered to her.

These days, Jagori was upset about the way she was perceived by people who do not know her. 'It was written in newspapers that I could jump from the first floor of a building, brandishing firearms in both hands and firing at the same time. Is it possible to do such a thing?' she made a face as she asked. She felt that everyone—those who know her and those who have only heard about her—detests her to the core.

Now that she had 'surrendered' before the police, she thought that they hated her even more. Jagori brought her head closer to mine and whispered in my ear, 'What is your perception of those who join the party or those like me who have now surrendered?' She paused and then risked a little more, 'Do you really *hate* them?'

I assured her that people do not all 'hate' the Maoists and surrendered Maoists. She hadn't been able to shed the feeling of being a social outcast. The feeling had grown within her over the years.

One of the reasons she wore the various 'signs' of marriage was that this was acceptable in the 'society' in which she lived. 'We are tribals [Santhals], but Hindus, and we have to follow the rituals of wearing all the "signs" of marriage.' Back home, it may not have been an issue, but in that town, surrounded by Hindu married women who all wear sindoor and shakha-pola-loha bangles, Jagori did not want to stand out.

Why did she leave home in the first place? Jagori said that living at her Bakdoba home—a remote, sleepy village bordering Purulia and West Midnapore districts—had turned into a nightmare. That was more than a decade ago (though she wouldn't specify the year).

Her two older sisters were already married. She and her

younger brother lived in their home along with their parents. But her uncles—her mother's brothers—'used to torture us no end'. There were land ownership issues—her father was living in her mother's house and the uncles feared they might lose out on the land completely if their sister's children continued to stay there. 'So all they wished for was that we should leave. Or simply out of anger, they tortured us.'

For over a decade, she had been flitting, floating and living multiple exiles, away from parents, siblings, and the place she used to call home, roaming the forests, walking miles moving from one village to another, evading cops on the prowl, and often sleeping under the star-studded sky…

For years, her 'home' had been moving with her, there were no locked rooms to experience privacy, or a secure, comfortable private space for bathing. Instead, there were plenty of arms-toting comrades around—people who decided a lot of things for her, for her family and even whether or not she could have children.

'I did insist on having one child from the start,' said Jagori. Not that it was encouraged but she went ahead, risking everything. 'I could not foresee how my own life would change after the child came into this world. But when he came, I decided to choose my path and do everything in my power by prioritizing my child in our lives. So I left that world and that life.'

For a while, she did try and keep her child at the homes of different relatives, but she couldn't see herself doing it for the rest of her life. By 2010, Jagori had decided she was not going to continue the life of a Maoist—not only had she aged and was no longer calling the shots in the party the way she once used to, but there was something far more important in her life now: her child.

She was clear about the fact that she did not want to remain in the squad, but neither was she prepared to surface as a surrendered Maoist. At that time, her only concern was to think of a solution to bring up her child well. But that was only possible if she formally 'surrendered'. She and her husband would both get government jobs, they would get a place to stay, admit the child to a school, get a decent amount of money as a fixed deposit, and most of all, get police protection to ensure safety from her former Maoist colleagues. Finally, Jagori agreed.

Some people say that she had no choice at all and that her emphasis on the child's safety and upbringing simply coincided with her declining career and reducing importance in the Maoist ranks.

The domestic arrangements and married life of rebels may be very different from the way people outside experience or perceive it; but at its core, there isn't much of a difference after all. While the rebels' lives necessitate giving up the simple pleasures of parenthood and family life, those cravings—no matter how socially constructed these notions of pleasure are—still remain.

This is also what leads to disruptions in the rebellion. Those participating in the movement are ordinary people with extraordinary heights to achieve but not all have been able to rise to the occasion or deliver extraordinariness. They have left behind their homes and are filled with the ache of absence.

Three years ago, I travelled to Jagori's home in Bakdoba to meet her parents. The pucca road traversing through the thick saal forests of this region is so rugged that even expert drivers have a tough time negotiating the craters. It takes much longer than it should to reach Bakdoba, which borders West Bengal's Purulia and West Midnapore districts. It was afternoon and still as death all around.

There was a flurry of activity all over Jangalmahal—the three forested West Bengal districts of Purulia, Bankura and West Midnapore—where Maoists still have a base, though far less powerful than what it used to be four to five years ago. State and Central government funds were being poured generously for everything—from roads to subsidized food grains, bicycles to new school buildings, and organizing football matches to the surrender policy for Maoists. So why did *this* area still remain untouched by those signs of development? Perhaps because it was still in the back of beyond—and here patches of village clusters remain untouched by the marks of development.

One of the reasons behind the resentment against the Maoist movement in West Bengal was the feeling of alienation among the tribal population. This also explained why Jagori Baske, a tribal woman, felt increasingly sidelined within the party. Her role—instead of becoming increasingly important due to her experience, shrewdness, courage and sharpness—gradually became marginal as the non-tribals began to dominate the party in Jangalmahal.

There have always been undercurrents of tension between the tribals and non-tribals over leadership issues. The Maoists initially realized the importance of winning over tribals in order to get a foothold over Jangalmahal, and they did so. But soon, the non-tribals took over and their opinions became the final say when it came to major decision-making. This led to a major fissure between the tribals and non-tribals even within the Maoist ranks—and once this gap was visible, it kept widening.

Shobha Mandi, a tribal Maoist leader, was apparently arrested in 2010 while she was riding pillion on a two-wheeler, though officially she had 'surrendered'. Other tribal leaders like Lalmohon Tudu were killed and Sukshanti Baske was arrested: and so, with all these tribal leaders no longer part of the Maoist movement in Jangalmahal, there was a feeling of alienation in the group.[4]

Under the circumstances, there was little reason for Jagori to continue in the Maoist movement.

As I made my way to Jagori's village, the car suddenly screeched to a halt—the road ended abruptly at a CRPF 169 battalion's Gurpana camp. We were at the end of the motorable road. Beyond that, the path went on—but it was an elevated, undulating stretch of red earth , making its way through a thick mesh of forest, to cultivable land and a pond.

Perhaps there was no pucca road anymore because Bakdoba has thirty-one homes of extremely poor tribals, whose main livelihood is working in fields to cultivate seasonal paddy, preparing *babui* grass for coils or raising hens and pigs for meat and eggs.

I walked down the road, through fields, passing the tiny Bakdoba primary school, grazing animals and dry fields. Two children lazed around, waiting for lunch outside the school building—*khichuri* was being cooked on a big *handi* placed on an earthen oven while the teacher was off on a break to his home nearby. No one else was around. The fragrance of boiled rice and lentils blended with the strong smell of mahua—a heady alcoholic concoction prepared from flowers of the same name. Almost every adult male in the homes around would have already had a few swigs of mahua by afternoon. As I looked for Jagori's house, some of them came out of their homes with tottering steps and in slurring voices politely showed the direction. These were beautiful homes with hand-painted walls, some of them with goats, cows and buffalos munching on grass outside the entrance doors. The entire scene looked surreal and enchantingly beautiful.

Jagori's mother, a dark, thin woman, was chatting with a neighbour. A visitor brought a smile to her face. She went inside and appeared with a khatia—a bed made of coconut husk coils that doubled up as a comfortable couch in the courtyard.

The house was a mud hut with thatched roof and a sprawling courtyard surrounded by three rooms. It was spic-and-span, the walls daubed with colours of burnt brick, indigo and ochre along with beautiful motifs and patterns in contrasting colours. The wide courtyard had a *dheki* in one corner—a large plank of wood used to separate husk from rice or to grind rice and lentils into a fine powder. A few chickens ran amok and two huge black buffalos munched on hay. It was a poor household, but showed signs of gradually recovering from the trying times it must have gone through in the past.

'We have always been very poor. My daughter used to go to the forest to collect wood. And forests can be very treacherous. So how would I know what happened one day when she went out but never came back?' Jagori's mother Gurubari Baske said apologetically without even my asking. She had already had to offer explanations to too many people.

The story of a girl mysteriously vanishing into the woods isn't completely shocking in these parts. Jagori's parents and other family members could guess right away where their girl had gone.

A teenage girl—depressed and miserable after a tiff at home goes crying in the forest when a group of young women and men are passing by. They ask the girl why she is crying and she blurts out her troubles—there is, in fact, plenty to worry about. There is poverty at home, a satisfying meal is a luxury, there is back-breaking work, quarrels and abuses. The friendly strangers say she could come along with them, they are going to change the world into a better place and where they stay, there will always be some food for her. That is how scores of girls like Jagori have joined the Maoists.

She was about sixteen years old when she left home and joined the Maoists. For her, this must have been the only option if she were to survive. Poverty was like a curse and no one from the administration or from political parties came to their rescue.

Jagori had told me that her uncles had a hand in 'inviting' the Maoists as well as the police in the area. She meant that their sole purpose was to create trouble for Jagori, her brother and their parents so they would somehow leave the house.

By now, Jagori's mother had brought out a framed photograph of Jagori, Rajaram and their son.

In the picture—which the mother held lovingly—Jagori is dressed in a bright orange-and-blue saree, her hair neatly tied in a plait, decked in sindoor and teep (bindi). Soren is in white full sleeves shirt, black trousers; their little boy—standing between the parents—looks dazedly at the camera in a yellow tee and matching shorts. The backdrop is a kitschy, dark blue cloth that acts as the sky with tiny, white specks of stars printed all over.

Jagori's mother, sitting on the khatiya, looked fondly at her grandchild's photograph. 'Policemen came and told us about Jagori's surrender. Later, they took us in a car to meet them. I met my grandson too. My daughter is learning stitching and my son-in-law is taking driving lessons,' Gurubari Baske said, her eyes twinkling with happiness. 'Policemen came here yesterday as well,' she said. These days, people from the administration were regularly coming to visit. 'Now, I have no fear of cops.'

Jagori's father Thakurdas Baske has come back from the fields. Dressed in white shirt and a faded mustard coloured lungi, he sat on another khatiya listening intently to the conversation. The parents were waiting for their son, Subharam, to come back from the fields after which they would have lunch.

Their lives had changed considerably from the time the sixteen-year-old Jagori left home. They now had two buffalos and some hens in the home, Thakurdas and his son Subharam worked in the fields, their daughters Manjuri and Sabita were married and stayed in far-off villages.

* * *

I had heard all about Jagori's tantrums, about her not being willing to work as a home guard despite drawing a salary of Rs 10,000 per month. When I asked her about the nature of her work, she giggled and said, 'I was asked to supervise the junior girls who work at a police station. But I have not been able to do it,' she said, without explaining why she was unable to carry out the work.

Perhaps deep inside, she felt *entitled* to a monthly salary even if she did not work for it. The surrender of Jagori Baske was a feather in Mamata Banerjee's cap. Jagori was flaunted as a prized catch and led to many more surrenders in the state subsequently. In the same month, the Maoists suffered the greatest blow with the death of Kishanji.

How much did Jagori change after her surrender? A lot, actually. She looked very different from when she had officially surrendered in November 2011. Standing next to Chief Minister Mamata Banerjee was a soft-spoken, dark, thin woman. With her husband and four-year-old son by her side, she had explained how the Maoists had misled them to the path of violence and killing.

By the time I met her, she had shed the life of a rebel and taken up the role of a mother and domesticated woman whose sole purpose in life was to give her child the best that she could. Her whole life was centred around the boy and she kept raving about him all the time. She had spent a lot of money to give the child all the comforts: her flat was furnished with an air conditioner, television, fridge, computer, even closed circuit television. She had admitted him to an 'English medium school', hired a car for the child's transportation between school and home and ensured that he got private tuitions. 'All this costs a lot of money. We end up spending a large part of our salary on him,' she said. 'Then there is Complan... we must ensure he is not deprived of *anything*.'

She fretted that he did not like to eat rice. '*Ami ki* every day *bhaat khabo?*' he keeps asking her (Will I eat rice every day?). She fondly stressed on the words 'every day' to indicate how his language was a mix of English and Bengali—a result of his studying in an English medium school.

As we sat chatting, Jagori and Rajaram told me they had tarka-ruti for breakfast and would soon go home and do the cooking. 'My son will be home at 2 p.m. Do you know what he does the moment he enters the room?' Jagori asked.

Apparently, he started watching television (the cartoon channels) while changing his uniform, then rushed to the computer room. 'We have to plead with him to get back to the bedroom and sleep a bit. Then he eats, fiddles with the mobile phone till he falls asleep,' Jagori said. Some more TV after getting up, then to the tuition classes. Jagori said she had to spend more than Rs 1600 as school fees, in addition to the fees for private tuitions, drawing-class fees, and a lot more. 'My son asks me, "why don't you let me play a bit?" There is no time for him to play, no companions either.' For security reasons, she had fitted her room with CCTV and kept track on the monitor through the day.

Rajaram and Jagori both said that they chose to live far from their homes in Purulia because they wanted to be physically away from the memory of the past. 'There are no forests here, no friends. But we chose this place because there is a good missionary school around and our sole purpose is to educate our son,' Jagori said.

'At one point I had decided not to ever get married. Not just to him (pointing to Rajaram), but to no one. Ever,' she said. 'But then I was told that there is a certain age when you must get married. So I did. And he has been very caring and protective of me.'

* * *

Durgapur, Burdwan. An isolated four-storied house.

In 2012-13, the West Bengal government—like all other state governments 'tackling Maoists'—had devised training programmes for the surrendered Maoists where they were trained in almost the same way as they were in their squads back in the forests. Jagori Baske and Rajaram Soren were trained in one such programme along with twenty-nine other surrendered Maoists.

In 2013, I visited a building in Durgapur, West Bengal, which housed thirty-one surrendered Maoists. They had been training for a month at the time. Subsequently, the government held several programmes to train surrendered Maoists to work as home guards, but this was the first of its kind in the state.

Bawling babies, toys and English nursery poem books strewn all over a bed, the smell of breast milk, a heavily pregnant woman walking around with her toddler, pots and pans scattered around the floor, water for tea boiling in the kettle in one corner of a room, a radio playing old Hindi film songs in the background, salwar kameez, undergarments and khaki uniforms hanging on clotheslines made out of coconut husk rope that cut the room into corners and crannies, tiny beds in two rows... There was something endearing about these images because there was a semblance of a home here—in this four-storey building guarded like a fortress round the clock.

In July 2011, at her first public meeting since she took over as West Bengal chief minister, Mamata Banerjee at a public meeting in Nayagram, appealed to the youths of Jangalmahal to lay down arms, saying, 'If you have to take up arms, take them up for the government.' She announced there would be 10,000 jobs in the National Volunteer Force, police and home guards for youths from Jangalmahal.[5]

The appeal to take up arms for the government rings true in every state—nowhere in India is the government policy to *discourage* violence, instead, it is justifying its own power and stance *against* the Maoists. Villagers in these same areas are wooed by Naxal leaders as well. The methods, approaches and tactics are otherwise uncannily similar. It is a matter of whose appeal the villagers will succumb to and it is usually guided by who is stronger at a given point in time.

The transition from a Naxal soldier to a home guard does not take much time and effort. All it needs is the government's stamp of approval. The job is exactly the same.

Here, in this Durgapur home, the former rebels were turning into representatives of the state. It was too tempting to resist equating this to a factory where Maoists were processed, churned and labeled with the state's stamp of approval. Most of them had already participated in daring operations, kidnapped and killed policemen, government employees and civilians. Now, their enemies would be their former colleagues.

I met Jagori thrice (and I was present at the press conference when she surrendered). The first time I met her was before her surrender, the second time I had sneaked into the building in Durgapur where she was being trained to be a home guard (in 2013), and the third time we met where she now stays (in 2015), which I have been requested not to mention by name.

The building where I met her in 2013 housed the living quarters for the former rebels. Jagori , her husband, and their son (who was six years old at that time) had been offered a separate tiny room with a large bed. There was a lot of happiness and warmth around.

The other surrendered rebels had been given dormitories to stay in. Women were on one floor, and men in another. A carrom board and a common television for all of them were on the men's floor.

Everyone was up as early as 4.30 in the morning, and got ready for the morning parade and practices. There was physical training, parades, games and sports, a quick lunch, and then more practice. They were given three weeks of physical training and then arms training.

In the evenings, there was a lot of adda over muri and chanachur. Many of them had worked together in the same squads, so they had common groups of friends, and even neighbours. The women sat around chatting over their tea. Khaki uniforms had been washed and left out to dry.

'We are very happy here. That is for everyone to see. Life has changed for all of us. One must look at life beyond this moment. We must all think about our lives ahead, we should look forward,' Shobha Mandi said. She had made newspaper headlines, making allegations of sexual harassment against her former Maoist colleagues.[6]

These women and men have since joined the police force in different districts (chiefly Purulia, Bankura and West Midnapore, their 'home districts') as home guards and senior home guards. They have also been living at residential quarters at the district police lines.

The state governments have taken a go-slow stance on the cases of these Maoists. 'The government does not have the power to waive charges already filed against the Maoists. The courts take the final call,' said a senior officer. So what happens to the pending cases against surrendered Naxals? In most cases, charges have been filed against more than one person in a particular case (the number is often as many as seven to eight). It is illegal for the State to lift charges against only some people in a case (i.e. those who have surrendered) and continue with the charges against the rest (i.e. those who have not surrendered). Therefore, the cases have to proceed to their logical conclusion.

According to the Central government's Guidelines for Surrender-Cum-Rehabilitation Scheme of Left Wing Extremists in the Affected States,[7] the 'trial of heinous crimes may continue in the courts' but in 'minor offences, plea bargaining could be allowed at the discretion of the State authorities. The States may consider providing free legal services/advocate to the surrendered LWE cadre as per the policy of the State concerned. Fast track courts may be constituted by the States for speedy trial of cases against the surrenderees.' All this, to allow the rebels a breather and to encourage them to lay down arms.

The situation is tricky for state governments because most of these are not minor offences, but 'heinous crimes'. The Guidelines also mention that 'the States may also consider withdrawal of prosecution on a case to case basis depending upon the antecedents and merits of the individual surrenderee.' This is usually not applied because the offences are of a serious nature and the state governments want the surrendered Maoists to be under their control.

As a temporary solution however, the states have decided to go slow with these cases. When the cases come up, the accused (surrendered Maoists) are produced in court, but the government usually does not object to their bail applications. 'That's what the government can do on its part,' said the officer. However, most of the charges are non-bailable, and there is little chance the courts won't order jail custody.

It is due to this aspect of the law that the West Bengal government has converted some existing homes like the one at Durgapur and some portions of certain police lines into 'prisons' for the rebels to live in protection and isolation, as well as enjoy a certain amount of freedom. The concept of these prisons is like 'open jails', whereby the rebels have been technically 'confined' but are free for all practical purposes.

* * *

After her surrender on 17 November 2011, Jagori had said (standing by the side of Chief Minister Mamata Banerjee at a press conference) that the party (CPI-Maoist) had led her to the wrong path. They had promised freedom to the people, but had instead taught her to use weapons and kill people. 'They [the Maoists] are even opposed to the development the government wants. I wanted to get back to the mainstream,' Jagori had said meekly that day, at a press conference at Writers' Buildings, the West Bengal government's administrative headquarters.

Her husband, Rajaram, who had surrendered along with her, had said: 'They [the Maoists] had said they would work for development of tribals. But they were killing tribals instead and I realized this was a wrong path'.

But when I talked to her in July 2015, Jagori certainly didn't think she had taken a wrong path at any point in her life.

'I am nobody, an uneducated person, someone of no importance. But what about those like the educated Kishanji and Arnab Dam [the latter an IIT Kharagpur dropout who was a senior Naxal leader, now in jail]? They had the best of education, and they still understood the plight of the poor. Why did they join the Maoists?' Jagori asked me.

Give them prisons or give them freedom, give them training, money or jobs, you can't imprison or rein in their thought process.

'In my heart I know I did no wrong. Neither in leaving home to join the Maoists, nor in surrendering,' she told me before she left during our last meeting in 2015.

It was time for her son to get back home from school. Now, there was not a second Jagori could spare for anyone or anything else in this world.

10

Ipsita Mukherjee

Ipsita is not her real name. I changed it, promising her that I wouldn't mention anything else about her that would give away her identity. But this book would have been incomplete without her story.

Ipsita played an important role in the Maoist movement of West Bengal as a student leader. However, she is in denial about this to herself. But it is only through this woman, now in her 30s, that it is possible to fathom the way in which the police have scuttled every possible form of students' protest against the State.

Her story appears in this book because the State's efforts at the 'surrender' of Maoists and Maoist sympathizers or those from the banned organization's frontal groups, has not been restricted to rural areas. The methods of 'surrender' of these educated women and men living in the cities have been different and that story needs to be told, too.

Mostly, those who have officially surrendered before the State and taken the surrender and rehabilitation schemes, are from extremely poor families in villages or small towns. In the official list of surrendered Maoists there would be none hailing from cities. Yet, the Maoists have a strong city connection with money, sympathy and camaraderie pouring in from the country's urban areas. To put an end to this support from the urban centres, the methodology for 'surrender' has been 'unofficial'—these are tactics that vary widely from one state to another. It is generally assumed that the city-bred Maoists or Maoist sympathizers would be difficult to woo with money and jobs. Therefore, pressure tactics work better here.

Through Ipsita's story one can see how Maoist sympathizers and those from frontal organizations have been pressured into what are also surrenders, just that these surrenders are nowhere written in government policies, nor 'officially' discussed by the government.

* * *

I met Ipsita one hot summer afternoon in the heart of the city. She took me to her home, where the rooms were filled with sunshine and her mother's full throated laughter. The laughter, she used as a shield to hide everything else about herself; it was her way of ridiculing her sorrow, a way of reiterating to herself that she had decided not to lose the battle she was fighting. Even if her daughter had been to prison and was now out on bail, there were a lot of things that had made their lives a tough battle. I cannot give away too many details as that might lead to revealing their identities.

Ipsita and I talked for hours. Her mother kept walking into the room and asked me to stay back for lunch, fed me sweets with her own hand, and when I had finished the interview and stepped out of the main entrance, called me back into the house from a window of the first floor, saying that the tea was almost ready and how could I have forgotten that she had told me a couple of minutes ago that she was boiling the water?

Ipsita was a bit embarrassed by her mother's childlike expressions of affection. But she allowed it, perhaps because she herself was just as warm at heart.

She wanted to make it clear at the very outset that she was *never* a Maoist. 'Ideologically, what they were fighting for and what I was fighting for were one and the same. But I was myself never a Maoist.'

As a student of a renowned university in West Bengal, Ipsita was upset about the way events were shaping up at Nandigram over a proposed site where the then Left Front government was keen on a chemical hub (a Special Economic Zone) to be set up by the Indonesia-based Salim Group.

Villagers were jittery about losing their land (especially due to the West Bengal government's lack of clarity on the project),[1] and the CPM which had been in power in West Bengal for the seventh time on the trot was confident that nothing could stop them from going ahead with the plan.

A people's forum, Bhumi Uchched Pratirodh Committee (BUPC), meaning committee against displacement from land was formed which had the tacit support of the Maoists, and a direct confrontation between the people of Nandigram and the State (along with the ruling CPM cadres) ensued. A police contingent was sent to Nandigram and opened fire on protesting villagers on 14 March 2007, which left fourteen people dead.[2]

'When the ruling party was grabbing land from innocent, unwilling villagers, I felt that students needed to do something. Some of us at college decided we had to get together for the people of Nandigram,' Ipsita said. 'We weren't sure how to go about it. But one thing we were certain about: we had to protest against this as students.'

Ipsita was well aware how students were always ridiculed for staying in ivory towers. 'I knew if I meant to do something for the people, I had to visit Nandigram, and I did.'

It was a good lesson for her. 'The common response of people living in cities to a disaster in rural India is to raise money "to help the poor". But the first thing I learned when I landed in Nandigram was that a lot of these people neither wanted nor needed money. They could feed me, if they wished to, for the rest of my life. For them, it was a matter of pride and honour. They wouldn't let the government force them to give up their land.'

Ipsita stayed on for days in Nandigram. The situation was tense. Villagers had by then united under the banner of BUPC.

The Maoists had been backing this committee actively along with the direct support of the opposition Trinamool Congress, and armed clashes with the CPM's armed goons were routine affairs. The state police was keeping an eye on the goings-on in Nandigram and the villagers were afraid to offer shelter to these young visitors.

There was a day, Ipsita recalled, when she was all alone in Nandigram, as her friends had by then all headed back to the city. Evening turned to night and Ipsita realized no one would offer her shelter in their home.

'All of them were afraid. Tired and hungry, I waited outside a hut. It was dark and cold and I had no idea how I would spend the rest of the night there.'

But then, eventually, well past midnight, someone came out and asked her in 'on the condition' that she would be out of the house before sunrise. 'That way no one knew I had been offered shelter,' Ipsita remembered. 'The people in the house were in a terrible dilemma. They could neither call me in, nor let me sleep outside in the cold. In the end, they risked a lot and called me in.'

The police lodged a FIR against her, claiming to have got her name while interrogating other Maoists. She was arrested, lodged in prison for some months, then released on bail. When we met she was still appearing regularly for several cases at various courts throughout the state.

In a matter of four years, Ipsita had decided to withdraw from it all. The fire, the gutsiness seemed to have mellowed down. She no longer looked like the firebrand leader whom I had first met years ago at a public meeting, where she was addressing people and enjoying the attention and affection of those surrounding her.

She had no easy answer when she was asked why she had 'backed out'. 'My answer is just three words—*ami parlam na* (I couldn't do it),' she said. But the three words are loaded with meaning.

'I've told this to many—to explain why I just drifted away—but they don't understand. Why is it so tough to believe that I couldn't take myself to the finishing line?' Ipsita said, giggling, trying to make light of the situation. 'Young female students going all the way to Nandigram, leading some people, rendering all our support—all this had been glamorized by the media,' she felt. 'But I don't think I had done that much. And today I feel that if I am able to find some meaningful work, I'll still do it. But I'd prefer to do it quietly.'

Did it mean she was no longer the confident, selfless youngster afraid of nothing? Or did she speak this way because of the enormous social and State pressure on her? Again, there was no easy answer. 'I didn't go to Nandigram or anywhere else because it was glamorous to hold a microphone and to organize people. I genuinely wanted to work for the people. But in the process I lost a lot of things.'

Ipsita realized she had hurt her family along the way. 'There were months when I didn't return home. I never bothered to think what my parents were going through. My parents' world was centred around me. I am partly to blame for the way they are suffering today. I should have been more responsible towards them. I cannot be ruthless anymore because they have constantly stood by me.'

She said she was doing her Master's now. 'After a gap of several years, I decided I had to complete my Master's. I was not getting any job. No one would employ me because of the pending cases against me. I was being asked bizarre questions at job interviews. I decided to take a break from all that, and continue with studies. Now I stay away from my earlier circle of friends, acquaintances and the places I used to visit. My friends felt that I had "surrendered", and I couldn't make them understand my line of thought. Now, I don't even try.'

Today, Ipsita doesn't have too many friends and she is cautious about making new ones.

She was also confused about the word 'surrender' in the first place. 'I have taken neither money nor a job from the government, my cases are still pending. Only, I have quietly come out of the movement and away from the people involved in it.'

She could not explain her logic to people who were once closest to her and to those who had led the students' movement. 'Leading a movement or being a part of one is not easy. One of the greatest challenges that you have to constantly face—and this is a matter you must handle every single day—is the different lines of thoughts within yourself and between you and your close associates. There are questions you will face from your inner self and you have to answer them. If there are no answers, you cannot move ahead.'

How did she react to the way the police kept and continues to keep a constant eye on her?

Ipsita smiled. 'Earlier, I had no idea how much the police knew. Or how it was that they knew so much about me. But now, I have some idea.

'The subtle pressure is there all the time. I know that my phone is being tapped, mails and messages are being read. The police intelligence system penetrates everything. We underestimate how much the State and the police know about us only because we have no knowledge of this system,' she said, matter-of-factly.

'When we had to plan something, we would be cautious about not discussing the plans over the phone because of surveillance. But the information would still leak out. How? Because one of these people in the close-knit circle was actually working for the police. These realities struck me much later. It is not easy to continue fighting against the State. It drains you and you need an enormous amount of strength to continue.'

She told me how the police intimidate in bizarre ways—'They asked me about my relationship with my boyfriend. In doing so, they were not really asking me anything. It was their way of telling me that they know so much about me already. They wanted to intimidate and scare.'

Most of the cases against Ipsita have been revived by the Mamata Banerjee government. These were allegedly committed by her during the Left Front regime that ruled the state before Banerjee, at a time Ipsita and her friends in the movement were actually close to the Trinamool Congress.

'It would be wrong to say all this does not scare me. But that's not the reason why I drifted away from the movement.'

Ipsita however, still hadn't changed her position on the armed movement though she did not associate herself with it. 'I can still justify armed movement, but people who hold the arms must know why they are taking up arms. Otherwise it can degenerate into hooliganism.'

Ipsita had at one point been an integral part of a Maoist frontal organization based in Kolkata. According to the police's claim, she had travelled to secret Maoist hideouts and met senior Maoist leaders with whom she would discuss how to organize movements in the city.

Two top officers of the West Bengal's Criminal Investigation Department (CID) and the State Intelligence Branch (SIB) have confirmed to me that some of Ipsita's friends in the movement have also drifted away only to become police informers. Whether this happened voluntarily or under pressure is irrelevant. There is actually no such thing as 'voluntary' when it comes to working as police informers.

One of Ipsita's friends, a student leader from a renowned college, was harassed so much by the police that 'she was compelled to disclose a few things', said one of their associates. The police would visit her home every other day, she would be interrogated, her home searched, her parents questioned (all of this in 2013). Her passport was seized and her family members too began to put pressure on her to snap ties with the pro-Maoist union in her college she had long been associated with.

After she passed out of college, it was actually possible for her to disassociate herself both physically and mentally from the movement. Now that the cases against her have been closed, she has turned into 'a completely different person altogether', said one of her friends. 'It is as if she is not the same person we knew. We wouldn't be surprised if she goes abroad, settles down there or takes up a job in a multinational company. She is going all out to make it clear that she has changed,' said a friend. 'You can make out from her Facebook wall.'

A few others are possibly in touch with their old 'Maoist' mates, but the Maoists' city unit at present lacks the leadership for police to suspect anything remarkable is brewing.

* * *

The change in the Trinamool Congress position, from being a sympathizer of students' movements to a powerful ruling party determined to scuttle every form of protest, is not unusual.

From being the opposition party sympathetic to people's rights over land, the Trinamool Congress soon turned into the ruling party that ensured the voice of protest against the government was scuttled completely. It's a mind game. Whoever has more power and influence, wins.

After the Trinamool Congress formed the government in West Bengal in May 2011, discussions began between Chief Minister Mamata Banerjee and civil society representatives to start talks with the Maoists.[3]

Names of interlocutors were finalized, but the talks led to a dead end. By November 2011, suspected Maoists had gunned down two Trinamool Congress men in Purulia and Banerjee called the Maoists 'terrorists, murderers, jungle mafia and supari killers'.[4] She said that she had made enough efforts to bring the Maoists to the talks table, appealing to them to abjure violence and not to indulge in killings. She also accused the Maoists of having a nexus with the CPM.[5]

Soon, students who had led the movement in Nandigram

and Haripur (where a nuclear power project was to be set up) and subsequently Nonadanga—had come under the government scanner.

Students' movements have always been an important aspect of the people's protests against the State. But some of the students who have been part of these 'movements' say that the State's most favourite position has been to call every form of protest against it as 'Maoist'.

Sanhati, a forum of human rights activists based in Kolkata, published on its website an appeal from a group named 'Forum Against Eviction and Mal-Development' and the United Students Democratic Federation (USDF), the latter a students' union, in 2012 April, which said: 'A year back, the Left Front government faced their first defeat after thirty-four years and Mamata Banerjee assumed power riding on the popular strength of anti-displacement movement giving people a new ray of hope. Now, the same government has become the oppressor of any voices of dissent and forcefully evicts the marginalized in the interest of the corporate and other so-called development projects without even considering rehabilitation of the displaced.'[6]

The note was written in the context of Nonadanga, where hundreds of so-called 'illegal' settlers were removed forcefully by the police. To protest against this, social activists and civil rights groups held a demonstration on April 4, 2012 in the city, where they were beaten up by the police. Nearly seventy persons were arrested. But while most were released immediately, seven activists hadn't been released when the note was issued by Sanhati.

By 2012, civil rights groups and students' unions who were once supporting the Trinamool Congress in its fight for land rights of the poor, had turned severely against the party and its leadership.

The Trinamool Congress felt the same way. Cases filed earlier were revived, the homes of these students and rights groups members were raided, their passports were seized and phones were tapped, accompanied by both threats and polite pleas asking them to side with the State and help the police. Refusal would mean that the pending cases would be treated sternly, while helping the police would make the State treat their cases lightly.

One of the main thrusts of the CPI (Maoist) in the recent past, has been its focus on urban areas. And for this reason, labour unions, students' unions in colleges and universities have been more of a focus for the party.

Not just West Bengal, other states, too, have taken to various methods to counter this plan. There are police cells specifically used to keep track of people with Maoist 'leanings', 'sympathisers', those associated with 'frontal organisations' and so on. Activities on social media are tracked, phone lines are tapped, and former Maoists 'won over' by the State are planted among the groups to get regular feedback of the activities. This is just the tip of the iceberg.

There may be differences between the thrust of the Naxalbari movement during the 1970s and the way it has changed over the past couple of decades. But the ways in which students from urban areas who were once a part of the movement gradually drifted away (or moved away under threat) over the years, are eerily similar.

* * *

The Naxalbari movement was primarily led by the urban intelligentsia. Charu Mazumdar came from a family of zamindars; he and his colleagues Kanu Sanyal and Jangal Santhal inspired the youth. Mazumdar and Sanyal had both inspired the educated youth from West Bengal (and even beyond) to join the war against the State.

The idea was to empower the poor and downtrodden through a class war. The warriors had no training in arms, they used traditional arms used by the farmers and tribals to wage war against the rich, exploitative landlords and the State.

But it was the brutal killings and violence that eventually disconcerted them. 'While I supported Maoism, I did not have a taste for the cult of violence that Charu Mazumdar preached. Also, I did not have the courage to face the prospect of police torture,' admits Dipesh Chakrabarty[7]. Chakrabarty was among the brilliant students in their 20s who had joined the movement.

Around that time, some criminals from the underworld also joined the Naxal movement, and this was encouraged and instigated by the police. It added to the violence in the movement, leading many others to get disillusioned.

Eventually, many students who were once part of the Naxal movement either went abroad to pursue their studies or quietly drifted away.

Ipsita—whose story I have narrated in this chapter—and many others like her may have been drawn towards the Maoist movement during the agitation against the government over land rights of the poor in recent times, but the same reasons that quietened the rebels of the yesteryears can be applied here too.

Ashim Chatterjee, who has no links with the CPI (Maoist) now, told me during a chat at his home in the northern fringes of Kolkata, 'The Naxalbari movement was dependent on the people. The terrain for the rebellion was not important; it was never limited to forests.' According to Chatterjee there are major differences between the Naxalbari movement and the Maoist rebellion that has unfolded, especially over the past couple of decades.

Chatterjee pointed out that for the Naxalbari movement, the class contradiction was most important, but to the new breed, sophisticated and modern arms are important and so is the terrain. The most important difference however, is the reliance on arms instead of the people (which is why the movement has become restricted to the forests). 'Not to take the responsibility of class struggle, but overindulging on the killing spree, to create free zones (*muktanchal*)—that is the major, in fact, complete shift in the present Maoist movement,' he said.

He said that it was primarily the Maoists' detachment with the people's causes in recent times that had led it to somewhat of a dead end. There are no ideological fights, no taking on the powerful State force on serious, significant issues. "You cannot survive only by creating free zones alone. You cannot survive only by killing people. An armed movement is not about targeting individuals. The Naxalbari movement was about class struggle, it was strongly attached to people's emotions. No matter how much you improve your technology now, or improve your firepower, for a movement to sustain, there is need for strongly associating with people's causes. There is need to inspire and to make a difference at the social and political levels," he said.

Chatterjee felt that this element was sorely missing in the Maoist movement in West Bengal in particular. "Yes, there was Nandigram, Lalgarh, but even there, it was restricted to a particular terrain. For a movement to influence a huge number of people in the long run, you cannot restrict yourself to a specific area and become dependent on squads and firearms," he feels.

It is true that the movement has failed to inspire the middle class and appeal to students' unions in recent years.

Very few from the new generation of rebels are from elite universities and colleges who join the war on ideological grounds, sacrificing high paying jobs and a comfortable life.

Added to this, is the West Bengal government's 'extreme position' on Naxalites, said Chatterjee. 'When the Left Front was in power in the state, the Trinamool Congress and the Maoists were *shahajoddha*s (soldiers fighting the same war). But after the Trinamool Congress came to power, the party came face to face with the Maoists in an armed war.'

The fallout of this was Kishanji's death, the tough stand taken against Chhatradhar Mahato (the spokesperson and convenor of the PCPA who was arrested during the Left Front regime, but who continues to languish in jail), and the way voices of dissent are constantly under pressure from the police and authorities, he said.

Mahato, who was the face of the Lalgarh movement (the movement continued between 2008 and 2011, though Mahato was arrested in 2009), was sentenced to life imprisonment for waging war against the state along with five others, in May 2015. Mahato along with Sukhsanti Baske, Sambhu Soren and Sagun Murmu were charged under the Unlawful Activities Prevention Act (UAPA). The other two are Raja Sarkhel and Prasun Chatterjee.[8]

Mahato, Baske, Soren and Murmu have been booked under the Unlawful Activities Prevention Act (UAPA) for their alleged links with the Maoists. Mahato was arrested by the police in September 2009. They posed as journalists wanting to interview him.[9]

Mahato's wife, Niyati, and others who were part of the PCPA agitation have, at various times, alleged that the Trinamool Congress leadership, including the party supremo Mamata Banerjee, who had once held meetings with Mahato, turned against him from the time the party came to power in West Bengal.[10]

Because of the tough stand taken by the Trinamool Congress against the CPI (Maoist), it won't come as a surprise if the rebels—who have, since Kishanji's death, gone into hiding in a neighbouring state—reorganize themselves and stage a comeback, Chatterjee said.

Whatever the future may hold in terms of comeback by the Maoists in West Bengal, the fact remains that the urban youth of today have—even if temporarily—drifted away from the Maoist movement in Bengal.

The State applies different formulae to contain the protestors in different places. For these youths based in the city, a rehabilitation package may not have been essential (since most of them are educated and come from relatively privileged backgrounds), but there were various forms of pressure to scuttle their voices of protest.

This is the case with student union leaders or other young sympathizers based in the urban areas (like Kolkata). But these are surrenders nonetheless, in the strictest sense of the word, even though one wouldn't find Maoist leaders from the cities accepting rehabilitation packages and government jobs. But they have 'moved on' for sure.

For them there are far more options to move on to, than the poor villagers. So, for many urban youth, the best available way out has been to concede by working as police informers if it means the government agrees to treat the cases being tried in court in a 'sympathetic' way.

11

Pinki, Mallika and Laxmi

Suchitra Mahato and Jagori Baske are high-profile women cadres who surrendered due to a range of reasons. But we shouldn't forget the numerous ordinary women foot-soldiers. These women may not have had any senior Maoist leader for a partner and possibly never rose up the ranks. They were not extraordinarily brave soldiers. In the party, they lacked any sense of direction. They could even be called reluctant soldiers whose foray into the Maoist movement was almost accidental. Yet the involvement changed their lives forever and in profound ways.

Pinki Kaude (neè Vadde)

Pinki Vadde was about 25 or 26 years old and preoccupied with her phone. The phone rang almost continuously while we tried to speak in the gaps between its ringing.

The first thing she told me as she disconnected a call was that now she was Kaude. '*Mein* Pinki Vadde *thi*, madam! *Abhi mein* Kaude *hoon*. Pinki Kaude.'

She was married to Mukesh Kaude, a police constable. I found the fact of a former Maoist married now to a police constable fascinating and was curious to learn more about their story. Yet, Pinki and Mukesh were not in the least surprised at what seemed to others to be an unlikely match. The two came from similar impoverished backgrounds and only chance had made the two lives take different paths.

Pinki was born in Chhattisgarh's Wadapenda village.

She was the eldest of five children of Saiko and Manirao Vadde. The family owned some land, but all four of their sons Budhu, Birsi, Dinesh and Santosh were sent off to Narayanpur town, some 60 km from their village, to study and stay at a government-run school-cum-hostel when they were barely six or seven years old.

This was an arrangement worked out by the couple to keep the sons away from Maoists who regularly visited their village on the lookout for young recruits. 'Those who did not want their children to join Maoists would send their sons away to hostels while the girls stayed back,' Pinki said. 'So I remained with my parents.'

Pinki did not go to school. 'My parents wanted to send me to school, but the Naxals discouraged it. They discouraged anyone who wanted to send their children to schools run by the government. At that time, my parents could not disobey them,' Pinki said.

Pinki is one of those rare former Maoists who bear an out-and-out grudge against her former colleagues and organization. All the others I have met and interviewed were tilted in favour of the Maoists despite walking away from that path. Pinki's version was different from theirs. She had nothing kind to say about the Maoists. It could be a cleverly worked-out strategy because of her current association with the police force—she was working in the force, as was her husband. Therefore, she did not want to leave any room for doubts that she secretly bore a soft corner for the Maoists.

In any case, as a child, Pinki remained in the village, and as the parents had feared, she had to be 'given away' as a young recruit to the Maoists. She was possibly thirteen or fourteen, then. She was first inducted into the *bal sangathan*, the children's wing of the Maoists. Bimanna, a dalam leader from Andhra Pradesh came and took her away, Pinki recalled.

Pinki mostly enjoyed herself in the bal sangathan—she made friends among children her age and practised songs, dances and plays that she and her friends enacted during their visits to villages in and around the forests. She was a part of the bal sangathan for five to six years.

This stint, however, was soon followed by physical training along with other girls approximately her age along with rifle training for two years. Pinki was also taken to Maharashtra's Wala (in Renapur tehsil of Latur district), where she got specialized training for ten days that involved learning to use different kinds of rifles and grenades. In addition, she even got special training to prepare explosives.

She was mostly moving through the forests bordering Maharashtra and Chhattisgarh. The forests and hills, and the tribals living within them, know no man-made boundaries. For those in the dalams, movement through the forests and hilly terrains was not limited to a particular state. They easily moved between one state and another, and sometimes also travelled to other states far from where they were usually based, for specialized trainings.

Often, Pinki would be on sentry duty and moved through the forests with others in the group carrying arms. While the women and men (and even children in the groups) walked, the arms and ammunition used to be carried on horseback. 'We had five horses in our squad—two white horses and three brown horses—that were used to ferry the arms and ammunition,' she recalled. If elderly women and men or little children who lived in villages inside forests asked for rides, the Maoists would kindly offer to take them on horseback. Moving through villages in the forest areas was difficult—one had to toil hard to collect firewood and tendu leaves or to visit markets to buy food. The Maoists helped people as much as they could.'

Did the police not notice people moving through the forests on horseback ferrying arms and ammunition? I asked. Pinki snubbed me, offended by my off-the-cuff remark: '*Madam, wahan pe police nahin jati thi… uss time pe woh log kabhi jungle ke andar gaye hi nahi…'* (Madam, the police had never ventured into the forests in those days…) She talked about a time when the civil administration or the police hadn't even ventured into the forests to provide either ration or other supplies for the villagers nor attempted to find out about the people's needs. They were beyond the radars of government plans and programmes. The Maoists were the real friends of the people.

Yet, even though Pinki had been 'forced' by the Maoists to accompany them, surrendering never occurred to her. 'I was part of that reality and did not know it was possible to have any other way to live life than what had come my way,' she said. Then, she went to a village fair with a colleague at Ghamandi village in Narayanpur's Orchha area in 2008. The police took her male colleague away for interrogation and she too was picked up sometime later.

Pinki says she was allowed to go home after this. 'Since I had been mostly part of bal sangathans, the police allowed me to leave after I was caught, as there was no major 'case' as such against me. They asked me to go back to my village. But, madam, I was very scared.'

She pleaded to be allowed to stay. Therefore, she was given a gun ('sometimes an SLR, sometimes a small gun') by the police and turned into an SPO in 2009. This transition was so quick that she was a bit shaken initially. But Pinki knew she had to survive. She wanted to do a job with the police because that was her only option.

She made her decisions prodded by survival instincts. Her Maoist friends quickly turned into foes and the policemen were the people she was supposed to now help, all this for a salary of Rs 1,500.

It was only after she had joined as an SPO that Pinki began to study, since 2010. 'I went to school and studied in class V and VI. The officers said I should study more, but I didn't, as I got married,' she said, giggling. (There is, however, no explanation for how she was able to start from class V instead of a junior class. Possibly, the government sent many like her to schools so they could get school certificates in order to continue to work with the police.)

Why did she stop studying after she got married? What's the connection between studying and marriage? I asked.

She took it in good humour, saying that her husband wanted her to study as well, but 'I was shy that I was quite old already, was married and had a child, and still going to school.' She blushed and said, 'So I quit.'

As an SPO, Pinki was asked to venture into the forests and villages to hunt down her former colleagues. She would be asked to disclose information on their secret dens and to take the police contingent there. She would also be asked to talk to the arrested Maoist soldiers and make them 'admit their crimes'. She helped in the interrogation by acting as an interpreter—helping the interrogators translate from Gondi (spoken by the locals) to Hindi (which is spoken by most officers).

'Even though I was an SPO, I didn't burn the homes of people. On the contrary, I saw the Naxalites punishing those who did not follow their instructions. I saw them burning homes of innocent villagers,' she said.

After a couple of years, Pinki's salary was increased to Rs 3,000, though her work remained exactly the same. She continued to go inside forests, helping the police in combing villages and forests in search of Naxalites.

After the Supreme Court verdict of 2011, the SPOs were re-designated as *sahayak arakshak* (assistant constable) and Pinki's monthly salary was increased to Rs 8000. In mid-2015, her salary became Rs 14,940.

The Supreme Court order of 2011 deemed the appointment of SPOs in Chhattisgarh as unconstitutional. 'We hold that appointment of SPOs to perform any of the duties of regular police officers, other than those specified in Section 23(1)(h) and Section 23(1)(i) of Chattisgarh Police Act, 2007, to be unconstitutional.'[1]

The court ordered that: '(i)The State of Chattisgarh immediately cease and desist from using SPOs in any manner or form in any activities, directly or indirectly, aimed at controlling, countering, mitigating or otherwise eliminating Maoist/Naxalite activities in the State of Chattisgarh; (ii) The Union of India to cease and desist, forthwith, from using any of its funds in supporting, directly or indirectly the recruitment of SPOs for the purposes of engaging in any form of counterinsurgency activities against Maoist/Naxalite groups; (iii) The State of Chattisgarh shall forthwith make every effort to recall all firearms issued to any of the SPOs, whether current or former, along with any and all accoutrements and accessories issued to use such firearms.'[2]

The Court also said that 'The State of Chattisgarh shall take all appropriate measures to prevent the operation of any group, including but not limited to Salwa Judum and Koya Commandos, that in any manner or form seek to take law into private hands, act unconstitutionally or otherwise violate the human rights of any person.'[3]

Two months later, the Chhattisgarh Assembly passed an Act authorising an 'auxiliary armed force' to 'assist security forces dealing with Maoist/Naxal violence', and legalised existing SPOs by inducting them as members. The Chhattisgarh Auxiliary Armed Police Force Act came into retrospective effect from July 5, 2011, the day the Supreme Court passed the order. This made the SPOs stay in the post.[4]

The SPOs were recruited as *sahayak aarakshaks*, or assistant constables, on better terms and conditions.[5]

As Pinki Kaude told me, her work remained exactly the same just that her pay and the designation had changed. During the months following her arrest, Pinki had met Mukesh, a constable. 'I used to see her come to Balod police station,' Mukesh told me over the phone. (I couldn't meet him during my visit to

Narayanpur because he was down with a fever, but had long chats with him and Pinki over the phone later.) He wanted to marry her and told the 'sirs' about it. They got married and now Mukesh and Pinki have a three-year-old son, Sahil.

After Pinki's arrest, Saiko and Manirao Vadde, Pinki's parents, along with their children Budhu, Birsi, Dinesh, Santosh and sister Rinki (who is five years old), were forced to leave their land and village. They now live in Narayanpur town. 'My parents had gone back to Wadapenda after coming down to Narayanpur to meet me after my arrest. But the Naxalites asked them to take me back to the village. I didn't want to return and urged the police to give me a job here.

'The moment I changed sides from being a Maoist to becoming an SPO, the lives of each of my family members became unsafe,' Pinki said. Now that the entire family has moved from Wadapenda, their neighbours have informed them that the Maoists have 'taken over the village land, and use it for cultivation'.

Her father had had a lucky escape. 'How can we even dare to go back and claim our land? The Naxals had come to kill my father. He had a lucky escape and scraped through with a bullet injury on his palm.'

Pinki's husband Mukesh on the other hand, was all alone in the world till he met her. He wouldn't disclose much about his past, and I didn't t have the heart to ask.

Mukesh and Pinki told me how tough it was for so many of them to survive on such a meager salary. 'My brothers are still studying. It is difficult to make ends meet in a small town. Back home, we were struggling. Now too, it isn't much different.'

Since Pinki was picked up and arrested, the government did not have much to offer her. She got the job but there was no special rehabilitation 'package' offered to the surrendered Maoists. Apart from the job, she got a two-decimel plot of land (offered by the government under a scheme for the poor), and Rs 10,000 to build a house.

'That is nothing special. Almost every poor person living in Narayanpur got land from the government,' Mukesh said. Manirao and Budhu have rented a room and stay close by while the rest of the family live in the house that they built. Little Sahil was already going to a play school.

Just before Pinki had to leave, to go home, I asked her, 'Do you like this work that you do now?'

In my earlier conversations with her Pinki had been easily offended if my questions were a bit obtuse. She raised her right eyebrow now and said, '*You* tell me what I can say to that! Earlier I used to love the work I had to do, now I do this work, I like this too.' (*Ab iska jawab mein kya doon? Pehle jo kaam karti thi who bhi achha tha, ab yeh kaam karti hoon, yeh bhi achha hain…*)

Did she ever have a choice?

Mallika

The names of her village and post office are as fascinating as her name. She comes from a village called Mahadebsinan—meaning a bathing place of the Hindu god, Lord Shiva, or possibly where devotees pour water on the Shivalinga. The post office is called Meetha-aam or succulent, sweet mangoes.

Since the young woman didn't want me to disclose her name, I had to name her Mallika.

But life hasn't been as sweet, nor her circumstances as pristine as the imagery these names suggest. In a queer turn of fate, she is a home guard with the West Bengal police and teaches toddlers in a government-run school.

Mallika was wearing a batik-printed red and brown salwar-kameez with a white dupatta wrapped around her neck. She was sweating in the humid rainy season of south Bengal. Her hair was tied in a plait but some strands hovered around her forehead making her blink from time to time.

A few minutes of talking to her and I realized she was extremely intelligent, observant and cautious. Now in her thirties, Mallika regretted the way her life had turned out. 'I had a lot of dreams. I wanted to complete my graduation, take up a job and wished to get married. Now, those dreams will never come true,' she said. 'That's because I have been stamped as a Maoist. I don't think anyone will want to marry me. I asked my mother to look for a groom for my younger sister instead.' She hoped her own social ostracism would not make her sister an unsuitable match.

Her maternal uncles are highly qualified—they are 'mostly doctors and engineers', Mallika informed me proudly. She too, would have followed their path and done something outstanding. She was doing a course in fashion designing from a private institute at Salt Lake—a satellite township adjoining Kolkata. In 2009, after appearing for her BA final year exams, she came back to stay at home, in Mahadebsinan, after a long absence. So far, she had mostly stayed away from home at different hostels in order to complete her studies.

'Our neighbours were extremely hostile towards us. They were jealous because we were more educated than most of them and also because of our political inclinations. It was a CPM area and we were supporters of the Trinamool Congress. We were also relatively better off financially than our neighbours.

'With the Lalgarh movement on in full swing, women leaders from Kolkata's Jadavpur University came down to our village and asked us to join them. At that time, *everyone* was involved in the movement—they were speaking against police atrocities on Chhitamoni Murmu (in 2008), who had lost an eye when police raided the village and tortured helpless women like her. We were told by the women leaders who had come down from Kolkata that educated ones like me must join the movement in order to bring about a new political order.'

She did feel inspired, but also a little pressured, to join the movement, Mallika told me. 'It is one thing to support a cause and another to actually walk in a protest march, shout slogans and put pressure on the government for certain demands.' Mallika said she was always a bit shy and not one who would feel comfortable being part of a protest meet. 'In my heart I was one with the movement, but I was unsure about the slogan shouting and protest marches. Yet, there was a pressure on me. I was told by the didis from Kolkata that it would be silly to remain so passive. There were so many women and girls like me who had joined the protests. I didn't think it was such a wrong thing to do. Therefore, I too went out in groups, along with other women, visiting different villages.'

Some villagers had become cautious. Sensing trouble, many parents had sent off their boys to other states—some went to different parts of Maharashtra, or to Gujarat or neighbouring Odisha and even to other parts of south Bengal to work in factories—because they did not want them to become part of this armed movement.

'But where could the women go? The leaders of the movement were persistent that educated women like me should influence other women. We were told not to allow the police to enter the area because they were coming only to torture and molest women.'

She did not know how, despite not handling arms, nor having any case pending against her, she became 'Wanted' in police records. 'I could not figure out how this happened. There were so many women in our groups. But when I became a 'Wanted' person, I did not know what to do. I was compelled to go underground. I stayed at different relatives' places for several months.'

Then the police came and took her sister away. It was probably a ploy to draw her out and bring her into the police net. It worked. She realized it would be impossible to be on the run for the rest of her life. 'I had to pay the price for my association with the Maoists. Sooner or later, I would be arrested. So I decided to surrender. My maternal uncles got in touch with a CPM leader who helped me get in touch with the police.'

Yet, this surrender turned out to be hardly what she had expected it to be. 'I had thought that surrender would mean the police would listen to the circumstances under which I had worked with them (the Maoists) and I would be allowed to go home because the charges against me would be waived. But I am surprised by the way I have now been almost imprisoned here,' Mallika said. She got the job of a home guard, and teaches at a government run school, but is unable to go home. Security personnel guard her because it is a rule to provide security to surrendered Maoists due to the threat to their lives from their former colleagues, or perhaps so she cannot run away. She is surprised that she is treated like the other Maoists who had surrendered to the police. 'It is a little difficult to believe that I can be a Maoist simply because I participated in some meetings and demonstrations with some frontal organizations. I had hoped I would be set free if I told them everything.' This might appear a bit too naïve, but that's the way she is.

Initially, Mallika stayed at a 'safe house' (a shelter offered by the West Bengal Police) for seven months and then she was trained along with thirty other surrendered Maoists to be a home guard. She learnt to handle SLR, Insas and 9mm. There, she met many 'hardcore' Maoists like Jagori Baske, for the first time. The irony wasn't lost on me—her association with 'arms and hardcore Maoists' began only *after* she surrendered and became part of the police force.

Mallika got Rs 1.7 lakh under the government's surrender scheme which was deposited in her name and draws a monthly pay of Rs 2,000. The Maoists who surrendered in West Bengal trained for three and a half months as home guards, but in practice, they do not have much work to do. Some have been assigned work as gardeners, while others teach toddlers in nursery classes at government schools.

Unable to clear her B.A. examinations, and not having finished her fashion designing course either, Mallika is stuck teaching at the school and broods on why her life took such a bizarre turn. 'Tell me Didi, what was so wrong? Is it not true that the police came and tortured women in villages? There were so many like me who had protested police atrocities. So why am I still suffering for it?' she asked. 'Actually, it is the *situation*—let me tell you, if you were in my situation, you too would have been a Maoist.'

Now, Mallika only hopes she can enroll again and clear her B.A. examinations, save some money and buy a computer so she can write about her anguish and experiences in a book in the Santali language, her mother tongue. Her wish to get a good job and to get married will never come true, she reiterates bitterly.

By the time I met her next, her sister had been married and Mallika's salary had increased a bit. That's about all the change that had taken place in her life. She continued to live in the same cramped room as earlier. Ten home guards share the same accommodation with her. The two fans, one on the table top and the other on the ceiling were able to make their room only slightly cooler during the summer heat. Some inmates lit their own kerosene stoves on a tiny slice of a verandah and cooked rice and curries, some pooled in to prepare common meals.

In the end, Mallika's story was that of a perfectly simple and well behaved girl—who did her best to leave her village, gave wings to her ambition, fluttered and flew like a butterfly traversing villages and cities to get a formal education in order to become a professional—gone horribly wrong.

Her wings were clipped and she became almost a social outcast, unable either to realize her ambitions professionally or find a suitable groom. She was a misfit in the movement, and now she stands out in the society she so desperately wanted to belong to.

Laxmi

I met Laxmi at a police station in Odisha's Raigada. Raigada is not your run-of-the mill town. Bustling with cars and people—though much less in number than bigger cities—it is cocooned by tall hills all around. The air is chilly and there's something beautiful about this small, clean, hilly town during the months leading up to winter.

We were sitting in the sprawling police station's enormous conference room. It had newly done up walls, artificial plants and a plasma TV. The garish curtains were drawn. The air conditioner was on full blast and Laxmi's tiny frame shivered in the cold from time to time. But she seemed unaware of this physical discomfort, for she was looking elsewhere—not at the TV (which was switched off, anyway), nor at the artificial plants, nor the table nor the chairs. She was looking somewhere beyond the room.

She was in her thirties, dressed in a red, yellow, black and green cotton printed saree, her hair tied up in a plait exposing her rather broad forehead. Her bindi and nose-pin glittered as the sun's rays played hide and seek through the curtains in the shadowy darkness of the room. Her eyes rested in the depths of their sockets shadowed by high cheekbones. She was quiet and shy, sombre even. She dwelt in her inner space—looking away wistfully, and frequently flitting in and out of the real world. It was difficult to make her speak, and even by the end of the interview, I hardly got to know anything about her.

Laxmi's disposition was like that of many women I have met who are never encouraged by their family members to speak up. They are usually quiet and remain in the periphery of the normal goings-on of life, as if they do not actually exist.

Born and brought up in Raigada, Laxmi was always a simple girl. 'Akash, who eventually became my team leader, used to come regularly to our village. Some of the girls were encouraged to join the Naxals. I readily went, along with some of my friends.

No one forced me to go, it was a call from within,' Laxmi said after much prodding. Most of her answers were monosyllabic.

Now she draped the pallu of her saree around her thin frame and continued: 'We did a lot of exercise every day, trained in arms. Sometimes I would carry an SLR, sometimes it was an Insas.'

It is no mean task to carry guns and heavy rifles and move from one part of the forest to another, walking eight to ten kilometres a day at times. It was hard work. A majority of people in the camps were like Laxmi—with a thin frame and low weight. Most Maoist recruits are from financially disadvantaged families, where poverty is acute. If poverty and malnutrition afflicts most villagers in these backward areas, the move to Naxal dalams primarily solves the problem of food. There is always food to eat, something they missed back home. But when it comes to work, it either remains the same or it increases manifold.

Laxmi reminded me of a Naxal cadre I had met at a Gaya correctional home in Bihar. The frail young man, I was told, had killed several policemen—something his quiet, calm eyes had not disclosed. I draw this parallel here in order to indicate that irrespective of gender, those in the Maoist camps face the uphill task of doing very hard manual work in spite of their tiny, frail frames. All of them (including younger boys and girls) have to walk miles through the hilly and forested terrain and carry guns and other belongings tied in bundles of cloth.

When I asked her why she had quit, she didn't hesitate. Simplicity was her forte. 'It was not an easy job, madam. These were very heavy guns. It was very difficult to walk for miles together without food or water in the tricky terrain with mountains, rivers, wild animals, and the constant fear of police on your mind.'

I had never expected this to be the main reason why a person could quit the life of a soldier. Poverty and the lack of a choice had led her to take up the life of a Naxalite. She took up the work hoping it would change her life. But she missed home and it was back-breaking work. 'It is a life most ordinary people cannot take in their stride. After a while, one doesn't want to die in an exchange of fire,' Laxmi said, the stillness of her face betraying no hint of emotion. 'And it takes a toll on your health.'

Now that she had left that life behind, Laxmi felt happier than ever before, hoping that finally, she would not have to go through such a gruelling routine again. The difference between her life before she joined the Naxalites and after her surrender is huge: she has bagged more than Rs 1 lakh and doesn't have to worry about many things for a long time. If she uses her money judiciously, perhaps she doesn't have to worry about finances any more in her life.

She surrendered before the Odisha police and was now married to a young man belonging to her neighbourhood who was never in the party, she clarified.

At this same police station, I also met S. Dharma Rao (47) and his wife Uma (alias Ramna). They both hailed from Andhra Pradesh but worked mostly in bordering Odisha's Raigada. The couple had a three-year-old son and a two-month-old daughter.

'It was a very tough job. There would be no food for days. We had to walk in the forests and cope with difficult weather conditions, and even stay hungry,' said Uma. 'We realized that it would be impossible to have a family like this, and raising children within the camp was out of the question. But at the same time we were also sure we wanted a family life.'

The prospect of regular meals at the Maoist dalams or squads could make the recruits feel good only initially. But it's usually difficult to sustain in the absence of something brighter and better to look forward to in the long run.

* * *

During the course of my visits to the 'Maoist areas' of Chhattisgarh, Odisha, Bihar, West Bengal, I met and spoke at length to many SPs—superintendents of police. An SP posting is extremely crucial in the career of an IPS officer—she/he is in charge of the law and order of an entire district; it involves taking prompt decisions and is in general a baptism by fire. You are on a tightrope and have to strike a balance between the demands of ordinary people, pressure from political parties, the administration and businessmen working in the area (certainly not in that order). For districts where Maoists are a major presence, it is all the more tricky. There would be no information in the district that the SP wouldn't know about.

Therefore what SPs divulge in private conversations tends to be 'trustworthy'. Most of the SPs I spoke to, said that sexual exploitation by Maoist male cadres of their women colleagues is extremely common. In many cases, the arrested, surrendered cadres have 'admitted' and 'disclosed' these things. Interrogation reports mention instances where the arrested persons express anger and disgust about women's exploitation in the groups. These reports however are not legal documents and are to be taken with a pinch of salt. It might be just what the police would want a Maoist cadre to say and not what she/he would have wanted to say in the first place.

This is why I have taken resort to only one interrogation report, to indicate what these often say. But I changed the names in order to protect the identity of the girl.

Take the case of Renu Malik, from Odisha's Kandhamal who was arrested in 2011. According to Renu's interrogation report, she was leading a life of extreme poverty and the Maoist movement breathed new life into her. Once she became an integral part of the group, Renu was sent for arms training to Kotagarh in 2009, to Gilima (village in Odisha's Ganjam district) and Patuma (village of Gajapati district) in 2010.

Later, she revealed that Alok—a 30-year-old cadre who was married and was ten years older than her—had exploited her sexually. He wanted to take her to Chhattisgarh and had used his power to make the organization order her transfer to that state. Renu was also upset about the fact that senior cadres from Chhattisgarh, Jharkhand and Andhra Pradesh always had an upper hand over the local Odisha cadres who were used mostly for manual labour and the women exploited sexually, even forced to marry senior cadres from these states.

Many former Maoists who had worked in Chhattisgarh, Jharkhand, Odisha and West Bengal, told me how difficult it is for a single woman to work in the organization. 'It is easy to work if one has a male partner, then the other men stay away from you,' said a woman from Maharashtra's Gadchiroli.

'Most of the time, a woman would agree to be with a man, but then, if he fell in love with another woman or she fell for another man, there would be pretty messy situations to handle. It is difficult to ascertain what the nature of the sexual crimes are; there is often consent, but also jealousy, misunderstanding and false accusations,' said a former young Maoist soldier from West Bengal.

In February 2014, former minister of state for home affairs R.P.N. Singh had said in the Rajya Sabha[6] that 'Many instances of exploitation of tribals by the Naxalites/Maoists has come to the notice of the government. Such atrocities primarily include sexual exploitation of tribal women cadres in the Maoist camps, which have been disclosed in the statements of several surrendered women CPI (Maoist) cadres of Odisha, Maharashtra, Bihar, Jharkhand and other states.'

Nearly four years before Singh's statement, in August 2010, Shobha Mandi, (alias Uma, alias Shikha), then twenty-three years old—a CPI-Maoist Jhargram area commander—surrendered before the Midnapore district administration (in West Bengal). She had apparently fled under the pretext of seeing a doctor. Shobha was in the party for seven years and was at that time commanding nearly thirty people under her. There is, however, another version which says she was arrested by the police when she was riding pillion on a two wheeler and was later 'made to surrender' on the condition that she would make these accusations.

So what were these accusations? According to an interview Shobha had purportedly given to two newspapers 'before' her surrender,[7] 'They [Maoists] committed injustices against which they claimed they were fighting. As a recruit, I protested against the habits of some leaders in the presence of Kishanji. Nobody liked it. The leaders instructed the squad members not to speak to me. I was isolated and warned of dire consequences if I protested.' Later, she also wrote a book, *Diary of a Maoist*, where she made the same allegations, and which contain her personal observations on the movement of which she was once an integral part.

Shobha alleged that after a year of joining the Maoists, she was put on night-long sentry duty at a forest camp in Jharkhand, when a senior leader, Bikash, went up to her and asked for water. Then he grabbed and raped her, threatening to strangle her if she raised an alarm.

She told Akash (one of Kishanji's closest aides and a state committee member) about it, but he did not do anything. According to Shobha, Akash's wife, Anu was in a live-in relationship with Kishanji.

She also said that a recruit, Seema, had confided in her that Akash had raped her too, and Rahul (alias Ranjit Pal) had raped Belpahari squad commander Madan Mahato's wife, Jaba. Rahul had been punished by the party for this apparently, and was removed from the regional committee for three months. State committee secretary Sudip Chongdar was also apparently punished for similar acts and transferred to Jharkhand's West Singhbhum district, according to Shobha.

Kamal Maity, a Bengal-Jharkhand-Orissa regional committee member had, at a meeting attended by Kishanji and other top Maoists, proposed a relationship with Shobha. The leaders agreed to this. At this point, because she was so insecure, Shobha agreed to this proposal thinking it would 'protect' her from subsequent sexual exploitation by other leaders. It did change her life—she began to rise in the ranks.

According to Shobha, there was rampant sexual exploitation by senior leaders and if someone became pregnant, she had to undergo abortion because the presence of a child would hinder the group's movement.

She said Maoists also rape women when they take shelter in villages and the women are too afraid to disclose it. During the interview to the two newspapers she had spoken to, Shobha also said that senior women leaders have many sexual partners because it is a certain way to rise up in the Maoist ranks.

This then, confirmed—in the public domain, beyond the pages of interrogation reports—the allegations the police had been making for years. There are several other instances of surrendered Maoists making such allegations, but Shobha Mandi's statements have been the most explicit and also the most shocking.

Shobha's male colleagues didn't take kindly to her accusations. Her words angered the Maoist cadres—not only because they portrayed them in a bad light and put them on the same level as the police whom they had been accusing of rape and sexual crimes for years, but also because many felt the charges were false. One of Shobha's former colleagues told me, seething: 'Shobha had consented in the relationship. It is only later that she made false accusations to suit her purpose'.

The Naxals say that theirs is a fair organization where any sexual assault or show of disrespect—let alone rape—is severely punished. No one, however, says it doesn't happen. It is easily comparable with the stance taken by the state and central forces where officers say departmental proceedings are on against jawans who have allegedly raped/sexually assaulted women in villages. Or the curious silence of corporate offices where sexual harassment panels don't even exist.

When it comes to power and authority of men over women, it takes place across different groups. Whether it is the police executing their authority over women in villages during raids or on female rebels in the Maoist groups when they are arrested, whether it is men beating up women in their homes, or the Maoist cadres exploiting women in their own groups. It is the same story—that of the assertion of male power over the female.

In the 9th Congress of the CPI (Maoist) in 2007, one of the resolutions taken was on 'State Violence against Women':

> The Unity Congress-9th Congress of the CPI (Maoist) condemns the increasing atrocities against women all over the country, especially the repression and atrocities of the State forces and state sponsored vigilante groups. The most widespread and brutal attacks have been on Adivasi Women in Dandakaranya in the name of Salwa Judum. Both the paramilitary forces and counter revolutionary vigilante Salwa Judum groups have resorted to raping and killing many women in inhuman ways in their campaign to crush the revolutionary movement and the spirit of the people.

It also mentions incidents of killing and gangrape—especially on Adivasi women of Bastar, how thousands have been 'forcibly driven out of their homes and villages and detained them in relief camps which are in fact concentration camps.'

'Even teenage adivasi girls recruited as SPOs by the government are being subject to sexual exploitation.' There is also mention of the attempt to 'suppress the revolutionary peasant struggle in West Midnapore, Bankura and Purulia the police and social fascist CPM goons are perpetrating different types of heinous crimes against women.'

It mentions women being arrested in large numbers and kept in jails of Bihar, Jharkhand, Chhattisgarh, Maharashtra and Odisha and that '...the ruling classes and their armed forces are using violence against women as one of their weapons.'

According to a Maoist cadre who used to work in Purulia

district in West Bengal, 'In our squad, our leader Bikram used to tell us that we must always treat women and men equally.' Pointing to me, he said, 'The clothes you are wearing show your neck. We, at the squads never wear anything like that—neither women, nor men. Just as men on seeing women's skin feel aroused, women too can feel the same. So we were all dressed from head to toe, only our faces were visible.'

In private conversations, rebels—male and female—admitted to instances of sexual misdemeanor, but they were always careful to add that even in cases of sexual assault, *what you hear about are matters of consent and love.*

It is easy to be judgmental, chase the wrong story and fall into the trap of taking uncouth interest in people's personal lives.

What should not be missed, however, are the undercurrents of gender politics here. The underlying truth is that women's exploitation does take place, but beyond that, the police and the Naxals are always trying to outsmart the other by using the female rebels. Despite this, there are unbelievable stories of women's survival, of women trying to rise through the ranks, love and betrayal, and severe disgruntlement over women in the Maoist workplace.

Like any other workplace, perhaps?

Many prefer to look at the Naxal world as an ideal system completely cut off from the rest of the world. But can one really believe that those who have taken up arms to bring about social change are groups of homogeneous, like-minded, educated and 'pure' men who are always respectful to women? Is the world of the Naxal not an extension of this world, tainted and diseased by men who rape, exploit and commit sexual crimes against women?

It is also true that the police constantly try to divert attention from the rapes and sexual crimes committed by their own men by focusing on the sexual misdemeanours of the Naxal cadres.

According to an officer of Chhattisgarh police, intelligence reports indicated that many leaders from Andhra Pradesh—

mostly from Karimnagar and Warangal—who were married, got into relationships with women, in the places away from their own home, where they worked. This caused major disgruntlement among the local cadres and villagers.

At Chhattisgarh's Narayanpur, two former Maoist cadres Lachchu and Kasru told me about some junior female cadres used as personal guards for special zonal committee members whom they were 'close' to. It was not something they were happy about.

Their comments on their women colleagues indicated that the camaraderie shared between junior female cadres and their senior leaders had been the subject of serious scrutiny among the juniors. Toofan Sahu in Odisha told me how upset he was with a senior male leader he used to respect, because this man shared a tent in their secret forest hideout with three women in the group. All these women were his bodyguards.

Not only Shobha Mandi, but many of her other female colleagues have been seen as people whose sexuality has caused turmoil in the normal goings-on of the Maoists' larger purpose of attaining their political goal.

Women like Suchitra, Nikita, Tara and scores of other lesser known junior Maoist militants have been looked at as those who have used their sexuality to rise up the ladder, causing anger and disgruntlement in their male colleagues.

In Arundhati Roy's article titled 'Walking with the Comrades', published in *Outlook* in March 2010,[8] she writes, 'I'm drinking tea with Comrade Narmada, Comrade Maase and Comrade Rupi. Comrade Narmada talks about the many years she worked in Gadchiroli before becoming the DK head of the Krantikari Adivasi Mahila Sangathan. Rupi and Maase have been urban activists in Andhra Pradesh and tell me about the long years of struggle by women *within* the party, not just for their rights, but also to make the party see that equality between men and women is seen as central to a dream of a just society. We talk about the '70s and the stories of women within the Naxalite movement who were disillusioned by male comrades who thought themselves great revolutionaries but were hobbled by the same old patriarchy, the same old chauvinism. Maase says things have changed a lot since then, though they still have a way to go.'

Narmada (or Narmadakka) and Shobha became central committee members, apart from Anuradha Ghandy. However, there are still no women politburo members yet.

Anuradha Ghandy, who died of cerebral malaria in 2008, was the wife of Kobad Ghandy (a politburo member). Narmadakka, who was killed in an encounter with the police in 2013, was the wife of politburo member and ideologue Sudhakar allias Kiran. Sheela Marandi (alias Shobha, alias Budhini Munda, alias Didi) is the wife of Prashanta Bose, alias Kishan Da, also a politburo member. These were the only three women to have ever become members of the Maoists' central committee.

Apart from them, other senior women leaders are Aluri Krishnakumari (alias Sujatha, Sujatakka, Sarita, Shanti), wife of Ganapathy, general secretary CPI (Maoist) who is a member DKSZC and secretary, Northern Regional Committee. Padma (alias Sujatha, Sujatakka, Manekabai, Manekakka) wife of the late Koteswar Rao (Kishanji) is member DKSZC.

Those like Narmada, Sujatha, Manekakka and Sheela, married to top Naxal leaders, have been revered and looked at more as mother figures. But it is no secret that compared to the male members, women still occupy less important positions in the party.

Sheela Marandi (more commonly identified as Shobha), who hails from Jharha village of Jharkhand's Giridih district was given the name 'Budhini' by her party, while the foot-soldiers called her Didi. She worked in the Nari Mukti Sangh (NMS) for many years and had organized and mobilized women from the grassroots. She developed units of NMS at village, block and district levels at Gaya, Rohtas and Jehanabad districts of Bihar and Bokaro, Giridih, Hazaribagh and Ranchi districts of Jharkhand. She was more of a grassroots worker and leader, not a party ideologue. She married Kishan-da in 1992 and was arrested in July 2006.

Narmadakka (46), the other central committee member of the Maoists, hailed from Andhra Pradesh. A divisional secretary of south Gadchiroli, she later went on to become the chief of the women's wing of CPI (Maoist). She was killed in police firing, near Hiker village, bordering Abujhmarh of Chhattisgarh, in south Gadchiroli, in 2012.[9]

In recent times, Naxalites have been facing an acute crisis in senior leadership. Top leaders like Ganapathy have admitted to this vacuum. There has been a steady change in the composition of the soldiers—several senior leaders have been arrested and killed while more women are being recruited in the organization. This has led to women comprising over 60 per cent of the organization. Under the circumstances, it may seem only natural that women would occupy important positions in the organization. But that has not been the case.

Most women have had difficulties in getting respectable, senior positions in the party.

It is ironic that many women joined the movement carrying in their hearts sadness at the lack of love and equality at home. In the face of acute poverty, many felt they were loved less than their brothers. A girl from Malda—now married, and in her 20s, who was part of a squad in West Bengal's Purulia district, admitted: 'I used to feel that my parents loved my brother more. He was sent to school, but I wasn't. On the contrary, my parents expected me to go through manual labour and earn money in order to fund my brother's education.

'Not that he fared badly in studies, but he wasn't a very keen learner. Yet, I had to toil in the fields to earn money so he could study in school.' To escape this situation at home she started desperately looking for a life where she would get more love and respect. 'So I joined the Maoists. I wanted to leave the situation at home. No one had forced me to join the party.'

* * *

How do the Maoists themselves view their women soldiers? Anuradha Ghandy—a central committee member of the Maoists—worked with women from different cross sections and had expressed her party's position on women through her writings.

In a memorial piece on Anuradha Ghandy, a CPI (Maoist) document mentions how she was 'instrumental in the preparation of the Women's Perspective of the CPI (Maoist)'. This was published after Anuradha Ghandy passed away on April 12, 2008. The writer in the memorial piece mentions how the CMSC (Central Mahila Sub Committee) went on to rewrite the party document *Our Approach Towards the Women's Question*, which was first released in 1996.[10]

In the 1960s and 1970s, when the Naxalbari movement had influenced thousands of people throughout Bengal and beyond, both women and men were simultaneously drawn to the movement. Women, no longer restricted to homes, had joined the Naxal movement, but their roles remained restricted to that of couriers, cooking, cleaning and nursing—an extension of the work they were doing back home.

In her essay, 'Philosophical Trends in the Feminist Movement' Anuradha Ghandy addresses the issues of gender, patriarchy and class struggle. She writes, 'The Maoist perspective on the women's question in India also identifies patriarchy as an institution that has been the cause of women's oppression throughout class society. But it does not identify it as a separate system with its own laws of motion. The understanding is that patriarchy takes different content and form in different societies depending on the level of development and the specific history and condition of that particular society; that it has been and is being used by ruling classes to serve their interests. Hence, there is no specific enemy for patriarchy. The same ruling classes, whether imperialists, capitalists, or feudal, and the state which they control, are the enemies of women because they uphold and perpetuate the patriarchal ideology within that society. They get the support of ordinary men undoubtedly who imbibe patriarchal ideas, which are the ideas of the ruling classes and oppress women. But the position of ordinary men and those of the ruling classes cannot be compared.'[11]

My own reading from this observation is that the Maoist society is not free from the patriarchal order either. Ghandy does mention in her various writings how women from Dandakaranya, parts of Jharkhand, Maharashtra, Bihar, have come forward and participated in the war. But if this order has at all witnessed any change, it is not too different or free from influence from the 'outside world'. The Maoist order, and its ideological stance on the progress of women has not been able to differentiate itself from the order of the dominant ruling classes it is fighting against. The so-called empowerment of women in the CPI (Maoist) is a misleading notion.

This has perhaps been one of the greatest fallacies of the Maoist movement—a war fought to end class war and economic disparity has overshadowed and ruthlessly scuttled marginalized female voices.

Part IV

THE COUPLES

~

'According to Sumita, many couples in their groups were not allowed to have children. This is the reason why, just months into their marriage, Chhota was made to undergo a vasectomy. Chhota and Sumita both claimed they had no clue what the operation was all about. It was only later that Chhota was told it would be the best precaution for not having children.'

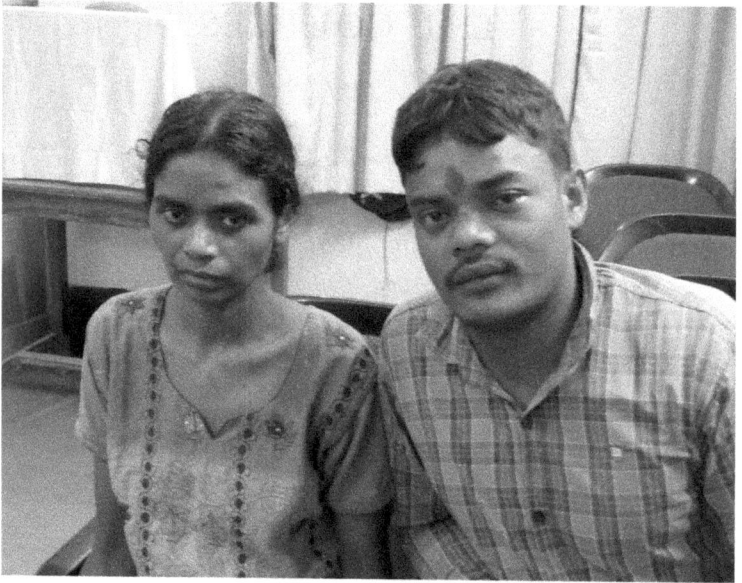

Champa and Hemanta Hembrom

12

Chhota and Sumita

Guerilla dalam lopoye marmi,
Lavey tora marmi.
Kiya koley, dada!
Mundaye soota hileyo, dada!
Kamkayo sindoor hileyo, dada!

A marriage in the guerilla dalam,
A marriage of the fighters.
We get married like this, brother!
With neither ring nor thread, brother!
No turmeric or vermillion, brother!

Somewhere in the forests of Maharashtra's Gadchiroli in a village called Tapali, Sumita and Chhota got married as their comrades sang this lilting Gondi song. Chetana Natya Mancha commander Shankara from Andhra Pradesh had written this beautiful song for them.

As the coy bride and bridegroom—both around twenty or twenty-one years old—stood facing each other, feet shuffling on the ground, hearts pounding, the song was sung in chorus by their comrades. Amidst the chirping of birds and the smell of the wild, wet forest, they vowed to be with each other till the end of time. Then, they exchanged their arms—he gave her his AK-47 and she surrendered to him her SLR.

Someone cracked a joke, the others laughed. They all sipped tea, and the ceremony was over. The memory of the day keeps coming back to Chhota and Sumita (their names changed here according to their wish) now. The exchange of arms was a marriage ritual and they ensured that, once it was over, they quickly returned their arms and ammunition to each other and went about their business as usual.

Was this exchange a mockery of the traditional exchange of gold rings and flower garlands? Or was it an affirmation of their treasure—the guns—that helped form their bond and gave purpose and meaning to their lives?

Sumita was a section commander and led a group of seven, and Chhota was a platoon commander leading a group of thirty women and men.

Sumita was born in Gadchiroli's Kalamtola village. Daughter of a middle-rung farmer—a *madhyam kisaan*—she lived a hand-to-mouth existence. Her father owned a small plot of land but was too poor to grow crops in it. Life was all hardship for Sumita, her younger sister and three brothers.

'When I was thirteen, Maoists visited our village. When they sang and danced, we were asked to join them in the performance. After it was over, my friends Lalita, Junki and I were asked to join their group,' Sumita recalled.

Her parents and siblings were opposed to the idea. How could their girl leave home and follow a band of armed women and men? How could she move around from one village to another singing songs, stay in forest hideouts and eventually take up arms? But it wasn't really a matter of choice, she said. Her parents were at that time assured that Sumita would only remain part of the cultural wing of the party.

After the initial two years, she joined the Chetana Natya Mancha—this too was a part of the Maoists' cultural wing that went from one village to another to make poor villagers aware of their rights and how the government had been exploiting them for decades.

Under her leader Ranita, Sumita went from village to village, singing songs, enacting plays, enthralling people. The groups were spread across different Marh villages—Kondagaon, Permeli, Aheri, Sironcha, Etapalli, Dhanora, Tipagarh, Chatgaon, and so on.

Marh, or Abujhmarh, is a 3900 sq. km area of dense forests spread over Narayanpur, Bijapur and Dantewada districts of Chhattisgarh and also borders Maharashtra. Abujhmarh means a forest not understood, it is so dense and deep, its people so untouched by civilization. The forest and its people are, indeed, hardly understood by the government and people from outside.

The main tribes in this area are Gond, Muria, Halba, and a few others. There are nearly 17,000 people living in over 400 villages in the area. Many villages are still outside the government or the local development authority's radar, where Maoists run the administration for all practical purposes.

Sumita was in the Chatgaon CNM, where her commander was Sima. They would announce the war cry—'PLGA *ko mazboot karo*', strengthen the Jantana Sarkar and ask people not to be with the government.

Their home was out in the open, their food was what people offered them in villages. 'If people were happy with our performances, they would offer us food which we ate heartily. Otherwise, we would go without food.' That happened only if there were no performances or they travelled for hours on end without stopping. Otherwise, people blessed them and they always struck a pleasant chord with the villagers who saw their own angst reflected in the performances of these gritty girls and boys.

Sumita was all of sixteen years at that point. Then, Shankaran, who hailed from Andhra Pradesh, got her inducted into the military wing of the party. That's how Sumita moved—like many young Maoists—from the cultural to the military wing of the party. She was in military platoon number 15 when she was seventeen years old—and beginning to train in 12-bore gun at Gadchiroli's Marh region.

At nineteen, Sumita was inducted into the military company number 4 (which had 25 women and 35 male cadres). In 2010, she went on a month-long training in arms, preparation of plans and executing operations. Well versed in Gondi and Marathi, she also picked up Hindi gradually.

After spending over seven years with the Maoists, she became part of company number 10 in 2010—part of a group of 65 cadres (30 women and 35 men). In tents and camps, the cadres would split into seven-member batches with either three women and four men or four men and three women.

Her first operation was fortuitous—a sudden attack by the police on their camp. Sumita was in a camp in the Gatta area—a village in Marh—doing PT drills when the forty of them who were in the camp got surrounded by the police. Somehow the police had got wind of their presence. The raid came without the slightest warning, but Sumita and others instantly managed to take up their arms and started firing randomly at the cops. Though panic stricken, Sumita and her mates showed how well-trained they were. In a matter of few seconds, they fired shots at the policemen and gave them the slip. Some of her mates died, but a majority fled, unscathed.

Then, a couple of years later, she got married. Marriages among cadres can sometimes take place if you are in love with someone in the same camp—which is common—or with someone in another camp—which is rare but not unheard of. There is a third reason: when there is a rumour about two persons in a particular camp seeing each other and even if this has no grain of truth, the two have to get married if the seniors come to such a conclusion. This is more the norm.

The area zonal commander, Aitu—under whom Sumita and Chhota worked—decided that the two must get married. Sumita said she wasn't too keen about marriage at that point, but there were strong rumours about their courtship and she had no idea who had spread them. However, there was enormous pressure on her and she eventually accepted the fact that she had to get married to this boy, Chhota. The good thing about this marriage, though, was the fact that Chhota was, and continues to be a soft-spoken but brave soldier, a good soul.

Chhota remembers how, as a little boy, he and his two brothers and sister would watch Naxals visit their village, asking children to join bal sangams. 'The first job of such a boy would be to work from home and inform Maoists on police movement,' said Chhota, his small, bright eyes shining. That was how he started—as a ten-year-old. Soon, at twelve years, he joined a platoon—it had thirty-odd members. Chhota did not get initiated into the group through the cultural wing—that is more common for girls. After he was a part of a platoon, he began to travel from one part of the forest to another with a walkie-talkie in hand.

He was soon arrested by the Marh police and taken to a juvenile home—a rehabilitation centre for those below eighteen years. Chhota's resolve grew stronger there—he missed life in the forest and promised to himself he would get back where he belonged. He was quick to persuade other boys in the juvenile home, who were moved by Chhota's resolve and the cause for which he was fighting. The boys helped him escape the home and raised Rs 200 from among the inmates for the difficult journey he was going to undertake.

After escaping the juvenile home, Chhota took a bus and went to Markegaon village in Dhanora tehsil of Gadchiroli district, where he could meet the Naxalites. This time, he joined a different platoon and soon became the 'in-charge' of a section. He began leading a team as a fourteen-year-old. This portion of Chhota's story bears enough testimony to the fact that children as young as fourteen are not only part of Maoist groups, but they even use arms, lead armed groups and conduct dangerous operations.

In 2009, Chhota was involved in an operation at Markegaon

village in which fifteen policemen were shot dead. It was one of the most gruesome killings ever—the policemen were not only gunned down, some of the dead policemen were also beheaded and their bodies were dismembered.[1]

'This was my first major success as a leader. My bravery and success was appreciated by my leaders. People would sometimes look at me and take me for a little boy, but when they heard about the operations I had participated in or had led, it would change to awe and respect,' Chhota told me.

'After five to six successful operations, I became platoon commander. In 2004, I was trained in AK-47. From SLR, I quickly moved on to using the AK-47. Things were going smoothly for me, and I was steadily rising up the ranks. Then, a couple of years later, I got married.

'Each one among us is dedicated to the work. But at the end of the day, it is very hard work. There is a lot of pressure and tension. The constant fear of getting killed or being caught by the police is taxing. This is no ordinary job and there is immense satisfaction despite the pain of separation from one's family.

'The soldiers live on the edge, get emotionally drained, there is also the fear of being backstabbed, a constant dread of being suspected as a police informer even if one has done no wrong.'

Chhota told me how the pressure of the job took its toll on several comrades. Pyarelal—from Gadchiroli—committed suicide in the camp. It happened probably because a senior comrade scolded him. 'No one knows what was going on in his mind. He simply shot himself with his own gun,' Chhota said.

'Then, a woman in our group committed suicide suspecting her husband was having an affair with someone. She took some pills that cure malaria, and was dead before anyone could do anything,' Chhota recalled.

'Not that all this does not happen in the outside world. But in the camps life is very, very tough. Not everyone can handle the pressure. Most of us tread this path because there is not much of an option, but they burn out and get frustrated about several practical aspects of the movement. Any minor physical or psychological pressure can even lead to death. It's a very precarious life out there.'

There have been instances of someone stealing money and leaving the camp for good. 'But you cannot blame the movement for someone who has fallen from grace and succumbed to the lure of cash. I know of a DVC member from Andhra Pradesh had once fled with Rs 3 lakh, and then he surrendered to the police. The government has a surrender policy and he took Rs 8 lakh from the police as he surrendered with arms. He must be a rich fellow now!' said Chhota, laughing.

What about the fact that Chhota himself surrendered to the police as well? Revolutionaries aren't immutable after all, I counter.

'For us, it was different. It was a difficult decision. We had no option but to surrender,' he said.

I was talking to Chhota and Sumita at Chhattisgarh's Rajnandgaon—an area bordering Gadchiroli, where the couple was based. Chhota was dressed in cargo pants that looked like army fatigues and a matching tee, while Sumita wore a green salwar-kameez and dangling earrings.

Day-to-day work as an armed soldier is back-breaking labour, they told me. An ordinary woman or man is likely to tire after a while. Perhaps the only stimulus and solace can come in the form of marital love or companionship.

'Marriage isn't so disappointing (which I used to think it was), even if a woman is not in love with the man she married,' Sumita said. She had already told me that she was neither in love with Chhota nor too keen on marrying him. 'But marriage gives you security; the woman knows she has a man to protect her from the other men in the group and if he is senior and is known for his bravery, then she feels protected and less vulnerable to abuse or attack from other men in the group or from other groups.'

'But yes, over the years, we have grown attached to each other,' she admitted.

A man and a woman, once married, are allowed to see each other only once or twice a month even if they are in the same group. These rules however, vary across groups. In any case, the work is so tough, there's hardly much time left in a day to spend with each other.

According to Sumita, many couples in their groups were not allowed to have children. This is the reason why, just months into their marriage, Chhota was made to undergo vasectomy. Chhota and Sumita both claimed they had no clue what the operation was all about. It was only later that Chhota was told it would be the best precaution for not having children.

Chhota's case is a bit unusual because Maoist leaders are known to explain vasectomy to their lower level cadres who are made to undergo the operation. Also, it usually takes place before the marriage and is voluntary. However, in Chhota's case, he claimed he had no clue what the outcome of the operation would be. Still only a twenty-one-year old, Chhota did not crave for a child desperately yet, but was sure he would want to be a father some day.

'When I became a soldier, I had never foreseen the nature of the job. There was no scope to ponder that eventually I would be married, would wish to lead an ordinary life with my wife and children,' Chhota said. Sumita's version was much the same. But when the real nature of the job unfolded before them through their growing years—from children to teens and then stepping into adulthood—even for devoted homespun Maoists like them the attraction seemed to diminish, bit by bit.

However, it wasn't years of hard work and stress that had led them to surrender. For Chhota and Sumita it was because they felt cheated by their leaders who deprived them of parenthood. Using this sentiment to woo the Maoists for surrender has now become a major strategy for the Maharashtra and Chhattisgarh police (the Marh region covers both states). The state governments have been promising Maoists a 'reverse vasectomy' operation that would enable them to bear children.

'I think the only future we saw for ourselves was dying in an encounter. It was never a question of 'whether', but 'when'. The larger context of the war was lost to us in the fear of uncertainty,' Chhota said. 'Not fear per se, but the fear of uncertainty,' Chhota clarified. He is normally as quiet as a mouse, but his words could be quite a revelation when he opened up and put things in perspective. 'The time had come to change that for the better.'

According to a report by the IANS, the ministry of home affairs had sent out 'advisories' to nine 'Left-wing extremism affected states' to 'facilitate vasectomy reversal procedures for surrendered rebels so that they can have children after marriage and lead a fuller [sic] normal life. The ministry also asked Andhra Pradesh, Bihar, Chhattisgarh, Jharkhand, Madhya Pradesh, Maharashtra, Odisha, Uttar Pradesh and West Bengal to address the issue of vasectomy, a procedure that can be reversed, within the ambit of their policy for surrender and rehabilitation of Maoists.'

According to the advisory, 'forced sterilization of the lower rung and tribal cadres of the People's Liberation Guerrilla Army of the CPI-Maoist by the top leadership has been in practice for a number of years... The Andhra Pradesh leadership resorts to this practice to keep the tribal cadres perpetually battle-fit and also to foreclose the option of alternate family life away from the Maoist fold. In view of the above, there is a need to address this issue within the ambit of the existing surrender and rehabilitation policy for Maoist cadres.'

No rehabilitation is complete if the Maoist cadres cannot return to normal family life and have children...This process will also reduce the temptation of the cadres to return to the Maoist fold. Hence, the state governments should consider facilitating vasectomy reversal operations of willing Maoist cadres.'[2]

The police have been following this advisory by the book. In Chhattisgarh, where high numbers of such cases have been found, the Director General of police (DGP) of Chhattisgarh, Ramniwas, had instructed all SPs to 'encourage Naxalite couples to undergo reverse vasectomy surgery'.[3]

For the past few years, posters have been printed in Gondi and Hindi and distributed in Chhattisgarh and Maharashtra (centred around Gadchiroli) asking Maoists who have undergone vasectomy to surrender before the police and get their sterilization reversed.

Military action is a severe way to fight the war so the state governments have in recent times also gone for remedies that work at a relatively slower pace. Unlike the armed path, some of these are clever strategies to win over a large number of soldiers.

Therefore, the police have been arranging marriages, offering surrendered Maoist soldiers quarters to live in, armed security for high profile and senior surrendered leaders as well as for their family members, free plots, money to build homes, jobs and so on.

If the government can offer all of this to surrendered Maoists, then why not grant them the joys of parenthood as well? This logic has worked well for the state governments. Many former Maoists have flocked to get their vasectomies reversed.

A teenager in one of the Maoist areas had observed wisely: 'I always tell my friends that the Maoist movement has been a blessing in disguise for the people in this area. It is only after the movement that the government began to take notice of us.'

I haven't remained in touch with Chhota and Sumita. I did not get back in touch with them perhaps because there was a need to keep their story full of possibilities. Perhaps they have already become parents, live a quiet and peaceful life in a home of their own? The very thought is comforting. All stories need not end in despair.

13

Akori Sahish and Duryodhan Rajowar

Akori is a giggly girl all decked up in a pretty brown salwar-kameez with matching sandals. Her hair is well-oiled and tied into a plait. The parting of her hair has a huge lump of sindoor.

Was she just about eighteen years? Or perhaps all of sixteen? She didn't know it herself, she told me, smiling an infectious smile.

Ask her anything under the sun and she would flash that gorgeous smile. Akori Sahish was not like this before, ('so, so happy!' as she is now) back in her village at Ghatbera in Purulia's Balarampur block. Her family of four sisters, an elder brother and parents almost always had nothing to eat. *'Bari'r abostha emon, na khatley bhat jutbey na* (the condition of our home was such that there would be no rice without labouring hard)', she told me in her heavy accent, characteristic of the Bengali spoken by the residents of a large part of this West Bengal district.

They would all be looking out for work in others' fields—ploughing land, planting paddy saplings or running tractors. But, in the predominantly dry and backward Purulia, finding work in others' land was tough and the pay very poor.

When the Lalgarh agitation was brewing in the adjoining West Midnapore district in 2008, the Maoist movement throughout Bengal got a shot in the arm. Even prior to 2008, Purulia's Ayodhya Hills had always been a strong Maoist bastion, having carried out some of the most daring operations under the leadership of Bikram, Ranjit Pal, Rajaram Soren and so on. Akori hadn't heard these names, of course, but she had witnessed some meetings in her village, where some leaders had spoken about fighting against the system to improve the lot of the poor.

Akori was tempted to be a part of the group who wielded so much power and always had something to eat. 'I thought it would be a good idea to go into their group and to work there. I could eat regularly and perhaps make some money to send home,' she said.

She took it up as a regular job, though she never made enough money to send home, she said. Initially, she was doing the job of a cook, but later she 'slowly learned to do other things that are required when you are part of such a group', Akori said with a smile and a twinkle in her eyes. She would usually carry a SLR while moving through the heavy forested and mountainous areas of Purulia. She had learned to use firearms, hurl bombs and fit into the system.

The darkness and gloom at home had been exchanged for the real darkness of forests, but this, she knew instantly, was way better. In this group, she met Duryodhan Rajowar, a squad member in his forties.

Duryodhan had once been part of the Forward Bloc—one of the constituent political parties of the Left Front that ruled West Bengal for thirty-four years since 1977. But at Tilai village of Purulia's Balarampur block, where he lived, the supporters of 'big brother' CPM (the largest constituent of the Left Front) and those of the smaller Forward Bloc were always engaged in violent clashes. There would always be some pretext or the other for such fights, like grassroots level elections in local schools, land or crop issues. In reality they were a show of political strength.

'It was frustrating to live such a life. No matter what, CPM men would just hound you and beat you up if you belonged to a smaller party,' Rajowar said. He tried his best to continue living in the area and work in the fields. The family had approximately four bighas of land where they grew paddy in one season and tomatoes and cucumbers during the rest of the year.

However, with clashes becoming a regular affair, Duryodhan decided to strengthen his ties with Maoists like Rajaram Soren, whom he 'had known for some time'. Villagers often have such casual interactions with Maoists, each providing support and empathy for the other. But since the police and supporters of the ruling CPM keep a constant eye on every villager, it isn't easy to keep a growing friendship like this under wraps for too long.

Duryodhan's village was located between two police camps—Kerua on one side and Kunwarigram on the other. Therefore, if he tried to escape from the police from one side it would mean falling into the trap of the other.

His friendship with the Maoists—which had gradually grown over the years—now began to cost him dear. There was no escape now from either the Left political party cadres or the police. In 2005, Duryodhan decided to leave home and began to live in a Maoist squad. Just prior to that, he had a particularly bitter brawl at home involving his brothers, parents and wife. He went away leaving behind his wife Malati and three children—two sons and a daughter.

Those at home, in the neighbourhood and in the local political circles thought Duryodhan Rajowar had left home due to a family dispute.

* * *

At Tilai village of Purulia's Balarampur, Duryodhan's wife Malati was struggling to survive with the three children when I visited them in 2014.

Duryodhan's father Jyoti Rajowar, mother Sandhya, brothers Dhiren, Bhim and Biren, keep their distance from each other. Duryodhan's eldest son was in class IX, but mother and son were worried sick that there was no money for continuing his education.

She quickly ate some *panta bhaat* (rice soaked overnight in water, slightly fermented and sour) for lunch before rushing off to work in the fields with a sickle in hand. She had been working in others' fields—sowing rice, cutting the paddy when ripe, and doing all other sundry jobs to get a few rupees. But even a hard day's work would never fetch enough money to feed four persons.

The hut was a tiny mud room with barely three utensils and a khatia where her eldest son was resting. He was down with fever. His books and exercise copies were scattered on the floor.

'I have nothing at home as you can see. There is no food, no utensils. My husband left home many years ago, and now I hear he has married a Maoist cadre and surrendered before the police. But what about all of us who are rotting here?' an angry Malati asked. The other children were much younger and, blissfully unaware of their mother's ordeal, were playing in the homes of their uncles and grandparents,

The West Bengal government's surrender plan for Maoists involves Rs 50,000 cash reward immediately after surrender and Rs 1.5 lakh fixed deposit after two years. During these two years, the surrendered cadres get training to begin life afresh.

The cash rewards varied from time to time, and in Duryodhan Rajowar's case he got Rs 1.5 lakh after three years of surrender.

Duryodhan Rajowar left behind a spouse and children when he joined the Maoists. In a war where the only certainty is death and separation from family, soldiers desperately seek solace in love and relationships. Who is to judge whether this is right or wrong?

For many like Akori and Duryodhan, home was a morbid memory of sorrow and suffering. Here, in their new life they would live in secret hideouts, plan attacks, carry them out with precision and celebrate. In the squad, Duryodhan had learnt to prepare explosives and handle all kinds of firearms—from .303 to AK-47s. Akori was cooking, washing pots and pans and training in firearms.

In their heart, the duo did not carry the burden of any ideology. Their fight did not have any longing to translate dreams into reality in their lifetime. For one, it was an escape from a bitter battle with hunger and for the other an escape into a space where he didn't have to cower under political pressure nor buckle under the hardships of growing family responsibilities. It was a glorious escape that Duryodhan and Akori initially began to enjoy individually, not together.

In December 2010, Duryodhan and Akori were both said to be involved in the gruesome murder of seven Forward Bloc workers in Jhalda's Bagbinda village.[1] The fact that these were all Forward Bloc workers—Duryodhan's former partymen—wasn't perhaps a pure coincidence.

The following year—2011—was a year of sweeping changes throughout Bengal. Left Front rule ended and Mamata Banerjee led Trinamool Congress to form the new government in the state. Some months into the Trinamool Congress rule, the atmosphere turned vicious—there were clashes between the Maoists and the ruling party after talks with the new government and the rebels led to a dead end. Being a Maoist was fraught with major risks.

It was Akori who decided to quit. She no longer felt safe hiding in the forests and leading the life of a rebel. What if she got killed? Some of her friends in the group were already fleeing. There were internal clashes and she knew no one she could trust. The state government had announced a surrender-cum-rehabilitation scheme for the rebels, and some were already discussing amongst themselves if they should flee and surrender before the government.

Akori and Duryodhan came together during this time of crisis. Akori began to visualize a peaceful life where she wouldn't have to worry about food nor run around with the fear of getting killed in a gunfight. She was convinced it was impossible to have a secure life without a man—she was not a child anymore and could not ignore this important lesson that she had learnt.

Everything was controlled by men. Would Duryodhan be able to take care of her? He had a family back home; would he still want to be with her?

Duryodhan on the other hand, was excited at the prospect of leaving all the worries of his family life behind. He was willing to leave the party for this young woman who seemed to be drawn to him. For him, his home was associated with demands he had grown tired of fulfilling. He wanted to begin life afresh with Akori.

Akori and Duryodhan fled the group and got married in a temple. In November 2011, they surrendered before the then Purulia police superintendent, Sunil Chowdhury.

In July 2015, when I met Duryodhan and Akori, they looked like a perfectly happy couple. Their three-year-old daughter was in an English-medium play school, and they were elated that she spoke some English. It didn't matter that they had to shell out Rs 500 per month for the school.

Duryodhan told me that he was now 'blissfully happy'. He and Akori were earning Rs 20,000 per month (each had a salary of Rs 10,000 as special home guards) and had been rewarded with cheques worth Rs 1.5 lakh three years into their surrender. 'I have decided not to spend the money. I wish to see how much dividend I can earn by keeping the money in a fixed deposit.' Their monthly salary was enough to run the family and send some money back home. 'I send them (his ex-wife and children from the first marriage) clothes during festivals and money almost every month,' Duryodhan claimed. One hopes he was telling the truth.

Duryodhan himself hadn't gone back home. Neither could he remember how old his younger son was. 'If I go back home, it can be only for a day. There are security issues as my life is under threat. So what's the point taking all the hassle and spending all the money to go home just for a day?'

He preferred to stay within the confines of his current

accomodation, working as a home guard, earning a salary and enjoying domestic life. He was also head over heels in love with his wife. 'I had no intention to return to a 'normal life'. But she [Akori] wanted to. So I decided to leave that life behind. Now I am very happy. I don't even want to think about my life as a Maoist soldier. It is over for good.'

In this unusual 'love' story, there was one simple question which I asked Akori at the end of the interview when she and I were alone in the room: Why did she choose to marry a man so much older than herself, who was already married and had a wife and three children back home?

The girl had no glib answer. 'At that time, things were very tough. People were getting caught and being put behind bars. People in the group were fighting amongst themselves. I had to save my life and I had to run away…'

'Ar… eka to palano jabey ni… jabey ki? (and …one can't just run away all alone… can one?)' she asked with a giggle.

Who can answer this rhetorical question?

Champa Hembrom and Hemanta Hembrom

Champa Hembrom's appearance was quite alarming. She was reed thin, her eyes were sunk deep in their sockets, her cheekbones were jutting out, her lips were dry and hair dishevelled. The dark and morose Champa wore a salwar-kameez, but the kameez slipped off her frail shoulders every now and then. The clothes could barely hang from a body that was all bones. Like Akori, she too had no idea of her age but she must have been in her 30s, though she looked a lot older.

In 2014, she and Hemanta Hembrom were married inside the Purulia police lines. She had surrendered three years before that. Hemanta had surrendered too. He was a young man, fair, with a moustache, who looked perfectly healthy and reeked of alcohol at three in the afternoon when I met him. He routinely got drunk and beat up Champa.

The marriage of these two surrendered Maoists was quite a celebratory event for the security forces. It was attended by all the senior police officers in the district headquarters. They were married in a social function at a temple within the police line premises, followed by a feast.

Did her parents attend the wedding? Champa was silent.

Why were they unable to come? Champa was silent again. She struggled to utter words. She had withdrawn into a deathly silence from which she found it hard to come out and express herself in sounds and syllables.

Finally, after a few minutes, she said that the wedding was never accepted by her family. 'It is because Hembroms don't marry Hembroms.' She had flouted this rule and so they refused to accept their daughter's marriage.

She was born in Purulia's Maldi village in Balarampur block. Champa, her sister, seven brothers and parents lived in extreme poverty. All of them collected wood in the forests, but it wasn't enough to feed all of them. 'The Maoists came to our village, held meetings and said everything would be fine if we gave ourselves up to them,' Champa recalled.

Therefore, it wasn't really a matter of choice that she left home to be with the Maoists. It was a golden opportunity for her to be able to feed herself well after years. She heaved a sigh of relief that she could finally survive.

She left home telling her mother that she would be back after a week, but stayed on for three years. Things went smoothly in the Maoist squad that she was a part of. There was hard work, but also food. It was like a regular job, though there wasn't any salary or money to send home.

But the happiness was short-lived. In 2011, Champa headed back home. She had to go back because 'the party was in shambles (*party to bhenge gyalo*),' she said.

And it wasn't long before the police found her in her home and arrested her.

Once the police picked her up from her home, Champa said they were kind to her and had asked her to surrender instead. She could then get money under the rehabilitation package, they said. She agreed, since she always ended up doing things suggested to her. It wasn't such a bad idea, she figured. She got trained by the police, got the job of a home guard, began to earn Rs 10,000 per month and Rs 2.5 lakh was deposited in the bank in her name which she could withdraw after three years.

But things changed dramatically in a year. The young man in question—Hemanta Hembrom—also came to live in the same police lines after his surrender.

Back in Tanasi, Hemanta's village, under the Arsha police station area, there was an equally pathetic tale. Hemanta said the police arrested him for no fault of his and he was packed off to Purulia jail in 2009. 'I stayed in prison for seventeen months for no fault of mine. It made me so angry! I was out in 2011. But even when I was released, I had to appear regularly in the court,' he said. Every time Hemanta had to appear in court, he needed to spend Rs 200-250 for transport and other expenses to travel the distance from his remote village. 'Where would I get all that money from? It was sheer injustice. I had done no crime, and I still had to appear in court. I had to spend all the money from my own pocket. I decided there had to be a way out of this misery,' he said. Finally, Hemanta found the solution: the only place he could escape was to the secret hideouts of Maoists.

'*Raag-er mathay ami party te choley gelam* (I joined the party in a fit of anger),' he said. He remained a CPI-Maoist cadre in Purulia for close to three years. The Maoists were trying to regroup and reclaim their lost ground in the state. But no major turnaround happened. When Hemanta heard about the government's surrender package he decided to make use of it. Perhaps that could change his life?

He finally surrendered in February 2014, and landed in the Purulia police lines after a period of training. Five months after his surrender, Hemanta married Champa, in July that year.

'I did not have money those days. I would go to her room and ask for some money to buy tobacco. She always agreed happily to spare some money for me,' Hemanta said in a slurring voice. He wore a green shirt, coughed every now and then and his left eye was red and swollen perhaps due to an injury from a fall. A child about four or five years old was walking around the room. 'He is my sister-in-law's child. I want to bring him up,' Hemanta said.

Champa was silent as usual. She didn't want to sit by Hemanta's side even for a picture. She was angry and upset with him. Finally, with extreme reluctance, she came and sat next to him. After Hemanta left the room, I asked Champa why she had agreed to marry him in the first place. She told me that he had smeared sindoor on the parting of her hair ('*Sindoor ghosey dilo je*'). 'In our society, if someone smears sindoor on you, you've got to marry him,' she said helplessly.

This bit of 'scandal' hadn't taken long to spread. Apparently, Champa was also eager to marry Hemanta at that point. One will never know. But now, she suffers miserably, and has been staying separately from Hemanta, away from the quarter offered to the couple by the West Bengal Police. But he still manages to steal her money and restrict her movements.

Hemanta had asked her not to visit her parents (Champa's father passed away recently). 'If she goes to her place, I will go there too,' Hemanta insisted, obviously angry about the fact that her family had accepted neither him nor the marriage. And perhaps for this 'insult', he takes out his anger on her by beating her black and blue.

Drinking is unmentionable in the Maoists' strict regimented life. Beating a partner is unheard of as well. There is punishment for those who flout the Maoist way of life. But Hemanta, who neither joined the party on ideological grounds, nor adhered to its 'rules', has made 'wife-beating' his favourite pastime.

When I asked him why he beat her up, Hemanta insisted

that Champa had also kicked him on the thigh. It is difficult to make him see logic in the fact that she must have done so in a desperate attempt to save herself from his blows. He wanted to take Champa to their quarter—she had been living away from him—but she was too scared knowing what lay in store for her. She was too broken to hope for anything miraculous to happen in her life.

As I left, I saw them going their separate ways. Champa was accompanied by some women. Hemanta couldn't have his way that day, but that would probably not dissuade him from bringing back his punching bag home at some point in the near future. He would keep trying.

Many wonder how Hemanta manages to sneak in alcohol to his quarters. He has been reprimanded, but not in a way that would make him afraid to do it again. He is being let off mildly—even when there is the Protection of Women from Domestic Violence Act, 2005, and he is surrounded by people whose job it is to implement the law. Since he is a home guard with the West Bengal government, he should perhaps be punished more severely.

'There is no end to my misery... I have been constantly suffering since childhood,' Champa mumbled before leaving. For some, an entire lifetime can be a long, dreary death.

Epilogue

The word 'surrender' is steeped in a sense of defeat. It conjures up the image of someone giving up pride, self-esteem, seeking forgiveness. Surrender involves an imbalance in power relations—it is all about the strong force crushing the weaker entity into subservience.

Suman Maiti eventually 'surrendered' before the State—something he had desperately resisted for four long years. He did not want to be known as a Maoist who surrendered before the government, availing funds under a rehabilitation package. He wanted to assert that he was not opportunistic, and felt that his 'change of heart'—from being a dreaded Maoist soldier to someone willing to help the State end violence in his village, Lalgarh—would be *rewarded* by the government with a job.

When he realised that the state government authorities would not do that, he regretted that no one in the police force gave him the option to 'surrender' when they arrested him in 2011, and slapped all those charges against him. Once the cases started, it was an ordeal for him to appear in court repeatedly and to plead innocence. All he wanted was to be exonerated from the charges slapped against him by the state government. Suman would have preferred to get a job with the Central Reserve Police Force (CRPF), where the pay is much higher than state police forces. He had helped officers of both the forces with information on the hideouts of his former Maoists colleagues and on hidden arms and ammunition.

But there were technical glitches (his height was not

permissible for a police constable's job in the Central paramilitary force), and moreover, apparently the CRPF did not want to recruit someone whose cases are still being tried in court.

'Getting a job for helping the police would have been respectable for me,' he said. 'But I got no job because of the cases. So the only way out was to plead with the officers to get myself enlisted for the rehab package.'

His audacity to demand respect from the State was successfully crushed. He was a proud youngster reduced to a compromising adult, who had to give up his pride in the face of the growing responsibilities of his family. His parents are in their late 50s, his brother is not doing particularly well in academics, and therefore a job—with the security of a monthly salary—was absolutely necessary.

Over the past few years, some police officers ensured he got some monthly allowance—but this help was offered entirely due to a personal liking for the boy—and asked him to patiently wait and keep trying for a permanent government job. In times of utter frustration, Suman even thought he might have to run away somewhere. But he was very sure he didn't want to get back to being a Maoist soldier again. He had very consciously and decisively given up that life.

In November 2015, Suman was one of 86 Maoists who 'officially' surrendered before the West Bengal government. The others were from Jhargram police district, Purulia and Bankura.

There was a buzz that the state government had offered this rehabilitation package to these young men with an eye on the Assembly elections of 2016 to keep 'Jangalmahal happy and smiling' (roughly translated into Bengali as Jangalmahal *hnashchhe,* a favourite Mamata Banerjee phrase). Some of the surrendered Maoists had been arrested earlier (like Suman), but most of their cases have not been pursued and pushed by the police, chargesheets were not filed, or the cases were on the backburner due to lack of 'adequate proof'.

In this manner, there was no escape from a formal surrender for Suman. Like all surrendered Maoists, he had to restrict himself within the paradigm set by the state, unable to move out to do any ordinary job due to the potential threat to his life.

He has now begun to write a book on his experiences as a Maoist, has undergone training and has been recruited as a home guard with the West Bengal Police force, and draws a monthly salary of Rs 10,000. He was married in July 2016 and now lives in a rented accommodation close to the police station where he is posted. Interestingly, he is posted at a place where the Maoists had held a major operation in 2009, where Suman himself (then Saontha) was involved. Sometimes, in some bizarre ways, life comes a full circle.

Suman is writing about those days of the rebellion in Lalgarh—how he and his Maoist friends visited villages and collected everything from warm and boiled to cold fermented rice, cooked rat meat and semi-cooked vegetables from the homes of villagers whether they were rich or poor, tribals or non-tribals. The food would then be mixed together. It was a melting pot of sorts—they would all eat the food along with the villagers—tribals and non-tribals, the poor and the relatively well-off. Then, they would participate in festivities, joining the tribals in their music and dance. Those were the glory days of a powerful movement, they were a cohesive force that could have changed at least their part of the world.

Though there was a change of government, the Maoists are now opposed to the political party that runs the present government. Has the paradigm of the ruler and the ruled changed? Does the State now welcome dissent? Are voices of protest from the poor and the tribals going to be heard henceforth? Will the rebellion be less bloody if the Maoists rise up against the state again?

* * *

Toofan Sahu—the boy from Odisha—still roams around forests, hills and the arid fields of his backward village, and sometimes works in a canteen run by a neighbour. He makes little money, and just hopes to get the principal amount given to him by the State that he has long been entitled to withdraw from the bank. He hopes to start a small business soon. Due to some technical problem, the money hasn't yet reached him, but that is hardly much of a surprise where government red tape is concerned.

* * *

Pinki Kaude's toddler has grown up a bit by now. That's about all the difference there has been in the life of this young woman from Chhattisgarh in the past few years. She hopes to get him admitted to a good school soon. Mallika still teaches toddlers in the West Bengal state-run school, lives in the same room shared with a score of other constables, cooks her food out of a small kerosene stove and hopes for a better tomorrow. Does she still hope a good man will marry her, *despite* knowing her past?

* * *

Lachchu has been promoted—he is no longer a gopaniya sainik, but an arakshak (constable). His salary has increased, and he seems happier, though often he has to venture into the forests in search of Maoists (along with the district armed police force) with an Insas rifle. But mostly, his duty is restricted to the police lines at Narayanpur, so he feels less threatened.

There hasn't been much of a difference in Kasru's (who is also a constable with the Chhattisgarh police) life either. Like Lachchu, he too goes into the forest from time to time to catch Maoist soldiers—only, Kasru's firearm is an AK-47 rifle. Back in the Maoist squad, he used to carry an Insas. '*Abhi utna dar nahi jitna pehle tha*,' a somewhat calm Kasru told me the last time we spoke in April 2016. He is perhaps assured and glad he has lived this long since his surrender. Or is it because he is aware of the current situation in Chhattisgarh where journalists and independent social workers are being attacked more and more these days and alleged to be siding with Maoists? Is he being guarded in his statements now?

* * *

I mentioned earlier that I haven't been in touch with Sumita and Chhota. However, a newspaper report about a Maoist couple who recently had a child after a reverse vasectomy caught my attention. On October 6, 2015, Bhagwat Jade and his wife Tijo gave birth to a baby girl, Aradhana, months after Bhagwat had undergone reverse vasectomy. Since 2012, the Chhattisgarh Police organised reverse vasectomies for twelve Maoist men who surrendered and wanted to have children. Aradhana is the first such baby among the twelve.[1]

The couple lives in Chhattisgarh's Rajnandgaon—that borders Maharashtra—the same place where Chhota and Sumita had surrendered, where I had spoken to them. One hopes they too will have a baby soon.

* * *

I haven't been in touch with Suchitra Mahato either. We never exchanged phone numbers because it would have made things complicated for both of us, with all the state government attention on her. Moreover, every time I wanted to meet her, it took time, but despite all the government restrictions and attempts to hide her from the media, I could always do so. I know I'll meet her again. I am supposed to get back to her and bring home a big jar of mango pickle made by her with fruits from her garden in Bankura.

* * *

Naveen is happy and not so happy. He says he has seen both sides—the Maoists and the police from close quarters. '*Khush to hai, par utna khush nahi,*' is how he sums up his present state, laughing. Perhaps he had hoped to be *bohot khush* (very happy). His salary had increased to Rs 22,000 per month by now.

Many ordinary villagers who have never had any connection with Maoists are being arrested by the State, it is alleged. The newspapers are full of reports on how the homes of journalists are being attacked in Chhattisgarh, activist Soni Sori was also attacked. Villagers are being picked up in the name of Maoists, but they are neither being brought under the rehabilitation scheme, nor offered employment.

There has been a distinct and forceful attempt by the State to create an atmosphere of fear in Chhattisgarh over the past few years. The government is out to scuttle every bit of independence, every voice of dissent, criticism, protest and will use every attempt to assert its own power and presence.

There is a bizarre parallel in the way the surrendered Maoists have been engaged by the Chhattisgarh government and the way the SPOs were deployed by the same government some years ago—the latter termed illegal by the Supreme Court.

The Supreme Court judgment of July 5, 2011 says:

> The State of Chattisgarh has itself stated that in recruiting these tribal youths as SPOs 'preference for those who have passed the fifth' standard has been given. This clearly implies that some, or many, who have been recruited as SPOs may not have even passed the fifth standard. Under the new rules, it is clear that the State of Chattisgarh would continue to recruit youngsters with such limited schooling. It is shocking that the State of Chattisgarh then turns around and states that it had expected such youngsters to learn, adequately, subjects such as IPC, CRPC, Evidence Act, Minors Act etc. Even more shockingly the State of Chattisgarh claims that the same was achieved in a matter of twenty-four periods of instruction of one hour each. Further, the State of Chattisgarh also claims that in an additional twelve periods, both the concepts of Human Rights and 'other provisions of Indian Constitution' had been taught. Even more astoundingly, it claims that it also taught them scientific and forensic aids in policing in six periods... Even if one were to assume, for the sake of argument, that such lessons are actually imparted, it would be impossible for any reasonable person to accept that tribal youngsters, who may, or may not have passed the fifth standard, would possess the necessary scholastic abilities to read, appreciate and understand the subjects being taught to them, and gain the appropriate

skills to be engaged in counter-insurgency movements against
the Maoists.[2]

The surrendered Maoists in Chhattisgarh have been given arms,
but there are many I have spoken to, who have got no training
from the state government before being employed as arakshaks or
constables. While there are those that have studied up to classes
five or eight *before* they joined the Maoists, there are surrendered
Maoists that have never been to school.

Take the case of Kasru. He never got any formal education
and learned to read Hindi in the Maoist camp. After he
surrendered, the Chhattisgarh government offered him a job as
a constable, but did not ensure that he was given some formal
education, nor trained him in arms or taught him about legal
provisions. 'I was in a Maoist group where I learnt to handle
arms and can read and write,' Kasru said. If at all there is going
to be any training, he says, '*Mera number abhi tak nahi aya* (my
turn hasn't come yet).'

Naveen (who completed class 8) and Kasru carry AK-47 rifles
as constables and have accompanied the state police on raids to
capture Maoists. The same goes for many surrendered Maoists
who neither received training nor got any school education. It
is difficult to figure out how the use of arms in the hands of
surrendered Maoists is not backed up by adequate education and
training when the Supreme Court had questioned this aspect
in the case of SPOs. It is also shocking to see how the state can
blindly rely on trainings offered at Maoist camps and not give
the surrendered Maoists basic training in arms before recruiting
them in their own force.

In West Bengal, the state government offers 'relaxations'
on educational qualifications to surrendered Maoists for their
appointment as home guards. So there may be some surrendered
Maoists-turned-home-guards who have received no school
education. There is a short-term training on arms, law, human
rights and so on, but no fixed time period for the training.

The training is simply on a given syllabus prepared by the state government and imparting it may vary from five weeks to a few months depending on the availability of trainers.

The redeeming factor in Bengal (as compared to the cases in Chhattisgarh) may be that home guards as a rule do not get to use firearms (only lathis if required).

Also, according to a senior officer in West Bengal, the surrendered Maoists are not given duties that require too much 'exposure' outside, but kept 'protected' by the government. This is also possible perhaps because the number of surrendered Maoists is much less than in Chhattisgarh. Mostly, their duties are restricted to offices, or, as in the case of Khagen and Mallika, they are given jobs of gardeners and teachers even if they are technically home guards.

In Odisha, the surrendered Maoists are offered training to be tailors, plumbers, mechanics and so on so they can take up jobs independently, or start a business. Many have found employment or started their own businesses. 'It all depends on police superintendents. The government has no fixed policy on this,' said a senior officer. He added that there are no relaxations for surrendered Maoists if they apply for jobs of home guards or constables.

'All those allegations that I had heard of about the police, which we discussed in our squads, turned out to be true. Now that I am part of the police force, and have seen it from close quarters, I know how true these allegations are,' says an associate of Naveen, who does not want to be quoted. Does Naveen feel the same? 'I cannot say such things officially. So I better not.' He is right. He may be pulled up by the government if he makes such comments, since he is after all, a part of the Chhattisgarh Police force.

But one does not miss the numbing sensation of sadness that engulfs all of them, some years down the line after their surrender.

It has also made them withdrawn. These women and men—who were once young and wanted to bring about the social change and rose up in arms against the State, were shocked by the cruelty of Maoist violence and disappointed at the pettiness of some individuals at the squads. Now, they are perhaps even more disillusioned about the way the State functions.

The soldiers—tired, bruised and cheated—got back home. Their hands have been 'dipped in the blood of class enemies', they have seen their dear ones being killed, they have lived without their parents, lovers and children for years, and had their dreams crushed.

But this time, exhaustion, not lethargy, has set in.

Which way must they go? Where is the honest path to a fair world? Now the only thing that matters to the surrendered Maoists are their families and, for most of them, to ensure that their children grow up and be happy. All of them want to steer clear of both the Maoists and the police force.

The enormous power of the State has made these former rebels quiet. Perhaps they are bitter inside. But at least they are quiet on the outside. It has thus taken the purpose of the State to its logical end.

For these women and men, the outrage has quietly ended.

For them, the rebellion has long been over.

Bibliographical Notes

INTRODUCTION

1. Rashmi Drolia, *The Times of India*, 14 April 2015, 'Maoists strike Chhattisgrh again; kill 5 jawans, injure 7', (http://timesofindia.indiatimes.com/india/Maoists-strike-Chhattisgarh-again-kill-5-jawans-injure-7/articleshow/46914217.cms)

2. Rashmi Drolia, *The Times of India*, 21 April 2015, '35 Maoists killed, 15 injured in April 11 attack in Chhattisgarh: surrendered Maoist claims', (http://timesofindia.indiatimes.com/india/35-Maoists-killed-15-injured-in-April-11-attack-in-Chhattisgarh-Surrendered-Maoist-claims/articleshow/47002084.cms)

3. Aman Sethi and D. Chandra Bhaskar Rao, *The Hindu*, 7 April 2010, 'Maoists massacre 74 CRPF men', (http://www.thehindu.com/news/national/maoists-massacre-74-crpf-men/article389303.ece)

4. Suvojit Bagchi, *The Hindu*, 26 May 2013, 'Mahendra Karma killed, V.C. Shukla injured in Maoist attack', (http://www.thehindu.com/news/national/other-states/mahendra-karma-killed-vc-shukla-injured-in-maoist-attack/article4750467.ece)

5. Press Trust of India (PTI), 'Over 15,000 killed in Naxal violence since 1980: Home Ministry, 14 June 2015', published in *The Indian Express*, (http://indianexpress.com/article/india/india-others/over-15000-killed-in-naxal-violence-since-1980-home-ministry/)

6. Ministry of Home Affairs, Government of India, website (www.mha.nic.in)

7. J. Venkatesan, 'Salwa Judum is illegal, says Supreme Court', 3 August 2011 (http://www.thehindu.com/news/national/salwa-judum-is-illegal-says-supreme-court/article2161246.ece)

8. Nandini Sundar, Ramachandra Guha and E.A.S. Sarma, in the Supreme Court at New Delhi, (public interest litigation petition) writ petition (civil) no. 250 of 2007 (under Article 32 of the Constitution of India) in the matter of: Nandini Sundar, Ramachandra Guha and E.A.S. Sarma

(Petitioners) versus State of Chhattisgarh (Respondents) (https://cpjc.
files.wordpress.com/2009/09/1nandini-sundar-and-ors-wp-250-2007.
pdf) [Also in Pleading for Justice (http://www.india-seminar.
com/2010/607/607_nandini_sundar.htm)—article by Nandini Sundar]

9. Shiv Sahay Singh and Ananya Dutta, *The Hindu*, 25 November 2011,
'Kishanji killed in encounter' (http://www.thehindu.com/news/national/
kishanji-killed-in-encounter/article2656599.ece)

10. Ananya Dutta and Shiv Sahay Singh, *The Hindu*, 26 November 2011,
'Claims, counter-claims on Kishanji killing' (http://www.thehindu.com/
news/national/claims-counterclaims-on-kishanji-killing/article2660289.
ece)

11. Ushinor Majumdar, 19 September 2013, 'Top Maoist leader Ganapathi
admits to leadership crisis in party', Tehelka.com (http://www.tehelka.
com/2013/09/top-maoist-leader-ganapathi-admits-to-leadership-crisis-
in-party/)

12. *The Economist*, 'A spectre haunting India', 17 August 2006, (http://
www.economist.com/node/7799247)

13. ANI, 23 November 2013, published in Indiatoday.in (http://indiatoday.
intoday.in/story/pm-manmohan-singh-asks-top-cops-to-root-out-maoist-
menace/1/326205.html)

14. Ushinor Majumdar, 19 September 2013, 'Top Maoist leader Ganapathi
admits to leadership crisis in party', Tehelka.com (http://www.tehelka.
com/2013/09/top-maoist-leader-ganapathi-admits-to-leadership-crisis-
in-party/)

15. Ministry of Home Affairs, Government of India, Annual Report, 2014-15,
page 21

16. Ministry of Home Affairs website www.mha.nic.in

17. Ministry of Home Affairs, Government of India, Annual Report, 2015-16,
page 27

18. Ministry of Home Affairs, Government of India, Annual Report, 2015-16,
pages 25-26

19. Ministry of Home Affairs website www.mha.nic.in

20. Ministry of Home Affairs, Government of India, Annual Report, 2014-
15 pages, 23, 22, and Ministry of Home Affairs, Government of India,
Annual Report, 2015-16, page 25

21. Ministry of Home Affairs, Government of India, Annual Report, 2015-16,
pages, 25 and 174

22. Ministry of Home Affairs, Government of India, Annual Report, 2015-16,
page 28

23. Ministry of Home Affairs, Government of India, Annual Report, 2015-16,
page 26

24. Ministry of Home Affairs, Government of India, Annual Report, 2012-13, page 21
25. Ministry of Home Affairs, Government of India, Annual Report, 2012-13, page 23
26. Ministry of Home Affairs, Government of India, Annual Report, 2015-16, page 26
27. India Resists, www.indiaresists.com, 18 August 2015, Arundhati Roy's note in solidarity with Soni Sori and Linga Kodopi and the people of Bastar, (http://www.indiaresists.com/arundhati-roys-note-in-solidarity-with-soni-sori-linga-kodopi-and-the-people-of-bastar/)
28. Staff Reporter, *The Hindu*, 23 October 2005, 'Woman Naxal surrenders' (http://www.thehindu.com/2005/10/23/stories/2005102309360400.htm)
29. Guidelines for surrender-cum-rehabilitation scheme of Left-wing extremists in the affected states, www.mha.nic.in
30. Abhishek Bhalla, 'Naxal boss has Rs 2.5 crore bounty: Top Maoist leader Ganapathy is now worth 10 of Dawood Ibrahim as states offer huge rewards for info', Mail Online India, 15 September 2014 (http://www.dailymail.co.uk/indiahome/indianews/article-2756983/Naxal-boss-Rs-2-5-CRORE-bounty-Top-Maoist-leader-Ganapathy-worth-10-Dawood-Ibrahim-states-offer-huge-rewards-info.html)
31. Bharti Jain and Anuja Jaiswal, 'Blow to Maoists, top leader Gudsa Usendi surrenders', 9 January 2014, (http://timesofindia.indiatimes.com/india/Blow-to-Maoists-top-leader-Gudsa-Usendi-surrenders/articleshow/28572700.cms)
32. Vivek Deshpande, 'Maoist chief admits to loss of leaders, weakening base, asks cadres to open fronts', 19 April 2015, (http://indianexpress.com/article/india/india-others/maoist-chief-admits-to-loss-of-leaders-weakening-base-asks-cadres-to-open-fronts/)

PART I: THE YOUNG ONES

Chapter 1

1. Naresh Jana, *The Telegraph*, 3 November 2008, 'Bombed: Buddha's consolation parade Paswan pilot car attacked', (http://www.telegraphindia.com/1081103/jsp/frontpage/story_10055857.jsp)
2. Sukumar Mahato, *The Times of India*, 2 December 2008, 'Probe ordered into "torture" of tribals', (http://timesofindia.indiatimes.com/city/kolkata/Probe-ordered-into-torture-of-tribals/articleshow/3782328.cms)
3. Swati Sengupta, *The Times of India*, 3 January 2009, 'Cops did commit excesses in Lalgarh: Probe panel', (http://timesofindia.indiatimes.com/city/kolkata/Cops-did-commit-excesses-in-Lalgarh-Probe-panel/articleshow/3929339.cms)

4. Naresh Jana, *The Telegraph*, 21 October 2009, 'At Maoist Mercy—Rebels kill cops in police station, kidnap OC and loot bank', (http://www.telegraphindia.com/1091021/jsp/frontpage/story_11639424.jsp)
5. Subir Bhaumik, BBC News, 16 February 2010, 'India Maoist rebels kill 24 troops in West Bengal', (http://news.bbc.co.uk/2/hi/south_asia/8517371.stm)

Chapter 2

1. Subir Bhaumik, BBC News, 16 February 2010, 'India Maoist rebels kill 24 troops in West Bengal', (http://news.bbc.co.uk/2/hi/south_asia/8517371.stm)
2. Ministry of Home Affairs, Government of India website, www.mha.nic.in
3. Suchitra Mahato is not named in the first information report (FIR) of the Silda case. It just mentions that 70-80 Maoists including 7-8 women were present in the attack. However, a district intelligence report mentions Suchitra Mahato and others like Tara and Durga as part of the attack.

Chapter 3

1. Rajaram Satapathy, *The Times of India*, 7 February 2004, 'Naxalites attack Koraput town, loot police stations' ((http://timesofindia.indiatimes.com/city/kolkata/Naxalites-attack-Koraput-town-loot-police-stations/articleshow/482576.cms)
2. Press Trust of India, Published in *The Indian Express*, 25 March 2006, 'Naxals attack Orissa jail, free prisoners, kill 3 cops', (http://archive.indianexpress.com/news/naxals-attack-orissa-jail-free-prisoners-kill-3-cops/1106/)
3. Prafulla Das, *The Hindu*, 17 February 2008, '15 killed in naxalite raids on Orissa police depots', (http://www.thehindu.com/todays-paper/15-killed-in-naxalite-raids-on-orissa-police-depots/article1203495.ece)
4. Debabrata Mohanty, *The Indian Express*, 18 July 2014, 'Top Maoist leader Sabyasachi Panda arrested in Orissa', (http://indianexpress.com/article/india/india-others/top-maoist-leader-sabyasachi-panda-arrested-in-orissa/)
5. UNI, published by *The Tribune*, 14 October 2000, 'Naxalites kill SUCI leader', (http://www.tribuneindia.com/2000/20001014/nation.htm)—news report of Madhi's death. Reference of the killing mentioned in Sabyasachi Panda's letter.
6. Subhashish Mohanty, *The Telegraph*, 25 September 2011, 'MLA shot in wheelchair', (http://www.telegraphindia.com/1110925/jsp/frontpage/story_14551840.jsp)

Chapter 4

1. District Census handbook, Bijapur, Directorate of Census Operations, Chhattisgarh (Census of India, Government of India) pages 14, 110 and 111
2. Nishit Dholabhai, *The Telegraph*, 27 April 2012, 'Calcutta "link" to Maoist arms', (http://www.telegraphindia.com/1120427/jsp/nation/story_15424600.jsp#.V8_3fE197IU)
3. Human Rights Watch, 'Dangerous Duty: Children and the Chhattisgarh Conflict', published September 2008 (excerpt published here with permission from Human Rights Watch)

PART II: THE MEN
Chapter 5

1. Suvojit Bagchi, *The Hindu*, 26 May 2013, 'Mahendra Karma killed, V.C. Shukla injured in Maoist attack', (http://www.thehindu.com/news/national/other-states/mahendra-karma-killed-vc-shukla-injured-in-maoist-attack/article4750467.ece)
2. Ejaz Kaiser, *Hindustan Times*, 27 May 2013, 'Chhattisgarh attack: Maoists danced on Karma's body after killing him, say survivors', (http://www.hindustantimes.com/india/chhattisgarh-attack-maoists-danced-on-karma-s-body-after-killing-him-say-survivors/story-gHbdngJ4vqaJ3U5jkLdXwN.html)
3. *The Indian Express*, 8 January 2014, 'Top Maoist leader, his wife, surrender before Andhra Pradesh police', (http://indianexpress.com/article/india/india-others/top-maoist-leader-his-wife-surrender-before-andhra-pradesh-police/)
4. 'A Few Words About Guerrilla Action', by Charu Mazumdar, quoted from *Liberation* (volume 3, February 1970), pg 17
5. Sougata Roy, 23 March 2010, 'Top Naxal leader Kanu Sanyal found dead in his house', (http://timesofindia.indiatimes.com/india/Top-Naxal-leader-Kanu-Sanyal-found-dead-in-his-house/articleshow/5715411.cms)
6. Pinak Priya Bhattacharya, *The Times of India, Crest*, 3 October 2009, (http://timesofindia.indiatimes.com/india/The-khatam-line-was-what-killed-us/articleshow/5083731.cms)
7. Dipankar Bose, *The Indian Express*, 20 November 2015, 'Chhattisgarh amends surrender policy for Maoists', http://indianexpress.com/article/india/india-news-india/chhattisgarh-amends-surrender-policy-for-maoists/

Chapter 6

1. Pronab Mondal, 20 March 2012, 'Rebels take Trinamul refuge—PCPA activists in Jungle Mahal join ruling party to avoid arrest', (http://www.telegraphindia.com/1120320/jsp/bengal/story_15271876.jsp#.V-uluCF97IU)

2. Romita Datta, *Livemint*, 5 May 2014, 'Dharampur: No more a dreaded battle zone', (http://www.livemint.com/Politics/RrwJWMJmlao43cIUROoaSK/Dharampur-no-more-a-dreaded-battle-zone.html)

3. Naresh Jana, *The Telegraph*, 9 July 2013, 'Curious case of change of heart', (http://www.telegraphindia.com/1130709/jsp/frontpage/story_17096819.jsp#.V-TuoSF97IU)

4. Romita Datta, *Livemint*, 5 May 2014, 'Dharampur: No more a dreaded battle zone', (http://www.livemint.com/Politics/RrwJWMJmlao43cIUROoaSK/Dharampur-no-more-a-dreaded-battle-zone.html)

5. Sougata Roy and Subhro Niyogi, 27 April 2009, 'Trinamool armed us to fight in Nandigram: Naxal leader', (http://timesofindia.indiatimes.com/india/Trinamool-armed-us-to-fight-in-Nandigram-Naxal-leader/articleshow/4452548.cms)

6. Suhrid Sankar Chattopadhyay, 'Lalgarh Battle', *Frontline*, Volume 26, Issue 14, 04-17 July, 2009, (http://www.frontline.in/static/html/fl2614/stories/20090717261412900.htm)

7. Times News Network, 11 March 2011, 'Jnaneswari Express accused Sashadhar Mahato shot dead', (http://timesofindia.indiatimes.com/india/Jnaneswari-Express-accused-Sashadhar-Mahato-shot-dead/articleshow/7676404.cms)

8. Sougata Roy and Subhro Niyogi, 27 April 2009, 'Fought Oppn then, battling CPM now', (http://timesofindia.indiatimes.com/city/kolkata/Fought-Opp-then-battling-CPM-now/articleshow/4452598.cms)

9. Press Trust of India, 20 May 2011, published in *The Times of India*, 'Mamata Banerjee sworn in as West Bengal chief minister', (http://timesofindia.indiatimes.com/assembly-elections-2011/west-bengal/Mamata-Banerjee-sworn-in-as-West-Bengal-chief-minister/articleshow/8459143.cms)

10. Biswajit Roy and Our Bureau, *The Telegraph*, 30 July 2011, 'Mamata green-lights Maoist talks', (http://www.telegraphindia.com/1110730/jsp/bengal/story_14309302.jsp)

11. HT Correspondent, *The Hindustan Times*, 13 August 2011, 'Mamata revises rehab package for Maoists', (http://www.hindustantimes.com/india/mamata-revises-rehab-package-for-maoists/story-e6vOftx0R42hutLySuYCzM.html)

12. Express News Service, 26 September 2011, 'JMM worker shot dead in Jhargram, CM says won't tolerate Maoists', (http://archive.indianexpress.

com/news/jmm-worker-shot-dead-in-jhargram-cm-says-won-t-tolerate-maoists/851773/)

13. Saibal Sen, *The Times of India*, 16 October 2011, 'Mamata issues notice to Maoist "supari killers"', (http://timesofindia.indiatimes.com/india/Mamata-issues-notice-to-Maoist-supari-killers/articleshow/10371561.cms)

14. India Today Online, 15 November 2011, 'Bengal to intensify anti-Maoist operations', (http://indiatoday.intoday.in/story/bengal-to-intensify-anti-maoist-operations-mamata/1/160008.html)

15. Express News Service, 14 November 2011, 'Jnaneswari mishap: Prime accused held', (http://archive.indianexpress.com/news/jnaneswari-mishap-prime-accused-held/875410/)

16. Times News Network, 19 November 2011, 'Dreaded Maoist Jagori Baske surrenders, slams rebels' wrong path', (http://timesofindia.indiatimes.com/city/kolkata/Dreaded-Maoist-Jagori-Baske-surrenders-slams-rebels-wrong-path/articleshow/10787364.cms)

17. Shiv Sahay Singh and Ananya Dutta, 25 November 2011, 'Kishanji killed in encounter', (http://www.thehindu.com/news/national/kishanji-killed-in-encounter/article2656599.ece)

18. Press Trust of India, published in *The Hindu*, 6 February 2012, 'Maoist squad leader killed in West Bengal', (http://www.thehindu.com/news/national/other-states/maoist-squad-leader-killed-in-west-bengal/article2863348.ece)

19. Shiv Sahay Singh, *The Hindu*, 2 March 2012, 'Kishanji replacement, 4 others held', (http://www.thehindu.com/news/national/kishanji-replacement-4-others-held/article2951580.ece)

20. Press Trust of India, published in *The Telegraph*, 8 March 2012, 'Kishanji's aide Suchitra Mahato "surrenders"', (http://www.telegraphindia.com/1120308/jsp/frontpage/story_15230038.jsp#.V-dsZyF97IU)

21. Shiv Sahay Singh, *The Hindu*, 24 May 2012, 'Biggest surrender by Maoists in Bengal', (http://www.thehindu.com/todays-paper/biggest-surrender-by-maoists-in-bengal/article3450930.ece)

22. Bureau, *The Telegraph*, 18 July 2012, 'Maoist top gun with IIT past arrested', (http://www.telegraphindia.com/1120718/jsp/bengal/story_15741734.jsp#.V-dxSiF97IU)

23. Madhuparna Das, *The Indian Express*, 12 September 2012, '"Dead" Maoist leader held from Kolkata with 2 others', (http://archive.indianexpress.com/news/-dead-maoist-leader-held-from-kolkata-with-2-others/1001694/)

24. Special Correspondent, *The Telegraph*, 3 April 2016, 'Maoist who planned Salboni blast and cop massacre arrested', (http://www.telegraphindia.com/1160403/jsp/bengal/story_78000.jsp)

25. Press Trust of India, 20 August 2015, 'CPI-Maoist says committed "mistakes" during Lalgarh stir', (http://indianexpress.com/article/india/india-others/cpi-maoist-says-committed-mistakes-during-lalgarh-stir/)

26. South Asia Terrorism Portal, West Bengal timeline 2015 (http://www.satp.org/satporgtp/countries/india/maoist/timelines/2015/westbengal.html)

27. South Asia Terrorism Portal, West Bengal timeline 2015 (http://www.satp.org/satporgtp/countries/india/maoist/timelines/2015/westbengal.html)

28. Tehelka Web Desk, 23 September 2015, 'Explosives found on Howrah-Secunderabad Falaknuma Express', (http://www.tehelka.com/2015/09/explosives-found-on-howrah-secunderabad-falaknuma-express/)

29. Express News Service, *The Indian Express*, 3 April, 2013, 'Cabinet clears civic police force for state', (http://archive.indianexpress.com/news/cabinet-clears-civic-police-force-for-state/1096435/)

Chapter 7

1. Census of India 2011, District Census handbook, Narayanpur, Series 23, Part XII-B, Village and Town Wise Primary Census Abstract, Directorate of Census Operations, Chhattisgarh, pages 78 and 79.

2. Bureau, *Business Line*, *The Hindu*, 12 December 2007, 'Chhattisgarh, Rlys, SAIL, NMDC tie up for new rail link', (print edition) (http://www.thehindubusinessline.com/todays-paper/tp-logistics/chhattisgarh-rlys-sail-nmdc-tie-up-for-new-rail-link/article1677158.ece)

3. P. Prabhat, Protect Rao, 2 August 2007 'Ghat Hills and the Mystical Tribals of Narainpur in Bastar district', Chhattisgarh, (https://www.gopetition.com/petitions/protect-raoghat-hills-and-the-mystical-tribals-of-narainpur-in-bastar-district.html)

4. ANI, published in *DNA*, 9 May 2015, 'Chhattisgarh government signs four MoUs in PM Narendra Modi's presence', (http://www.dnaindia.com/india/report-chhattisgarh-government-signs-four-mous-in-pm-narendra-modi-s-presence-2084452)

5. Malini Subramaniam, 8 August 2015, 'The Ghosts of Salwa Judum refuse to leave Chhattisgarh', (http://scroll.in/article/745397/the-ghosts-of-salwa-judum-refuse-to-leave-chhattisgarh)

6. Pavan Gahat, *The Hindu*, 1 January 2015, 'Surrendered Maoist killed in Chhattisgarh', (http://www.thehindu.com/news/national/other-states/surrendered-maoist-killed-in-chhattisgarh/article6745470.ece)

7. 'Ministry of Home affairs refers to the Salwa Judum as "a voluntary and peaceful initiative by local people against Naxalites in Dantewada district" in its annual report of 2006-07', Venkitesh Ramakrishnan, *Frontline*, Naxal Terror, Vol. 24, Issue 18, 18-21 September 2007 (http://www.frontline.in/static/html/fl2418/stories/20070921500400400.htm)

8. 'Being Neutral Is Our Biggest Crime: Government, vigilante and Naxalite

Abuses in India's Chhattisgarh State' (Human Rights Watch, extract published here with permission); 14 July 2008

9. Supreme Court of India, Justice B. Sudershan Reddy and Justice Surinder Singh Nijjar, 5 July 2011, Item number 44, Court number 9, Section PIL, Writ Petition (Civil) No(s). 250 of 2007 Petitioners Nandini Sundar and others versus State of Chhattisgarh [Respondent(s)] Page 54

10. Ashutosh Bhardwaj, 4 June 2015, 'In Chhattisgarh's Bastar, a front similar to Salwa Judum is taking shape', (http://indianexpress.com/article/india/india-others/chhattisgarh-salwa-judum-redux/)

11. Special Correspondent, *The Hindu*, 19 July 2006, 'Report sought on massacre', (http://www.thehindu.com/todays-paper/report-sought-on-massacre/article3107094.ece)

PART III: THE WOMEN
Chapter 8

1. Ananya Dutta and Shiv Sahay Singh, *The Hindu*, 26 November 2011, 'Claims, counter-claims on Kishenji killing' (http://www.thehindu.com/news/national/claims-counterclaims-on-kishenji-killing/article 2660289.ece)

2. Press Trust of India, published in *The Telegraph*, 8 March 2012, 'Kishanji's aide Suchitra Mahato "surrenders"', (http://www.telegraphindia.com/1120308/jsp/frontpage/story_15230038.jsp#.V-dsZyF97IU)

3. Subir Bhaumik, BBC News, 16 February 2010, 'India Maoist rebels kill 24 troops in West Bengal', (http://news.bbc.co.uk/2/hi/south_asia/8517371.stm)

4. Suchitra Mahato is not named in the first information report (FIR) of the Silda case. It just mentions that 70-80 Maoists including 7-8 women were present in the attack. However, a district intelligence report mentions Suchitra Mahato and others like Tara and Durga as part of the attack.

5. Press Trust of India, published in *Outlook*, 25 February 2004, 'Ultras strike with landmine, eight securitymen killed', (http://www.outlookindia.com/newswire/story/ultras-strike-with-landmine-eight-securitymen-killed/203759/?previous)

6. Press Trust of India, published in *Outlook*, 15 October 2004, 'PW landmine blasts kill six EFR, alert in western districts', (http://www.outlookindia.com/newswire/story/pw-landmine-blasts-kill-six-efr-alert-in-western-districts/255701)

7. Naresh Jana, *The Telegraph*, 21 October 2009, 'At Maoist Mercy—Rebels kill cops in police station, kidnap OC and loot bank', (http://www.telegraphindia.com/1091021/jsp/frontpage/story_11639424.jsp)

8. Agencies, published in *The Indian Express*, 28 October 2009, 'New armed wing of

PCPA behind Rajdhani hijack drama', (http://archive.indianexpress.com/news/new-armed-wing-of-pcpa-behind-rajdhani-hijack-drama/534412/)

9. Times News Network, *The Times of India*, 19 December 2009, 'Maoists kill 4 CPM men PCPA Torches Oil Tankers, Sponge Iron Unit & Forest Office', (http://epaper.timesofindia.com/Repository/getFiles.asp?Style=OliveXLib:LowLevelEntityToPrint_TOINEW&Type=text/html&Locale=english-skin-custom&Path=TOIKM/2009/12/19&ID=Ar00400)

10. *Muscular Nationalism: Gender, Violence, and Empire in India and Ireland* Sikata Banerjee, NYU Press (pgs. 101, 113, 114)

Chapter 9

1. Times News Network, *The Times of India*, 19 November 2011, 'Dreaded Maoist Jagori Baske surrenders, slams rebels wrong path', (http://timesofindia.indiatimes.com/city/kolkata/Dreaded-Maoist-Jagori-Baske-surrenders-slams-rebels-wrong-path/articleshow/10787364.cms)

2. Bureau, *The Telegraph*, 1 January 2006, 'Purulia Maoist carnage', (http://www.telegraphindia.com/1060101/asp/frontpage/story_5668244.asp)

3. Times News Network, *The Times of India*, 19 November 2011, 'Dreaded Maoist Jagori Baske surrenders, slams rebels wrong path', (http://timesofindia.indiatimes.com/city/kolkata/Dreaded-Maoist-Jagori-Baske-surrenders-slams-rebels-wrong-path/articleshow/10787364.cms)

4. Saugata Roy, *The Times of India*, 18 November 2011, 'Hint of tribal alienation?' (http://epaper.timesofindia.com/Repository/getFiles.asp?Style=OliveXLib:LowLevelEntityToPrint_TOINEW&Type=text/html&Locale=english-skin-custom&Path=TOIKM/2011/11/18&ID=Ar00201)

5. Madhuparna Das, *The Indian Express*, 13 July 2013, 'In Junglemahal, Didi asks youth to lay down arms', (http://archive.indianexpress.com/news/in-junglemahal--didi-asks-youths-to-lay-down-arms/816652/)

6. Rakhi Chakrabarty, *The Times of India*, 24 August 2010, 'Raped repeatedly, Naxal leader quits Red ranks', (http://timesofindia.indiatimes.com/india/Raped-repeatedly-Naxal-leader-quits-Red-ranks/articleshow/6423200.cms)

7. Ministry of Home Affairs, Government of India, Guidelines for Surrender-Cum-Rehabilitation Scheme of Left Wing Extremists in the Affected States, www.mha.nic.in (http://mha.nic.in/sites/upload_files/mha/files/SCRGuideline_22012016.pdf)

Chapter 10

1. Press Trust of India, published in *Outlook* magazine website, 9 January 2007, 'Buddha withdraws notification for land acquisition in Nandigram', (http://www.outlookindia.com/newswire/story/buddha-withdraws-notification-for-land-acquisition-in-nandigram/442549/?previous)
2. Livemint.com, 19 March 2007, 'The Nandigram story till now', (http://www.livemint.com/Politics/I1CAfbH2Und58UkVckctVP/The-Nandigram-story-till-now.html)
3. Biswajit Roy and Our Bureau, *The Telegraph*, 30 July, 2011, 'Mamata green-lights Maoist talks', (http://www.telegraphindia.com/1110730/jsp/bengal/story_14309302.jsp)
4. *India Today*, 15 November 2011, 'Bengal to intensify anti-Maoist operations', says Mamata, (http://indiatoday.intoday.in/story/bengal-to-intensify-anti-maoist-operations-mamata/1/160008.html)
5. Press Trust of India, published in Firstpost.com, 15 November 2011, 'Bengal to intensity anti-Maoist operations', says Mamata, (http://www.firstpost.com/india/bengal-to-intensify-anti-maoist-operations-mamata-131128.html)
6. Forum Against Eviction and Mal-Development/Lokeswari Dasgupta (USDF), published by Sanhati, 16 April 2012, 'Nandigram to Nonadanga—Onslaught Against Democracy Continues Unabated', (http://sanhati.com/articles/4887/)
7. Ronojoy Sen, *The Times of India*, 10 June 2007, 'Urban Guerillas', (http://timesofindia.indiatimes.com/home/sunday-times/deep-focus/Urban-Guerillas/articleshow/2112040.cms)
8. Our Correspondent, *The Telegraph*, 13 May 2015, 'Life term for Chhatradhar', (http://www.telegraphindia.com/1150513/jsp/bengal/story_19766.jsp#.V-55HyF97IU)
9. Our Correspondent, *The Telegraph*, 27 September 2009, 'Police stunt nets Mahato—Cops in media garb draw attention', (http://www.telegraphindia.com/1090927/jsp/frontpage/story_11547625.jsp)
10. Express News Service, *The Indian Express*, 13 May 2015, 'Lalgarh movement: Chhatradhar Mahato, five others get life in jail', (http://indianexpress.com/article/india/west-bengal-chhatradhr-mahato-three-other-lalgarh-movement-activists-convicted-under-uapa/)

Chapter 11

1. Supreme Court of India, Justice B. Sudershan Reddy and Justice Surinder Singh Nijjar, 5 July 2011, Item number 44, Court number 9, Section PIL, Writ Petition (Civil) No(s). 250 of 2007, Petitioners Nandini Sundar and others versus State of Chhattisgarh [Respondent(s)] Pages 54-55

2. Ibid
3. Ibid
4. Ashutosh Bhardwaj, *The Indian Express*, 10 September 2011, 'Chhattisgarh gets around SC order, clears law for anti-Naxal armed force', (http://indianexpress.com/article/news-archive/web/chhattisgarh-gets-around-sc-order-clears-law-for-antinaxal-armed-force/)
5. Malini Subramaniam, 8 August 2015, 'The Ghosts of Salwa Judum refuse to leave Chhattisgarh', (http://scroll.in/article/745397/the-ghosts-of-salwa-judum-refuse-to-leave-chhattisgarh
6. Ministry of Home Affairs, Government of India, Ministry of Home Affairs, Rajya Sabha, Unstarred question No. 2273 (http://mha1.nic.in/par2013/par2014-pdfs/rs-120214/2273.pdf)
7. Rakhi Chakrabarty, *The Times of India*, 24 August 2010, 'Raped repeatedly, Naxal leader quits Red ranks', (http://timesofindia.indiatimes.com/india/Raped-repeatedly-Naxal-leader-quits-Red-ranks/articleshow/6423200.cms)
8. Arundhati Roy, *Outlook* magazine, 29 March 2010, 'Walking with the comrades', (http://www.outlookindia.com/magazine/story/walking-with-the-comrades/264738)
9. Pradip Kumar Maitra, *Hindustan Times*, 28 December 2012, 'Woman Naxal leader killed in Gadchiroli', (http://www.hindustantimes.com/india/woman-naxal-leader-killed-in-gadchiroli/story-kjsNyMmSlHcvOgAGDtENrO.html)
10. Central Committee CPI (Maoist), *Advancing the Revolution With Great Sacrifices: Martyred Central Committee Members of CPI(Maoist)*, 21 September 2004, 'Comrade Anuradha Ghandy: Building Bridges between the Oppressed Social Sections and the New Democratic Revolution', pages 105-127
11. Anuradha Ghandy, *Philosophical Trends in the Feminist Movement*, published in *People's March*, Special Supplement, March 2006, Pg 51

PART IV

Chapter 12

1. Soumittra S Bose and Mazhar Ali, *The Times of India*, 2 February 2009, '15 Cops Killed in Gadchiroli: Deadliest attack by Naxals in Maharashtra Since 1992', (http://epaper.timesofindia.com/Repository/getFiles.asp?Style=OliveXLib:LowLevelEntityToPrint_TOI&Type=text/html&Locale=english-skin-custom&Path=TOIM/2009/02/02&ID=Ar00100)
2. IANS, published in Firstpost.com, 26 October 2012, 'Government's gift to surrendering Maoists—vasectomy reversal', (http://www.firstpost.

com/fwire/governments-gift-to-surrendering-maoists-vasectomy-reversal-504561.html)

3. Rashmi Drolia, *The Times of India*, 3 January 2014, 'Reverse vasectomy gives hope to surrendered Maoists in Chhattisgarh', (http://timesofindia. indiatimes.com/india/Reverse-vasectomy-gives-hope-to-surrendered-Maoists-in-Chhattisgarh/articleshow/28348369.cms)

Chapter 13

1. Agencies, published in *The Indian Express*, 17 December 2010, 'Maoists kill seven Forward Bloc members in Bengal', (http://indianexpress.com/article/india/latest-news/maoists-kill-seven-forward-bloc-members-in-bengal/)

Epilogue

1. Dipankar Ghose, *The Indian Express*, 1 February 2016, 'They call her Aradhana—Surrendered Maoist who did reverse vasectomy has child', (http://indianexpress.com/article/india/india-news-india/maoist-couple-call-her-aradhana-their-daughter-who-came-from-prayer/)

2. Nandini Sundar, Ramachandra Guha and E.A.S. Sarma, in the Supreme Court at New Delhi. Civil original jurisdiction (public interest litigation petition) writ petition (civil) no. 250 of 2007 (under Article 32 of the Constitution of India) in the matter of: Nandini Sundar, Ramachandra Guha and E.A.S. Sarma (Petitioners) versus State of Chhattisgarh (Respondents) pg 38, 39 (https://cpjc.files.wordpress. com/2009/09/1nandini-sundar-and-ors-wp-250-2007.pdf)

Acknowledgements

I would like to thank the following people for all their help and support:

Ravi Singh, Sudeshna Shome Ghosh, Paromita Mohanchandra and Shalini Krishan.

The police officers who gave me access to the surrendered Maoists, often helping me in complete secrecy. Thank you S, V, Z, A, M and R!

Varvara Rao and Ashim Chatterjee, who gave me time and cleared so many doubts in my mind.

Many present and former Maoists (you know who you are), who gave me such fascinating insights into their lives within and outside the party.

When I had started working on the book, it was meant to be something entirely different from what it looks like now. Subsequently, I abandoned the earlier work, sieved and picked up the gems I had found on the way and started writing this new narrative. This took a lot of time and patience, and I am glad Bitanu, my parents and Riddho were there all along.

www.ingramcontent.com/pod-product-compliance
Lightning Source LLC
Chambersburg PA
CBHW070710280326
41926CB00089B/3561